LIVING INDIGENOUS FEMINISM

LIVING INDIGENOUS FEMINISM
STORIES OF CONTEMPORARY
NATIVE AMERICAN WOMEN

CAROLYN ROSS JOHNSTON AND TERRI MCKINNEY BAKER

THE UNIVERSITY OF GEORGIA PRESS | ATHENS

EU Authorized Representative
Easy Access System Europe--Mustamäe tee 50, 10621
Tallinn, Estonia, gpsr.requests@easproject.com

Library of Congress Control Number: 2025938178
ISBN 9780820373768 (hardback)
ISBN 9780820373775 (paperback)
ISBN 9780820373782 (EPUB)
ISBN 9780820373799 (PDF)

Dedicated to Terri Baker, who lived Indigenous Feminism
and left this legacy of women's power for others.

Terri Baker. Photograph taken by Carolyn Ross
Johnston in Santa Fe, New Mexico, in 2017.
Courtesy of Carolyn Ross Johnston.

CONTENTS

HOW AND WHY WE WROTE THIS BOOK
SHARING INDIGENOUS WOMEN'S POWER STORIES

In 1994, in Lexington, Kentucky, Terri Baker and Carolyn Ross Johnston came to know each other when attending a six-week seminar presented by the National Endowment for the Humanities focused on southeastern Indians. During those weeks, along with the other ten participants, we read, argued, and laughed. Theda Perdue, a distinguished historian of Cherokees, and Michael D. Green, renowned historian of the Creek Nation, led us in this remarkable course. Terri, a member of the Choctaw Nation, one of the four American Indians in the group and the only literary scholar, beamed down into a clutch of historians and anthropologists, and so she was always asking for more details about dates and events to which the discussions referred. As the weeks wore on, we had the time of our lives in and out of the seminar. We chose to have a separate extra seminar each afternoon on American Indian women. No television, no radio, only conversation and long summer evenings in the backyard of our residence, the fireflies sparking in the bluegrass. We do not recall one angry argument, but only harmony and being high on the group's dynamic and energy.

Some of those Kentucky seminarians have remained friends over the past thirty years, including the two of us who wrote this book—a study of American Indian women's traditional power, which has continued and found expression in the modern era. This book began in 2015, though we have been talking about these issues for a long time. Over the years, we met in St. Petersburg, Florida, in Santa Fe, in Tulsa, in Little Rock, and in the Illinois River Valley, where Terri lived. Carolyn has spent weeks in Terri's family "barn" in Tahlequah, Oklahoma, while researching the Indian Pioneer Papers, a remarkable collection of oral histories of American Indians and other Americans collected during the Great Depression in Oklahoma. Numerous students have also accompanied Carolyn to do research and stay with the Bakers.

In 2016, while she was working at the Western History Collection in Norman, Oklahoma, and assisting with a senior thesis on Wilma Mankiller, Carolyn traveled through Tahlequah to see Terri and her husband, Tom, who graciously introduced her and her student Shelby Hall to many of their friends and colleagues from Northeastern State University. Amid one of our many enjoyable conversations about American Indian history and literature, Carolyn asked Terri to collaborate on a new book on Indigenous women's power, traditional and contemporary.

The text that has emerged from our collaboration is a bricolage of historical research and historiography, poetry, interviews, biographies, memoirs, and stories—both traditional and modern. This book poses the question of what southern and western history would look like if viewed through the eyes of a diverse sample of Indigenous women. Our choice for inclusion of women for this volume stemmed from Terri's network in Oklahoma and the Southwest, as well as the publications and activism of American Indian women in the Southeast. We found that these Indigenous women have been "living feminism" in ways that shed new light on these histories while showing how their lives and visions can offer fresh guidance for our turbulent present and the shared future we are making now.

This book features Native women of many different nations, cultures, and regions, including Cherokee, Choctaw, Comanche, Seminole, Seneca, Iroquois, Navajo, Salish and Kootenai, Kiowa, Muscogee, Creek, Yankton Dakota Sioux, Fort Sill Apache, Cheyenne, Red Lake Ojibwe, Ho-Chunk, Seneca, Tonawanda Band, Standing Rock Sioux, Lakota Sioux, Blackfeet, Laguna Pueblo, and San Ildefonso Pueblo. Our work is unique because of our thesis about Indigenous women's power: Indigenous women have always lived a pattern of gender power and balance, which the narratives of these women leaders confirm. Thus, Indigenous feminism is traditional and at the same time a source of fresh insights about how we can sustain balanced, inclusive, meaningful lives through times of challenge and change like those we live in now.

Drawing on their traditionally inherited powers, American Indian women in modern times continue to live their tribal values. They have worked to retain tribal identity over hundreds of years. While we think of this value-guided women's power as feminism, the term "feminism" was not widely used until the 1950s. Moreover, many American Native women reject the feminist label because they do not seek power as a source of freedom from male domination. They have always had power in the Indigenous economy, as mothers, within their tribal community's civic affairs and political life, within education, and within marriage.

By sharing the stories in this book, we hope to encourage the formation of coalitions of Indigenous American women who adopt and those who reject the feminist label to address the urgent needs of contemporary Native women's lives. The kind of problem-focused change process we describe and advocate for is Indigenous because it is communal and for the community's benefit. It spirals, as do the stories we share: people and events mentioned in one context reappear again later on from a different perspective and in relation to a different topic. Although traditional academic scholarship is an individualistic and solitary venture, ours is relational and organic, in terms of one another's scholarship, the living Indigenous women who shared their stories with us, and the Indigenous women who lived before us and whom we met on the pages of scattered historical records (and whose lives have left the textual traces that we bring together here). Their stories suggest powerful new meanings to what "living feminism" can do when we do it together.

NOTES ON TERMINOLOGY

"American Indian Women" and "Native American Women"
In the text, we have used the terms "American Indian women" and "Native American women" interchangeably, but in different contexts. For example, the term "Native Americans" became common in scholarship beginning in the 1960s, while generally, American Indians referred to themselves by tribal identification (if known). Some people, depending on age, preferred or still prefer the term "Indian" or "American Indian" (to distinguish Indians from the country India). While using some of these terms interchangeably, we have always been mindful of tribal identity.

"Indian"
In the text, we use the term "Indian" to refer to people living in North America in the territory that is now the United States before the Europeans arrived. We acknowledge that Indian identity is contested, with some individuals enrolled in the United States in federally recognized tribes, and other individuals not so enrolled, because their ancestors were not recorded on the Dawes Roll on which eligibility or membership in these tribes currently is based. Many other individuals believe they have Indian heritage, some residing on reservations and many off reservation, whether enrolled or not. Individual tribes determine blood quantum for membership. The term "Indian" is often used by people, especially older people, and we have left that term in interviews and quotations rather than changing it to "American Indian." The term "fullblood" indicates a child of two fullblood parents and is often used in American Indian country.

"Indigenous Feminisms" and "Native Feminism"
We have used the terms "Indigenous feminism" and "Indigenous feminisms" and "Native feminism" interchangeably. These terms imply plural manifestations and sometimes reflect historical moments of common usage. Indigenous feminism is a theory and practice of feminism that focuses on decolonization, resists patriarchal and colonialist ideas and values, and supports Indigenous sov-

ereignty and human rights for Indigenous women and their families. Our central thesis is that American Indian women have lived and continue to live what today is termed "feminism" while embodying traditional tribal values of gender complementarity and balance. "Living feminism" is a way of expressing the lifeways and values of their community. American Indian women have worked to retain tribal identity and values over hundreds of years. Native women are reimagining intersectional feminism based on their lived experiences. They face urgent crises that resemble those of mainstream white feminists.

"Feminism"

Our broad definition of feminism refers to an organized movement to eliminate social, economic, and political discrimination against women. Feminist consciousness is an awareness that women as a group have been discriminated against based on their sex, a willingness to fight male supremacy, and a belief in the possibility of a society in which men and women are equal.[1] Throughout this book, we distinguish the early women's rights movement from the successive feminist movements of the twentieth and twenty-first centuries. Moreover, we discuss the relationship of Indigenous women to these movements and their contributions and challenges.

"Matrilineality" and "Matrilocality"

Matrilineality is the tracing of kinship through the mother's line. Patrilineality traces lineage through the father's line. Matrilineality involves a social system in which inheritance is through the female line. Many Indigenous nations in North America were and are matrilineal. Matrilocality is the social system in which a married couple resides with or near the wife's parents and women of the clan family own the residence. Therefore, the husband goes to live with the wife's family.

"Matriarchy"

Matriarchy has been defined often as a social system in which females hold the primary power positions in roles of political leadership, privilege, moral authority, and control of property.[2] Most academics exclude egalitarian nonpatriarchal systems from matriarchies more strictly defined. The word "matriarchy," for a society politically led by females, especially mothers, who also control property, is often interpreted to mean the opposite of patriarchy. Peggy Reeves Sanday disagrees that matriarchies are a mirror form of patriarchies.[3]

Heide Gottner-Abendroth, a German feminist, has written extensively on matriarchal societies. She focuses on the involvement of Indigenous people. She offers a new definition of matriarchy as true gender egalitarian societies, and contends that matriarchal societies are founded on maternal values.[4] Gottner-Abendroth argues that a reluctance to accept the existence of matriarchies may be based on a culturally biased notion as well as conceptions of patriarchy.[5]

LIVING INDIGENOUS FEMINISM

INTRODUCTION
CULTURAL SURVIVAL AND INDIGENOUS
WOMEN'S TRADITIONAL POWER

When the Indigenous people of North America first encountered Europeans in the late fifteenth century, they shocked the Europeans for many reasons, including because Native women possessed so much power and exercised so much freedom over their sexuality. Many lived in matrilineal cultures and could easily separate from their husbands. These Indigenous peoples possessed culture-specific cosmologies that often featured female supernatural figures, and they rarely experienced rape or domestic violence. While there were many variations in the five hundred Native American nations that coexisted at that time, a principle of equality and balance of men's and women's roles generally characterized all their tribes. Indian women had more equity or equality than their European female counterparts, and Indian men accepted this as normal, deeply grounded in the ultimate nature of the cosmos.

In general, Native women have always learned what it means to be male and female from their mothers, from their people's creation stories and ceremonies, and from everyday tribal life. Femaleness has been greatly valued, greatly feared, and always respected in Indigenous nations. Medicine men and women have played a large role in their lives, and their thought has been cyclical and holistic. In contrast to Christianity, their spirituality has centered on nature, female and male divinities, and a belief that everything is connected and that they are related to all life, animals, plants, and stars. Women have been empowered by stories about female creators, warrior women, fire bringers, mothers who sacrificed so that their people could live, and female divinities who gave the gifts of corn and the sacred pipe—deities like Spider Grandmother, Selu and Kanati, Corn Mother, Buffalo Calf Woman, Changing Woman, and White Painted Woman. In addition to this shared female and male reverence for female divinities, Native women have held traditional policymaking power in the governing of their tribes. For hundreds of years, Native women have been dedicated to tribal sovereignty and the sustainability of their people's way of life, centered on maintaining healthy relationships with all live beings and nurturing the family and community.

In contrast, the European men saw this power of Indian women as pagan, dangerous, and uncivilized. Their goal of dispossession of the Indians' land was inextricably connected to their attempts to Christianize them and to alter their gender roles, so that men would replace the women who had been the agriculturalists, while taming and controlling their sexuality. To the Euro-Americans, bringing "civilization" to the Indigenous peoples of the Americas meant replacing the Indians' gender equality and balance with patriarchal values. "Civilization" also meant enslaving the Indigenous population.[1]

Before they encountered the Europeans, American Indian women did not have to strive for power, as later European American women did. They simply possessed power from their birth. They were born into cultures in which women possessed and exercised power as part of their daily lives. Women's power was and is a part of tribal existence. Although the assaults on their tribes were successful in many ways in the period of colonization, women always remained powerful, and in the twentieth century began to regain their political and familial power. Men's sacred knowledge prepared them for war and diplomacy while also acquainting them with the world of animals, which they needed for hunting and fishing. However, only women knew the prayers and songs that made the crops grow.[2] Women farmed, gave birth, raised children, cared for elders, managed domestic life, marketed surplus produce, and facilitated civil society. Both men and women passed on their gender's special kinds of knowledge to the next generation within families, in this way sharing the power of continuance of life and traditions within the group. This mutual dependence of men and women provided balance in their families and tribes.

In all these ways, Indigenous women's power differed significantly from that of European women who came to North America, and it continues to do so. Christian Europeans believed that women were the means by which sin and death entered the world. They were subject to the governance of men. However, as the following chapters show, the traditional power exercised by American Indian women largely has survived the violence of European invasion because their power survived within the family group. It was a quiet kind of power acknowledged as women's right, and they simply lived it. They did not have to discover it, fight for it, or be taught by Europeans what it means and how to use it to help their families and their cultures survive. Passed on from mothers to daughters, and generally supported by husbands and fathers, Indigenous women's power continues to sustain and transform the world in traditional, yet always-new ways.

Early Encounters with White Women's Rights Advocates

Iroquois women in the nineteenth century exemplified Indigenous traditional women's powers. For centuries before contact with Europeans, women of the Iroquois (Haudenosaunee) Confederacy, composed of Seneca, Onondaga, Cayuga, Oneida, Mohawk, and Tuscarora Indians, had lived in the Six Nations with gender equity, and they had traditionally exerted their own kinds of power and influence.[3] Because of their high status, these Haudenosaunee women inspired now-famous white American women's rights advocates of the nineteenth century, including Lucretia Mott, Elizabeth Cady Stanton, and Matilda Joslyn Gage. Lucretia Mott experienced these Haudenosaunee women's powers firsthand when she and her husband, James, served on the Indian committee of the Quakers and spent time on the Cattaraugus Reservation in New York, establishing a school and model farm there.

By the early nineteenth century, when Lydia Maria Child, Gage, Stanton, and Mott first encountered the Indian women of the Six Nations, their peoples had experienced colonialism, loss of land, and aggressive attempts to "civilize them" by missionaries and the federal government. Nevertheless, these Indigenous women remained powerful within their nations and inspired the leaders of the women's rights movement because of their greater freedom. They enjoyed easier separation from husbands and more control over their children, wore more comfortable clothes than the American women, and had more control over their personal property. They participated in political decision-making and discussion of issues.[4] Therefore, while the Indian women previously had even more power within their communities, in contrast with the American women, they still had impressive freedoms and exercised their agency.

Unlike most of their colonialist missionary predecessors, the Quakers did not intend to convert the Indians to Christianity, nor did they want to "civilize" them, convince them of the value of private property, or have the men take charge of agriculture. Rather, they aimed to help Native Americans preserve their land and improve their socioeconomic condition. Traditionally, Haudenosaunee women were the farmers in their tribes. This is one reason why Mott protested the colonialists' efforts to teach Iroquois women to stay home and cook while their men worked in the fields. In addition, she believed that the Indian women could be the "civilizers" of the tribe and ease their assimilation into American life.[5]

Mott spent a month at the Cattaraugus Reservation, during which she saw the power women were able to exert and the gender equity within their tribe. She observed a culture where rape and domestic violence were unthinkable. For

Iroquois women the concept of women's "rights" had little meaning; it was simply their way of life. They already lived the kind of feminism that Mott and her friends were just beginning to imagine.[6]

When Mott left the Cattaraugus Reservation in July 1848, she traveled to meet with Stanton, Martha Coffin Wright, Mary Ann McClintock, and Jane Hunt for tea in Waterloo, New York. Sitting around the table, they decided to hold a women's rights convention while the Motts were still in the area. Clearly, Stanton, Mott, and Gage all were inspired by the Iroquois women's political, social, sexual, and spiritual agency. All of them felt the need for similar freedoms and powers, not only for their own quality of life, but also to become effective agents of change in their own society, working for greater justice and democratic inclusion.

Other women's rights advocates were similarly influenced by Native women's freedom. Lydia Maria Child, a novelist, journalist, and activist, even "put forth the notion of Indian culture as an alternative to patriarchy and suggested that there was a natural alliance between white women and these people of color, based on their roots in similar matriarchal traditions and their common victimization under European patriarchy."[7] She endorsed this view in her book *History of the Condition of Women in Various Ages and Nations* (1835).[8] She contended that the Indians were not members of an inferior race and were capable of civilization—a radical claim in her time and cultural context. Child's writing influenced the thinking of Stanton, Sarah Grimké, and Margaret Fuller. She also influenced Matilda Joslyn Gage's views.

Gage extended Child's conception of the Indian culture as a matriarchal alternative to an American white patriarchy. Gage's friend Harriet Converse was an author and folklorist who was a close friend of Ely Parker, a prominent member of the Seneca Nation. She and other women's rights advocates also were aware of the American ethnologist Lewis Henry Morgan's work on the Iroquois, and that of noted anthropologist Johann Jacob Bachofen, both of whom extolled the "mother" right and matriarchal past of ancient societies. Later, due in part to Gage's influence, Stanton painted the Iroquois and other Native American nations as matriarchal in her address before the National Council of Women in 1891.[9]

Yet regardless of the admiration that Stanton, Gage, and others like Converse had for the Iroquois women's empowerment, their own class and white privilege led them to favor Indians' assimilating to American cultural values like private property while accepting allotment of their lands.[10] They thought the Indian women should adopt "civilized" white domestic skills and accept fee simple ownership (which is irrevocable) of lands in their hands.[11] Concerning their own society, these privileged white women favored both the rights of women and the imperatives of America's expansionist goals. Thus, they held contradictory views about American Indian women, just as they did about African American women. For example, after fighting in the abolitionist movement against slavery during the first six decades of the nineteenth century, by the century's end they were using the argument of expediency to exclude African American women from the franchise for which they were then fighting.

Like these earlier American feminists, Alice Fletcher, who was the first American scientist to live among the American Indians, had two conflicting perspectives on them. She saw the precontact male and female Indians as full-fledged adults, but she saw the same people after conquest as children who needed her as a mother. Postconquest Indian cultures were no longer an enviable alternative to her own patriarchal society, but people who needed to be rescued by women like her. Therefore, Fletcher advocated for "social motherhood." She helped write and pass the Dawes Act in 1887, which had the devastating effect of allotment of Indian land.[12]

Other mainstream American feminists who shared this dual perspective on Native Americans did equally great harms to them. In her 1904 Address to the National American Woman Suffrage Association's (NAWSA) Thirty-Sixth Convention, Carrie Chapman Catt, a prominent suffrage leader, used the expediency argument when she spoke disparagingly about the dreadful prospect of granting the ballot to "Indians upon the Western Prairies," while refusing it to women— by which she meant educated white women of her own class. Catt's statement was not only racist but misinformed as well, because American Indians were disqualified from voting because they were not U.S. citizens and generally would not become citizens until 1924. At the same time, contradictorily, other suffragists turned the Shoshone woman Sacajawea into a heroine for leading the Lewis and Clark expedition (1805–1806), and thereby helping to open Indian lands in the West for conquest.[13]

Catt and Anna H. Shaw, both major leaders for white American women's suffrage, were not above using racist and xenophobic rhetoric. Having portrayed the American Indian women as offering a symbol of matriarchy and a model alternative to patriarchy, they also accepted their Victorian culture's doctrine of separate gender spheres and they came to view the freer lifeways of Indigenous women as a validation of their views regarding the moral value of (white) women's unique qualities.[14] This did not mean that the early women's rights advocates accepted patriarchal roles. Rather, they thought it would be preferable to educate Indian women in adopting more modest dress and less sexual freedom while also adopting the principle of private property. These examples explain why many Native women of the nineteenth century had good reasons for thinking that American women were supporters of colonialism and conquest of their people, and therefore rejected other aspects of their belief systems. The consequences (and in part, the intention) of colonialism and the "civilizing" program of the missionaries and the American government were to disrupt gender balance in the tribal cultures, to promote patriarchal values, and to problematize Indigenous women's traditional powers.

Indigenous Women's Traditional Power Under Siege

Native women lost much of their power after contact with the Europeans because of forced removal from their traditional lands, America's Civil War, boarding schools, and the "allotment" of tribally held lands to individual Native American men. Southeastern Indians were forcibly removed from their homes after Congress passed the Indian Removal Act of 1830.[15] Many different tribes were forced into "Indian Territory," now called Oklahoma, during the early nineteenth century. The U.S. government pledged that these lands would be free of white encroachment, but this promise was never kept. The nations suffered the crises of the American Civil War and Reconstruction, with loss of lives and more territory. Then they faced the additional plunder of their lands through the government's "allotment" policy: the Dawes Act of February 8, 1887, and the Curtis Act of 1898 mandated that Indians register on the Dawes Roll and surrender all their land, except for allotted lands.[16] Thus, the Civil War and the forced allotment of tribal land to individual Native men both undermined tribal sovereignty and destabilized gender and family relationships. As Angie Debo writes, "The effect of allotment was an orgy of exploitation probably unparalleled in American History."[17]

Eventually Native women began to regain power and influence, which they had never lost entirely. They became educated in large numbers, entered professions, and became tribal chiefs and council members. Native women confronted governmental policies of tribal termination, challenges to sovereignty, and environmental degradation of their lands. They sought to re-establish the historical balance between men and women within their cultures.

Indigenous women's traditional powers, their peoples' respect for all women, and the effectiveness with which particular women have worked to maintain their cultures' deep background stories, as well as the ceremony and daily practices these guide, help us to understand how so many Native American peoples have survived across the generations, despite invasive colonialism, loss of their lands, "civilizing" miseducation, urban and rural poverty, and continuing, daily disrespect. "We are still here," many Native Americans note as the starting point for those who aim to understand this history and these continuing cultures. Just as Indigenous women's examples inspired the founders of American feminism in the nineteenth century, many contemporary scholars and activists who hope to empower all women—to create inclusively multicultural societies, to reshape our political economies in ways that will end poverty, and to care for the earth more effectively in times of ecological crisis—again seek to learn from these Indigenous women's wisdom.

Beginning in the 1970s, feminist anthropologists began to explore sexual asymmetry and to analyze the impact of colonization on American Indian women's status. Initially, the dominant interpretation was that women's power declined as their tribal populations were decimated, their lands seized, and missionaries and the government tried to "civilize" them. In the past twenty-five years, however, more scholars have emphasized Native women's agency, resistance, and adaptation. This book, *Living Indigenous Feminism: Stories of Contemporary Native American Women*, features examples of the exercise of their traditional powers of generations of Native women from various tribes and regions of North America. In their own words, they convey how and why they have made their unique contributions to their families, communities, and nations. As these stories reveal, Indian women have lived their power and led the way to a vision of freedom, sovereignty, and gender equality for their own peoples and for all Americans.

Their stories show how, after possessing gender equality before European contact and then experiencing some decline in Native women's power from the seventeenth through the early twentieth centuries, tribal women began to regain their influence during the second half of the last century. However, by that time, many of their communities were facing economic deprivation, sexual assault, domestic violence, alcoholism, teen suicide, and gangs. This is one reason why some Indigenous women joined and helped to lead the re-emerging American feminist movement's struggle for gender justice and empowerment of women inside and outside the home. At the same time, they also confronted governmental policies of tribal termination, challenges to tribal sovereignty, and public policies that caused environmental degradation of their lands. This is one reason why some Native women were ambivalent about embracing feminism, because they felt solidarity with Indian men in resisting colonialism and oppression—but they also wanted to re-establish the historical balance between men and women within their cultures during a time when many Indian men were adopting white patriarchal values.

Thus, since the 1960s, some Native women have been living their Indigenous power in ways that include their tribal identities, histories, and the fight for sovereignty, along with the goals of the American feminist movement. They have held an expanded and proud view of motherhood and the female sphere, as did the "social feminists" of the early twentieth century. They have been working to transform American society and its toxic influence within their own cultures in order to protect families and children, while focusing less on individualism and personal success. They have regarded their roles in the family as empowering while also seeing the need for equal rights as women, for reproductive control over their lives, for equal pay, and for equal opportunities for education, entrance into the professions, and political representation. Today, all Native women face the consequences of patriarchal colonialism on reservations, as expressed in alcoholism, rape, domestic abuse, and high rates of suicide. If they encounter sexism among Indian men, they may see it as a sign of these men's departure from their own people's traditional values and their assimilation to the colonizers' beliefs.[18]

The book's chapters lead the reader into a world of a colonial history's consequences, as tribal women struggle to hold on to their cultural lifeways, their Indigenous identities, and their tribes' political power. Readers will experience the structure of the book as a spiral, beginning in this introduction's depiction of Native American women's precontact exercise of grassroots power within their communities. Then the book circles in the first chapter to the story of Geraldine Hull McKinney, an Oklahoma Choctaw woman, who descended from those who were removed from the Southeast, who talks about the consequences of the boarding school experience she shared with millions of others for tribal identity, health care, and politics. Her life epitomizes the meaning of Native women's power and the ways in which cultural survival depended on women's action. Because the power of American Indian women is intergenerational, the second chapter presents a memoir of her daughter, Terri McKinney Baker, who lived Indigenous women's power in the academic world as scholar, teacher, and activist. During her long career, Terri worked with many tribal people and American Indian students as a canon-changing professor of literature and a Native American conference organizer at Oklahoma's Northeastern State University (NSU).

Chapter 3 tells the story of Terri Baker's friend, Wilma Mankiller, the first woman to become principal chief of the Cherokee Nation. This chapter includes conversations between them, including during Mankiller's last weeks as the Sequoyah Fellow at Northeastern State University in Oklahoma, formerly the Cherokee National Female Seminary. Mankiller's activism and leadership reflected a return to traditional Cherokee values of equality and gender balance, rather than focusing solely on women's oppression. Nonetheless, Mankiller was unapologetically a feminist, working closely with other well-known national leaders of the American feminist movement throughout her adult life. Thus, Wilma Mankiller embodied Indigenous feminism.

The next three chapters focus on the national and international work of the equally famous Indigenous feminist LaDonna Harris and her two daughters, Kathryn and Laura, who continue their family tradition of using women's power in leadership roles. LaDonna Harris was a founder and architect of the American women's movement in the 1960s, including the National Women's Political Caucus, and she has had a profound impact on the achievement of tribal sovereignty, women's issues, environmental issues, and civil rights. Across the years, she also has worked tirelessly at the grassroots level for Native women, families, and children. The stories of LaDonna Harris's daughters, Kathryn Harris Tijerina and Laura Harris, are explored in the following two chapters. Like their mother, they embrace their Comanche traditional values by living feminism in their own distinctive ways, preserving Indigenous cultures while lifting up new leaders who are well prepared to work both in tribal and in intercultural contexts.

As this bricolage of ways of telling stories about Indigenous women's traditional power and contemporary feminism spirals outward, chapter 7 focuses on American Indian women artists, including interviews with some of them, descriptions of their artwork, explanations of their techniques, memoirs, and literary references with historical connections. Chapter 8 takes an even wider view of Indigenous women who work on tribal sovereignty and cultural survival in the face of calamity. These contemporary American Indian women have maintained their tribal identities while embodying traditional gender equality, women's power, and resilience to identity suppression. The focus of their activism includes recovering Native women's history, tribal sovereignty, elimination of violence against Native women, and Native health care and reproductive rights.

In choosing the Indigenous women whose stories we include in this book, we spiraled outward from Terri Baker's intertribal women's network in Oklahoma and the Southwest to include those we learned about through publications on the arts and activism of American Indian women. Our focus on different regions, nations, and generations expanded as we did more research. Sometimes we followed suggestions offered by the women we interviewed. We listened.

Our conclusion emphasizes what these stories demonstrate: the past, present,

and future of American Indian women's power and resilience embodies memorable examples of what we call Indigenous feminism. We honor these generations of Native women from many different tribes and regions for the unique
contributions they have made to their communities and nations. As their own
words, creative voices, and life choices tell us, American Indian women have
lived their power and led the way to a vision of freedom, sovereignty, and gender
equality for hundreds of years, and they continue to do so today. The uniqueness
of Native forms of women's power stems from their roots in their lived experiences and their cultural traditions. American Indian women's power is organic,
originating in their tribes, rather than in the larger culture that surrounds and
still threatens them. Susan M. Williams and Joy Harjo describe the nature of
Native women's traditional power:

> Crucial to this tribal context are land and history as well as the belief that
> nothing is possible without the female and the power of the female to
> harbor and sustain creation. The female is sacred, as is the male. Both female
> and male energies are found in all life and these aspects coexist equally in a
> balanced universe. In recognition of the importance of women in sustain-
> ing tribal cultures, community takes precedence over individual women's
> rights yet conversely there are no human rights until femaleness is respected
> and venerated. These mandates in tribal social and religious thought form
> the backbone of tribal cultures that have lived in this country since time
> immemorial.[19]

We believe that everyone can learn from studying these stories of Native American women's traditional power across the generations, including the ways in
which contemporary Indigenous women are "living feminism" and are helping
to heal their tribal communities, as well as often-troubled relationships between
their cultures and other cultures with which they continuously interact, and human relationships with other living beings within Mother Earth's complex systems for sustaining life—all of which need Indigenous women's "love medicine"
right now.

CHAPTER ONE

MY MOTHER'S STORY
GERALDINE HULL MCKINNEY

My mother, Geraldine Hull McKinney, a member of the Choctaw Nation of Oklahoma, was born on September 3, 1916, in Bokchito, Oklahoma. She died on March 7, 2005. In this chapter, she recalls with me her experiences of attending Goodland, a Christian Indian boarding school, and her life devoted to the Choctaw Nation's health care and political process. My poem introduces her story about the boarding school experience, resilience, and identity in Choctaw country.

A Song for Two Voices and Four Worlds
—*Terri McKinney Baker*

Daughter	When Mother spoke
	In School
	She Spoke
Mother	From a well,
	From a Hill,
	From a sunny spot
Daughter	Against the wall
Mother	Saying
Daughter	Mother, I know you.
Mother	Mama, I love you.
Daughter	And my mother
	Closed her eyes
	To feel her mama's
Mother	Arms, the softness of her lips.
Daughter	When Mama slept
	At school
	She slept
Mother	In a large room
	Hollow with
	Home hunger,

Daughter	Echoing the stifled
Mother	Cries
	Of little girls
	In the good white peoples'
	Beds.
	In the good white peoples'
	Clothes.
Daughter	And she cried
Mother	In English.
Daughter	In English.
	When my mama laughed
	At school,
	She laughed!
Mother	And for a Chuckle's time
	Forgot
	Her wanting
Both	Her mama.
Daughter	When my mama learned
	At school,
	She learned
Mother	To survive.
Daughter	And she learned
	To help me learn
	And she learned
Mother	To remember.
	But she learned
	Hardest
	Deepest
	Proudest
	To love.
Daughter	And she
	Never forgot
	Her mama.
Daughter	Who are you?
Mother	You are
	Your mama's
	Child.[1]

As far as I know, my mother Geraldine attended only one reunion at Goodland Academy and Indian orphanage. I was with her, as we were returning from a family camping trip near Broken Bow. As we got closer and closer to the exit for Hugo that would take us to Goodland, I asked her if she wanted to attend the reunion at Goodland. She sat there silently, and then at the last moment, said yes. I careened on to the exit ramp at Hugo and we drove to Goodland, where my husband Tom, Daddy, and I sat off in the shade while Mother visited with people. There was a lot of turquoise jewelry and success at that reunion. As the afternoon wore on, the laughter increased as they shared memories. Mother would say to me again and again during the times she talked about Goodland as the years passed, "It was different for everybody." And because American Indians are people, their boarding school experiences were individually different as were the consequences.

Geraldine spent seven years at Goodland as a child and grew to adulthood, confident in her identity and possessing Native women's traditional power. Such power existed before European contact and the Europeans' initial assaults on lives, culture, communities, and ways of living, which differed markedly from European behaviors and beliefs. In holding on to their tribal identity, communities, and lifeways, American Indian women focused on survival of the family and the tribe. This inherited power sensibility nurtured women through contact, wars, removal, early nineteenth-century tribal resurgence, the American Civil War, post–Civil War struggles, allotment, the boarding school experiences, relocation, termination, nonconsensual sterilization, loss of children, tribal government renewal with accompanying financial success, and the twenty-first-century development of tribal financial diversity. While immigrants suffered, too, they generally did not suffer the attempts at genocide experienced by American Indians.

Since the days of contact, property has been the fundamental question. American Indians controlled what is now the United States and all that implies. Europeans wanted control of the land and the resources. Some few Native women managed either to hang on to property or retrieve it. The most famous incident involving this dynamic, perhaps, is De Soto's taking captive the Lady of Cofitachequi. Alvin M. Josephy Jr. narrates the meeting between De Soto and the old chieftain's niece, whom De Soto called the Lady of Cofitachequi, richly dressed and wearing a great strand of large pearls. The lady presented the pearls to De Soto with hopes that he would pass Cofitachequi by. De Soto took the lady captive along with her pearls. The lady escaped, later taking with her many of her pearls.[2]

Many others did not fare so well. From early contact, Europeans captured, raped, cohabited, or married with American Indian women to gain access to their wealth for trading purposes, for purposes of alliance, and for financial dominance.

As time passed, the Europeans' success in these arenas depended on terminating Native identity, because tribal traditions stood in the way of European success. American Indian boarding schools constituted one aspect of the attempts to excise tribal lifeways and replace them with European customs. Many works on the boarding schools focus on the negative experiences of students. In contrast, my mother found that her Choctaw identity was nourished by her boarding school experience. She agreed with K. Tsianina Lomawaima when she says: "The fact that schools often strengthened rather than dissolved tribal identity is not the only surprise tucked within alumni reminiscence."[3]

Why Mother attended a Christian mission boarding school is a story that begins before her birth with the story of my Great-Grandmother Lena. In the late nineteenth century, before Oklahoma statehood, Great-Grandmother Lena's traditional Choctaw parents required a bride price of a wagon load of corn and two mules from an old white Texan, aged forty-six, who negotiated for the hand of their sixteen-year-old daughter, Lena. In about 1890, Joseph L. Hull (called Old Man Hull by my family) married Great-Grandmother Lena to get her land near Caddo, Indian Territory, in what is today Bryan County, Oklahoma.[4]

Over the years, such interracial marriages altered the way American Indians looked and lived. These changes increased during the boarding school years (early 1800s through early 1980s) as tribal members married into other tribes and among non-Natives. Before Choctaw Removal, which began in 1831, from the Southeast to Indian Territory, now Oklahoma, white men were making alliances with Choctaw women, and their children were of mixed race and culture. Men who married into the tribe adopted Choctaw lifeways to varying degrees. Similar changes occurred in tribes with every ethnicity that came to North America.

Removal from traditional land areas constituted another assault on identity because of the large numbers of people who died as a result of removal. The Indian Removal Act was passed in 1830, and Andrew Jackson signed it into law. The number of Choctaws who died during removal, or immediately after arrival, are studied by scholars. Russell Thornton puts the percentage at 15 percent, which would be about 6,000 people out of the 40,000 Choctaws who left the Southeast.[5] Tribal people lost the young, the infirm, and the elders, who held priceless cultural knowledge and histories—regarding medicinal cures, songs, prayers, dances, rituals, ceremonies, genealogical information, plant identification, clothing construction, jewelry making, animal-grazing patterns, salt locations,

Lena Tabor, Geraldine McKinney's grandmother. She was the mother of Lafe, "Papa Hull." Courtesy of Terri McKinney Baker.

fresh water locations, negotiation skills, and farming cycles—all the elements of a viable living culture. Once in the new lands, all these kinds of knowing had to be reconstructed. Many of the details were lost. For tribal members, the consequences of removal were costly.

Some people think removal was a simple real estate transaction. It was not. Perhaps the cultural assumptions underlying the European worldview of land as individual property did not and still do not allow the European Americans to understand the very different worldviews of their American Indian neighbors. Whatever the case, removal certainly was and remains more than a land exchange. In addition, the tribal members who were removed could take only what they could carry.

The major Choctaw removal treaty is the 1830 Treaty of Dancing Rabbit Creek. It began the fraud that would finally result in allotment. Article 2 of the treaty, by which the Choctaw received land in Indian Territory (now Oklahoma), five hundred miles from their traditional homeland, in what is now called Mississippi and Louisiana reads in part as follows:

> The United States, under a grant specially to be made by the President of the United States, shall cause to be conveyed to the Choctaw Nation, a tract of country West of the Mississippi river in fee simple, to them and their descendants, to insure to them while they shall exist as a nation, and live on it.

Article 2 was not ratified by the federal government. Allotment of the land in Indian Territory to which the Choctaws had been removed took place 60 years later.[6]

How one views this and countless other American Indian experiences in American history depends largely on how it is presented and received—that is to say, how the moment is construed in museums, television programs, history books, school lessons, and so on. Regarding how history is constructed with words, my friend Wanda's story is instructive. Back in the 1960s, Wanda attended Haskell Indian Junior College, when Clara Sue Kidwell was a young professor there. At the college there existed a glass case of photographs, one of which was a picture of a horse with this caption: "The only survivor of the Battle of the Little Bighorn." Wanda and Clara Sue protested, and the caption was changed. During the 1990s, I would ask my students why the protest occurred, and what was wrong with this caption. After a pause during which you could hear student wheels grinding in young brains, lights would go on all over the room, hands would go up, gasps and then laughter would break out. I just stood there and smiled as they said all over the room, "American Indians survived the battle!" Still, for American Indian students attending Haskell, the message of that constructed caption shouted that they were not quite human.

Color is a part of the construction of history, also. Why color is important in the context of my mother's story has to do with identity. Colonization has resulted in much of our identity being based on color. However, the blending of colors itself results from the colonization. Consider the large number of mixed-blood American Indians today. That started long ago, long before Great-Grandmother Lena married the old Texan. Angie Debo notes that "the Cherokees, Choctaws, and Chickasaws also admitted intermarried whites to citizenship. There had been considerable admixture of white blood in all the tribes before the Removal, but for a time after the settlement in the West, white influence almost disappeared. After the Civil War, with the construction of the first railroads across the Indian territory and the rapid settlement of the Western frontier, this immigration and intermarriage began again."[7]

Debo presents the first U.S. Census of the Indian Territory (1890), which shows the racial composition of those people living in the territory of the Choctaw Nation:

WHITES: 28,345

NEGROES: 4,406

INDIANS: 11,057

TOTAL: 43,808

PERCENTAGE
OF INDIANS: 25.24[8]

Thus, even in their federally recognized territory, the Choctaws were outnumbered by whites, primarily because of the building of the railroads from Kansas through Indian Territory after the Civil War, though white people did live illegally in Indian Territory before the time of the building of the railroads. One can read about the railroads in the acts enacted by the Thirty-Ninth Congress (1866), specifically "An Act granting Lands to the State of Kansas to aid in the construction of the Kansas and Neosho Valley Railroad and its Extension to Red River." This involved not only the land on which the tracks ran, but "also all necessary ground for station building, workshops, depots, machine-shops, switches, side-tracks, turn-tables, and water-stations."[9] The railroad ran north and south and followed the Texas Road, now Oklahoma State Highway 69.[10]

Caddo, near which Lena's family lived, was a railway station on the Texas Road, which ran north and south. A few years later, rails were built running east and west. The railroad brought with it railroad workers, the majority of whom were white men, although some were freed slaves. And these workers also wanted land. So it was that in the late nineteenth century, white men were marrying American Indian women to get their property. This happened in many places in the United States. They married to get any kind of property.[11]

In Indian Territory, now Oklahoma, property meant land containing fossil fuels—oil in the case of the Osage, and coal in eastern Indian Territory.[12] Of course, property in Indian Territory also meant land suitable for farming and ranching, which was true for Lena and Old Man Hull. Mother Geraldine told me that the bride price for Lena was a good price—indicative of Old Man Hull's ability to protect his sixteen-year-old Choctaw bride in the lawless years of the late nineteenth century in the vicinity of Caddo, Indian Territory. Glenn Shirley, who treats those years in detail, refers to a list of "fifteen murders, most of them unsolved, some not even investigated, committed within a thirty-mile radius of . . . Caddo in 1873–74."[13] Although Old Man Hull and Lena married seventeen years later, lawlessness still prevailed.

By marrying Lena, Old Man Hull obtained tribal citizenship, as the tribes still controlled citizenship. That citizenship status conferred individual land rights under U.S. law, for Lena and Old Man Hull were married about 1891. Just three years earlier, the General Allotment Act, or the Dawes Severalty Act of 1887, had been adopted by Congress and signed by the president of the United States. It authorized a survey of American Indian tribal lands to divide them into allotments for individual Indians. Surplus land would then be opened to non-Indians.[14] Although the Dawes Act initially excluded the Choctaws as one of the five "Civilized Tribes," in 1898, Congress passed the Curtis Act, which amended the Dawes Act to include the five tribes (who had been removed from southeastern United States to Indian Territory, now Oklahoma) and "required that mineral lands be leased for the benefit of each tribe."[15] In the nineteenth century, news traveled rapidly to those who hungrily eyed property in Indian Territory. Old Man Hull had moved quickly and early into Choctaw country, which is right across the Red River from Texas.

Because sixteen-year-old Lena was an obedient Choctaw daughter of traditional parents, and even though she had already picked out someone else to marry, she married Old Man Hull about 1890–1891 and made a bargain with her husband. She would live with him until their children were adults, and then she would move into Bokchito and live alone. The bargain was accepted. Three children were born and grew to adulthood. Then Lena moved into a comfortable house in Bokchito. She had money each month for her expenses and enjoyed being the first person in Bokchito to have her own automobile.

Both Old Man Hull and Lena were listed on the Dawes Rolls, Old Man Hull as a "white Indian" and Lena as three-quarters Choctaw, even though she was a fullblood. She registered as three-quarters Choctaw in an attempt to evade being declared incompetent. Many people, even siblings, registered with blood quantum other than what they actually possessed. They did this because fullbloods were declared incompetent, and guardians were appointed to take care of their property. Some guardians turned out young children to live as best they could, robbed the assets in various ways, and charged exorbitant fees. Some guardians acted honorably.[16] By avoiding the uncertainty of an appointed guardian, Lena did manage her own allotment for some years.

The allotment years were hard years in what became Oklahoma. Allotment violated federal-tribal treaties by breaking up land that had been received in trade for land in the Southeast. Land which was declared surplus and sold no longer existed for the benefit of tribal citizens. The way allotment worked in Oklahoma is that after a set amount of time, taxes had to be paid on the allotted land, but many people were not informed about that and so lost their land.

After Old Man Hull's death, Lena married twice more—to a white man who physically abused her according to family stories, and to a Choctaw who, perhaps, did not. After the third marriage, Lena was through with men. In a studio portrait, the youngish Lena is dressed in the white way, which would have included a corset. This look continued until the 1930s, when a snapshot of Lena shows a woman who has "gone back to the blanket" (my mother's term), her body shapeless, with her long black hair blowing in the wind of southeastern Oklahoma. By the 1930s, Lena had lost her land. In neither the studio portrait nor the snapshot is Lena smiling. I don't think she had much to smile about.

During the early years of the Dawes Registration, as well as registering herself, Lena had registered her three children, including Lafe, who was my grandfather. Now I must tell you right up front, so there will be no romantic notions of Lafe. My Grandfather Lafe, "Papa Hull" as his daughter Geraldine, my mother, called him, was the scum of the earth, a man with few redeeming qualities, experiencing perhaps in rare moments of old age feelings of shame and regret for what he had done as a young father and hellion in Indian Territory. But my Grandmother Maud always loved him. She told me so.

You see, Lafe had met the daughter of one of the tenant farmers working for his father, Old Man Hull. Her name was Maud, and she became my grandmother, Geraldine's mother. According to the family story, Maud's mother, Laura Jane Linton, was Cherokee, purchased by a gambler William Walker Linton, who said he was of Choctaw descent. If he was, he was undocumented. When the Dawes Registration took place, Maud's Cherokee mother, Laura, was never allowed to enroll by her husband, William the Gambler. Nor did he enroll. Many people hid their American Indian heritage back then. My mother always claimed that Laura and the Gambler were married, though no marriage certificate exists. During the early years of their union, they had nine children and moved from town to town, as Maud's father followed the gambling money. The wife and children lived in the woods, while Father William the Gambler went into the towns, which were dangerous, violent, and often fatal. Such towns dot what today is eastern Oklahoma. In the late nineteenth and early twentieth centuries, the "hot action" gambling sites were railroad towns, agency sites, and tribal annuity locations—places where cash flowed along with bootleg whiskey; places peopled by whores, gunmen, outlaws, and gamblers such as Maud's father. Glenn Shirley calls the population of post–Civil War Indian Territory "the refuse of humanity."[17] Grandmother Maud's family was part of this "refuse."

By the time Maud had become a young woman, her parents had followed a trail once called the Osage Trace, then the Texas Road, now modern Oklahoma State Highway 69,[18] and settled as tenant farmers near Caddo, Indian Territory, in what today is Bryan County, Oklahoma, on land controlled by Old Man Hull through allotment. Old Man Hull had become a powerful banker and rancher in the area. Caddo was on the rail line. Lafe and Maud met, fell in love, and were married at Bokchito in the home of Lena, who had remarried. Maud probably insisted that Lafe marry her—Grandmother Maud was always stalwart in such matters. The couple lived with Old Man Hull on his ranch. Three children were born—Beatrice, Lodie, and Geraldine, who was my mother. By the time Geraldine was nearly four, in 1920, Maud the young bride had been replaced in dashing Lafe's affections by a local dressmaker. My family knew the family of the dressmaker in Bryan County; in fact, they attended the same church. But the relationship to that family was never a topic of conversation until I became an adult. Lafe, or "Papa Hull" as my mother Geraldine called him, mortgaged his allotment to the bank in 1920, took the money, and ran off with the dressmaker, leaving Maud with three young children, no money to pay the bank or anybody else, no income, and two sets of parents who had disapproved of the marriage.

An allotment was a quarter of a square mile of land.[19] How could it be mortgaged? Late in the nineteenth century, the white people decided that they had made a mistake in "allowing" all those Indians to have so much land, which by then had increased a good deal in value. So, they cried "do-over" and took most of it away one way and another.

The reforming white people deliberating the matter of the "Indian Problem" decided that American Indians were not greedy enough. Consider this quotation from the 1885 Annual Report of the Board of Indian Commissioners to the Secretary of the Interior. The speaker seems to be referring to Cherokees:

> The head chief told us that there was not a family in that whole nation that had not a home of its own. There was not a pauper in that nation, and the nation did not owe a dollar. It built its own capitol, in which we had this examination, and it built its schools and its hospitals. Yet the defect of the system was apparent. They have got as far as they can go because they own their land in common. It is Henry George's system, and under that there is no enterprise to make your home any better than that of your neighbors. There is no selfishness, which is at the bottom of civilization. Till this people will consent to give up their lands and divide them among their citizens so that each can own the land he cultivates, they will not make much more progress.[20]

This viewpoint, accepted by the Lake Mohonk Conference, a group of reformers who had been meeting since 1883 to discuss the "Indian Problem," is presented in some detail by Angie Debo.[21]

True, my Choctaw mother, Geraldine, had always encouraged generosity. Indeed, in 1847, during the Irish famine of 1845–1852, the Choctaw Nation of Oklahoma sent $170 to Ireland in hopes of helping to ease the suffering. This was only about fourteen years after removal, when so many of the Choctaw people had died on the trail. The Irish have since memorialized this generosity.[22] Among Choctaws, the ultimate condemnation of a person was that he or she was greedy.

But such was not the view of the powers in America. So, without tribal approval, the feds divided up the land into parcels and allotted it to individuals—heads of households and their children. If you were born one day after allotment ended, you were out of luck. Children born in succeeding generations had no allotments. After several years, the allotted Indian land was subject to the same taxation and freedom to alienate or sell it as white land. That "alienate" bit is how Papa Hull, my grandfather, mortgaged his allotment to the bank, which then attached it after nonpayment.

Land that was left over after individual allotment was declared "surplus" and sold, sometimes to the state (in this case the state of Oklahoma) and sometimes to individuals. Northeastern State University in Tahlequah, Oklahoma, where I taught for many years, was developed from such a "surplus" parcel, sold at a knockdown price to the state of Oklahoma. The main academic building at Northeastern originally was the Cherokee National Female Seminary, a beautiful and somewhat castle-like structure on the north side of Tahlequah, built by the Cherokees after the original Cherokee National Female Seminary burned in 1887. The new seminary was completed in 1889 "at Tahlequah at a cost of sixty thousand dollars."[23] Then the land and the building were declared surplus during allotment.

Clearly, what happened with allotment was simply a land grab. Most history books present this unsavory story in terms having to do with raising the poor savage to noble heights and providing free land to deserving white settlers. The fact remains that allotment is the story of a land grab and cultural erasure of tribal peoples—with their own understanding and tribal policies of how land should be used for the common good instead of for individual profit, which is the lack of selfishness that the Mohonk Conference attendees were talking about. Now today as I write this, many of the tribes are following tribal traditions, using money rolling in from their casinos for the common good—for hospitals, clinics, therapy centers, housing, assisted living, education, and so on. One can read about this practice, for example, in the Choctaw tribal newspaper, the *Bishinick*. Tribal resources are used for the common good.

That brings me back to my family story. So Lafe and the dressmaker ran off, maybe in a buggy, maybe on a train because there were trains there by 1919. Maud was left destitute, and her father-in-law, Old Man Hull, allowed her to work as a maid, cook-laundress-housekeeper at his ranch a few miles from Caddo. For a time, Maud worked in a telegraph office in Caddo. There were no nearby schools for the three children. Angie Debo says, "The census of 1920 showed that Indian illiteracy in the full-blood sections of the Five Tribes ran from 25 to 37.4 percent," and she goes on to say: "It is difficult to evaluate the general effect of the Federal educational policy; but it may be safely said that after a generation of this training the conservative fullbloods were no more fitted to cope with a competitive economic society than they were when they were first thrown upon the white man's mercy in 1900."[24]

All around her Maud could see the results of the "competitive economy," and she certainly had experienced the results firsthand. So of course, she wanted education for the children. At some point Maud discovered that she could send the children to a Christian mission boarding school for orphans near Hugo—about sixty miles to the east. For a little over two years Maud worked and waited for Geraldine (my mother) to reach the age of six, when she would be admitted to the boarding school. Tick tock. Tick tock. Wash. Scrub. Cook.

In the meantime, Lena and Maud became friendly. After all, Lena was grandmother to Maud's three children. Lena had a car. In 1922 Maud completed the documentation to get the children into Goodland Academy and Indian Orphanage near Hugo, Oklahoma, and took the children there. Goodland is a historical site, established within ten years of removal, and then during the Civil War serving as a mobilization site for two companies of the Second Choctaw Regiment, CSA (Confederate States of America).[25] It is situated in the Red River bottom land south of Hugo, Oklahoma.

My mother, Geraldine, arrived at Goodland on September 1, 1922, having turned six on September 3, and she stayed at Goodland for seven years. Mother told me that she could not remember how she got to Goodland the first time, but in later years she traveled in a friend's car (probably Lena's car) or went by bus. During the children's first year, Maud worked as a cook at Goodland, but her health failed because of the hard work and she was forced to leave her children, but she found less demanding work in a photography studio in Durant, some fifty miles west. Maud obtained a camera for Geraldine there, and Geraldine took pictures at Goodland. Several studio portraits in my possession exist from this time. I believe that it was Lena who drove Maud to Durant and helped her get a job at Truby Photography Studio. Lena's helping Maud equates to an American Indian woman working to preserve the family. After Maud had worked at the photography studio for several years, she trained as a practical nurse, and then worked for twenty-eight years at the Evergreen Sanitarium, the Bryan County Hospital, and the Durant Hospital.

There were several other Christian mission schools in Oklahoma focused on "educating the Indian out of the Indian." The government wanted tribal people to put away tribal lifeways and become white in their habits, and schools were a tool of this assimilationist policy.[26] Students were to assimilate, but not to forget their "place." In these schools, students were to be educated to become domestic servants, farm laborers, mechanics' assistants, laundresses, cooks, childcare workers, and so on. Students were recruited, sometimes kidnapped as was my Kiowa/Comanche friend's father and became students at boarding schools. On

Graduates of Goodland Academy and Indian Orphanage
with Superintendent Bailey Springer (*wearing hat*).
Photograph by Geraldine Hull (McKinney), 1922–1929.
Courtesy of Terri McKinney Baker.

Geraldine's friends dressed as flappers at
Goodland Academy and Indian Orphanage.
Photograph by Geraldine Hull (McKinney),
1922–1929. Courtesy of Terri McKinney Baker.

site at mission and federal boarding schools, the children's hair was cut, white foods replaced tribal foods, white clothing replaced tribal clothing. Students participated in structured exercise every morning. Rule-breaking was met with physical punishment or demerits that had to be worked off. Tribal languages were forbidden, and all courses were taught in English. Christian religious practices were required. Goodland, like most of the boarding schools, prominently displayed a picture of Jesus in the chapel. At the boarding schools, the American Indian children, led by the superintendent, worshipped and prayed in English to a white God.

The early mission schools followed a military pattern, later adopted at Carlisle under Captain Richard Pratt, and then at federal boarding schools across the nation. The schools themselves were staffed for the most part by white people, though as the years passed the mission schools sometimes had both white and American Indian teachers and staff. Whether kindness to students or abuse of students was practiced depended entirely on the individuals in charge. My mother told me many times that the experience was different for everybody.

I did not know the details of Mother's boarding school experience until I grew older and began to interview her with direct questions. Mother just didn't talk about the boarding school much when I was a little girl, because she didn't want to dwell on it, I think. I knew only that she had been to a boarding school. Friends of hers from Goodland Academy and Indian Orphanage peopled our lives. Her Goodland roommate was school secretary for the junior high school that I attended, and another Goodland friend traveled many times from Denver to spend Christmas with us. One Goodland friend attended our family funerals to help Mother bury her dead. Such people were her Goodland family.

Meanwhile, my mother's family by blood had been fragmented by allotment. Several years ago, I was in Phoenix, Arizona, and met with a cousin, the son of Beatrice, Mother's sister. Cousin George had found out that our Grandfather (Papa Hull) had lived in a small town near Phoenix, and we considered, briefly, going to the town to look around. But it was high summer, so we decided to just have another cold drink. Neither of us had much use for or interest in Papa Hull. As a little girl, I knew Papa Hull only as a slurred voice on the telephone when he would get drunk and call my mother, his daughter Geraldine, at Christmas time. The phone would ring, Daddy would answer and tell Mother, "It's Lafe." She would talk to him and then allow him to say something to my sister and to me. So it was that on Christmas Eve, Jesus, Papa Hull, and Santa Claus came to our house.[27]

As time passed, Choctaw history with the Presbyterian Church punctuated the song of my family's life. Consider that the Oklahoma Presbyterian College was first a boarding school in Durant, Oklahoma, that Mother's sister Beatrice attended after Goodland, and graduated in 1931. Then later in the 1950s, Oklahoma Presbyterian College was the site of my kindergarten. In the 1970s, Oklahoma Presbyterian College was owned by the Red River Valley Historical Society. The Red River Valley Historical Society arranged with Choctaw principal chief C. David Gardner to lease the north basement as a museum, and the Choctaws then got access to the rest of the building to serve as the headquarters of the Choctaw Nation of Oklahoma.[28] In 2017, the Choctaws used the outline of the OPC building as a Christmas ornament. The ties between the Presbyterian Church and the Choctaw Nation of Oklahoma are strong.[29]

In the late 1980s Mother came to Tahlequah, and I interviewed her. A friend videotaped the session. Other interviews took place at Mother's kitchen table, and I took notes. During the interviews, Mother was in her late sixties and early seventies. I simply asked her if she would agree to be interviewed, and she agreed. As we talked, we sometimes laughed. Sometimes I had tears in my eyes.

To begin, I asked Mother how she got to Goodland, a Presbyterian mission school.[30]

TERRI BAKER: Could you tell me about how you got there, when school started for example, and how you traveled from Durant? Was it Durant you travelled from?

GERALDINE MCKINNEY: Yes, from Durant. And school at Goodland, always, every year, it started September 1st. I can't remember how, how I got there the first year, but we would ride the bus, or some friend would take Mama and us down.

BAKER: In a car?

MCKINNEY: In a car, uh huh. Usually, an old Model T back then.

BAKER: When you say, "us," who else went with you?

MCKINNEY: I have an older sister, Beatrice, and an older brother, Lodi, and we three went there. Momma kept us at home until I was six, and then she put we three children in school at Goodland. Beatrice and Lodi only stayed there six years, but I stayed there seven years. Beatrice then attended Oklahoma Presbyterian College in Durant. That was the school for the Indian girls in Durant. And my brother . . . Lodi went to live with my father in Arizona.

After Mother died, in going through my mother's papers and photographs, I found a picture of three women standing by a car with a license plate that read "Bokchito." That was the town to which Great-Grandmother Lena, wife of Old Man Hull and mother of Lafe, moved when the children were grown to adulthood. The three women were Lena and her sister and half sister. I suspect that Lena drove Maud and the children to Goodland in that car. I also believe that the women were simply trying to find ways to survive the changing life patterns and hardships that had come their way and were looking out for the future of the children. The hardships were the consequences of removal, railroad development bringing white presence, and allotment. Women were intent on the survival of their families.

As the interview continued, I asked Mother where she lived at Goodland, and she described her dormitory.

MCKINNEY: We had dormitories there and I was assigned to what was called "Little Girl's Dormitory." And I stayed in that dormitory the seven years I was there. There were, oh, mercy—I would say there were around thirty or thirty-five children in the dorm. We were all upstairs in a big hall. It had a little room leading off it. It was a big hall, and it had a big center where we met, and that's where the matron would come up every night and we'd all congregate out in that hall, on the floor, and we'd have our prayers, our evening prayers. And, then we'd all go into our individual rooms. Of course, there were two. They were not private rooms. Two of us to a room.

BAKER: Please talk about your days at Goodland, the foods you ate and the work the students did, the tribal memberships of the students, friends you made then and later.

MCKINNEY: The best I can remember [is that] the majority of the students, I would say I believe all of them, were Choctaws, but I could be wrong. And the teachers were white and Indian and . . . I guess that's about the extent of our teachers. They were, most of them white, but . . . our superintendent was Bailey Springs, who was fullblood Choctaw. And we spoke English. I still have friends in Durant, who went to Goodland, who speak Choctaw fluently. And we could speak Choctaw if we knew how, but we didn't practice Choctaw. I wish we had. We took the basic classes: writing, reading, and arithmetic and English and . . . I remember spelling and learning to read.

I know we got up early in the morning; our matron would come around and she'd ring a bell. And we all got up and dressed. And we all went up to what we called "the Main Building," which had a sidewalk which was quite long, and everybody lined up on that sidewalk and we did exercise for maybe twenty or thirty minutes. Then we went in for breakfast and we had prayer again. And then from breakfast, we went back to our rooms and prepared ourselves for school. We should have already been prepared, but there was always something to do back at the buildings, at the dormitories. From there, we went to an assembly, and our superintendent spoke to us for just a few minutes, and then everybody was dismissed to go to classes.

For breakfast we had . . . nice biscuits, every morning. And we had, sometimes we had cereal, but a lot of times we had hot bacon grease and we would mix that with our cereal. We very rarely had butter. And we used the bacon grease on our biscuits, which were homemade. They were good. They were made there. And at noon . . . the seven years I went there, I think, every day at noon we had red beans, and I think, well, maybe that's why I like them so well today.

BAKER: Where did the food come from?

MCKINNEY: Well, Goodland produced most of their food. We had a dairy and we had fresh food, and they had their own hogs. They taught the boys how to take care of all that. And the girls had to work in the laundry. The first few years I was considered too small to work in the laundry, but the last year I went there I was assigned to the laundry to fold clothes. But everybody's name was marked on their clothing, and you had to be awfully careful when you folded a garment—you knew whose name was on there and what building it went to. All of us had our . . . we called it "details." You were given details every month, and of a morning when we got up, we had to make our bed and we all had little single beds, and they were the iron, little iron bed, looked kind of like what we'd call a cot today, but it's the kind that the legs would fold under. We were all allowed to have our footlockers, our little trunks, whatever, in our room. And we had a little closet. And when you went back to your room after breakfast, and if your cover was thrown back off the bed, you knew that Saturday you had what we called a demerit, and you walked a bull ring for how many hours they gave you for not doing your bed right. And they would open your trunk, and everything had to be organized. Your socks were in one place. Your underwear and everything were folded, and if it wasn't, you got another demerit.

We had a huge furnace in our, the small girl's dormitory. And one year, I've forgotten what month it was. I know it was real cold. Another girl and I were detailed to bring the firewood in, and the boys would cut the wood and rick it in the back, oh, outside the school, outside of our dormitory, but we had to bring it in to the basement. The furnace was in the basement. And we built a pretty good fire one night. We threw the logs on there and we forgot to turn the damper, and we all had to leave the building, that night. It filled with smoke and got too hot. And of course, I thought, "Oh, mercy. I'm going to get expelled." But the boys all came over. The building didn't really burn; it was just the stairs that got awfully hot that we had to walk down to get out of the building. They put rugs down on the hot steps. But it all worked out.

We had to keep our own building. We had to dust. That was one of our details, too. But our matron, Mrs. Nanny Riddle, our matron gave us [our work assignments]. They would rotate your details. Some of the girls would do the dusting, upstairs. Some of the girls did the banisters, which led downstairs to the floor where the matron lived. And Jimmy Belvin, who was the principal chief of the Choctaws for twenty years, or thirty . . . I've forgotten how long he was . . . twenty years I believe. He and Mrs. Belvin lived on the bottom floor, too. Jimmy Belvin taught while I was there. I really can't remember what Jimmy taught. I don't know. And they had a daughter, Louise, and she has moved back to Durant. She lives in Durant now.

We had a certain time to do our work. Like we cleaned our rooms every morning [when] we got up. When the matron sounded that bell, you bounded out of bed, and you got your clothes on, and you started putting things up and making up your bed. And then we got back from breakfast, we had to go to the basement. But we did have a lavatory in there where we could brush our teeth. And that's when we got through and went on to school. But through the day at different times, you would be detailed to do your detail work. We had outside work. We didn't get out of any classes. Usually, we did the work in the afternoons when we got out of school.

The work and discipline are also described in an address delivered by the adult Frank J. Self, who was a student in the 1930s. It was published in the alumna newsletter published by the Goodland Presbyterian Children's Home. Mr. Self describes the "Bull Ring": "It was a large square rectangle out in the middle of campus. If you committed certain infractions of the rules, you would be given one or more demerits. Each demerit equaled one hour walking around the bull Ring." Mr. Self goes on to describe the work of raising the food for the school on "180 acres of Boggy Bottom land which the students first cleared":

> I don't believe that any farm boy or girl worked harder or longer than we did. I remember one summer the boys picked and the girls canned 2000 gallons each of string beans and tomatoes. Oh lord how I hated canned to-matoes! To this day I have never eaten them. I don't believe that work hurt a single Goodland student. In fact, I think it helped to build self-pride in a job well done. It gave us something tangible to see as the result of our labor: acres and acres of corn, beans, sweet and Irish potatoes, peanuts, apples,

grapes, peaches, pears. How beautiful it was to be surrounded by all that
food we ourselves helped to raise.[31]

While Mother also talked about the bull ring and the campus, Mother had to
walk the bull ring only once. She said, "I had better things to do with my time."
As I was growing up, Mother required her children to be on time or early for
events, as she had been trained to do at Goodland. No "Indian Time" for her!
She also taught me and my sisters how to fold clothes and dust as she had been
taught at Goodland.

> BAKER: Please describe the campus.
>
> MCKINNEY: We had a regular building that was . . . We had a, what was called,
> "The Little Girl's Building," that I was in, and then the next building was for
> teenagers, and then they had the main building where the older girls stayed
> there. That's where the superintendent had his office, and we had a little store
> there that sold candies. It was just open during some part of the day. I mean,
> every day it was open at the same time, just for a few minutes. And they had a
> reception room and a piano. And the laundry was between two of these build-
> ings, and that's where they did all the laundry. And they had huge tables, that
> when the clothes were dry, then the ones who were detailed to fold clothes. . . .
> Had to fold them there. And then every . . . every Sunday Rev. Fireball, who was
> our preacher, had church on campus. Mrs. Fireball and our pastor had two sons,
> Robert and I can't remember that other one's name. But they lived just a short
> way . . . They lived on campus, but it was up a little way from our building.
> Rev. Fireball could have been Indian. He looked kind of like it, but I can't
> remember. But they had been workers. He had been a preacher among the Indi-
> ans for years and years. The school was a Presbyterian school.

Mother also described the games they played.

> MCKINNEY: Of course, I was quite a tomboy—played baseball if we could find a
> ball and a bat. We used sticks for bats. And we played house at the edge of the
> woods. We would put rocks to divide the rooms, and we had a "big room" and
> bedrooms, and a kitchen. One game we played was dangerous, I know now. The
> big kids would bend down a small tree, a sapling I think it is called. Then a little
> kid would grab on tight, and the tree would be let go and it would whip back
> and forth.

When Mother told me about the tree game, I asked "what if you got hurt or became sick?" She answered, "You didn't get hurt or sick. If you did, they took you away and you didn't come back." Mother said that Goodland had no health-care facility during the years she attended. Students who needed health care were taken to Talihina to the tuberculosis sanitarium. Such students didn't come back to Goodland. Angie Debo discusses the presence of tuberculosis in the Choctaw Nation in the early twentieth century and says:

> The last session of the Choctaw council requested that a tract of tribal land
> be set aside at Talihina and that $50,000 in tribal funds be appropriated to
> erect a tubercular sanitorium there, with the understanding that its subse-
> quent maintenance be provided by the United States. Congress accordingly
> made the appropriation of Choctaw-Chickasaw money, and the institution
> was opened for the citizens of the two tribes in 1916. It was an excellent
> sanitorium, but it never became popular with the Indians, and had very little
> influence in checking the ravages of the disease.[32]

As an Elder during the 1990s, Mother was on the Choctaw Health Board, serving for a time as chair. The health board oversaw the building of a large $27-million debt-free hospital in Talihina. The health board met in the old tuberculosis sanitarium. Mother said she thought of the Goodland children every time she entered that building. Later in the 1930s as part of the Works Progress Administration (WPA) program, a health clinic was built at Goodland. Mother's work for health care is just one consequence of her years at Goodland that resulted in her strengthened tribal identity, resulted in her determination in overcoming the hardships, and motivated her in working for the common good of the Choctaw tribe.

Mother's work for the hospital was also a part of her sense of women's power and responsibility—women helping other women and their tribes. Such work is the continuation of responsibility that comes with power—the traditional power of women that they were born into precontact and held on to in varying degrees in the five hundred years that followed. Women such as my mother also passed on the sensibility of power and responsibility to their descendants, as they talked about tribal history, taught courtesy protocols, showed how to form networks, and, in my mother's case, made sure her children and other Choctaws were enrolled members of the tribe.

My husband, Tom, and I went to the dedication of the Choctaw Nation Health Care Center in 1999, and the event was splendid. A BIA representative attended, dressed in a white Navy dress uniform. The Oklahoma chapter of the

Indian Masons was there. State politicians, tribal elders, preachers, tribal coun-
cilmen, local town leaders, tribal members—all came that hot summer day.
Young Choctaw men and women dressed in khaki pants and golf shirts guided
the immense crowd. The event was very well organized, and people were happy.
Health care had come to an area of Oklahoma where before it had been all but
absent for American Indians. Mother sat at the head table and remembered the
children she had known at Goodland: the children who had been sent away and
never returned.

The Choctaw Nation Health Care Center is a consequence of knowing
about the hardships of life without good health care, and the remedies for
those hardships provided by the tribe. Memories of hardships motivate tribal
members to work so that tribal members may enjoy prosperity and the advan-
tages of American life along with other Americans. Mother's work exemplifies
her power and dedication, both in working for tribal survival and in working
for tribal health care.

Mother was also aware of the many orphans who came to Goodland Academy
and Indian Orphanage. Allotment had torn up families, leaving orphans who
needed care. She talked about that.

MCKINNEY: There were a lot of children there who were orphaned. Their grandparents had them. They thought it best they be put in Goodland, where they
could have supervision, and the grandparents wanted the children to be educated in, I guess you could say, the white people's world. So they would know
how to survive. But then there was a lot who had parents that just wanted their
children to come there.

[Educationally] it was a wonderful experience. It's a terrible thing that children have to be away from their parents, but it gave you an independence that
you learn to look after yourself when you had to, and we had little ones there
who were almost too small to be there. We had one boy, I can't remember if he
was four, five, or six, but a taxicab drove up and left him at the gate and went on
back to town. And he lives in Durant now; he is a very good friend of ours. He's
just a wonderful person. But everybody helped him. You know. We showed him
what to do and where to go.

I, too, knew the little boy as an adult in Durant. He attended our family funerals as a part of Mother's Goodland family. Mother believed that the Goodland
educational experience benefited the children in that it taught them independence. Mother also required that I learn independence, as in this story from my
childhood: At Christmas I received a tether ball, and it hung on a pole in the

backyard. Two neighborhood boys would not let me play with it. They laughed at me, threatened to hit me, and drove me away and back into the house. Finally, my mother went into the yard and brought a stick to me. She told me to use the stick to drive the boys away from my toy, or she would spank me. I did drive the boys away and took control of my ball. Although I didn't know it, Mother watched from the carport, I suppose to rescue me if necessary. Still, I grew up with a sense of independence.

This sense of independent strength is a part of Indigenous women's power. And this Indigenous sensibility differs from the white interest in power of the 1960s, which stressed the individual. Within Indigenous women's power, the individual takes care of herself with aid from others, and also works in cooperation with others to help those in need and to help the tribe in general. This is not an abstract theory but rather a lived behavior.

Mother Geraldine's interview also included information about the summertime and indirectly describes the family fragmentation that resulted from allotment, and how women helped one another.

MCKINNEY: We went home in summer from school, but Mama had to work, and that meant that she had to find a way to take care of us. Beatrice stayed with our Grandmother Lena in Bokchito. Lodie stayed with our grandfather, Old Man Hull, on his ranch. Old Man Hull still owned and worked his allotment at that time. He raised cotton. On the Dawes Roll, he is listed as a white Indian. After Mama got a job in Durant in a photographer's studio, she lived in a boarding house, and got paid in money. There wasn't a place for me at the boarding house, so during the summertime when there was no school at Goodland for the boarders, I stayed with Papa Hull's Choctaw relatives—aunts, cousins. They were good to me.

Some summers I stayed with a fullblood cousin who lived in a house off First Street in Durant. Her house had two bedrooms, so I had a room. She was very kind, but there were strict rules about what I could and could not do. The major rule at Cousin's house was that I was not to clean up in the kitchen. I would be served my meals, and, of course, I wanted to be helpful, so she would like me and let me stay close to Mama. One time I cleaned up after eating, but I didn't do that again. I was allowed to pass through the kitchen, but I was not to touch anything.

You see, Cousin was a bootlegger, but I was not supposed to know. Cousin kept her jars of wildcat covered with dishtowels in the kitchen, and she didn't want me to mess with the bootleg product. Mounds and mounds of lumpy dishtowels covered every available surface in Cousin's kitchen. Customers would come to the back steps, and she would sell the jars out the back door.

Times were hard. She was very kind to me. I never let on that I knew what she did for a living. We never talked about it.

I heard this story for the first time immediately after Cousin Bootlegger's funeral, while Mother and I waited for the funeral procession to form. That afternoon she drove me to the house where Cousin Bootlegger had lived and pointed out the window to her room and the backdoor for the customers.

The children with families went home for Christmas, and Mother talked about that, too.

MCKINNEY: Most every Christmas we did [go home for Christmas]. We'd have . . . It was according to what day of the week Christmas fell on. And we would be out, maybe, a day or two before Christmas and then back the following week for school.

As I continued to talk with Mother about Goodland, I asked her about runaways. Of course, as at most boarding schools, children ran away and the older ones sneaked out of campus for country dances. Mother's brother, Lodi, was one of the runaways.

MCKINNEY: My brother, Lodi, left school and . . . well, he decided he just was going home to Grandpa. He knew my mother was living in Caddo, Oklahoma, and at the time, Grandpa lived ten miles east of Caddo, in the country, and that's who Lodi had always lived with. So, he took off and . . . But they caught him before he ever got to the highway. He didn't get more than three or four miles.

BAKER: Did you go out to dances that I have heard about?

MCKINNEY: And, yes, they had country dances around Goodland. Of course I'd never go. I was too scared to get out of the building after dark. And I was too young anyway, but the older boys and girls would slip out. Of course, we all knew it, but no one dared tell anybody.

Mother also talked about the social fabric at Goodland.

MCKINNEY: Some of the fullbloods were real good friends of mine, but you get all the fullbloods together, and they all spoke Choctaw. And I didn't speak Choctaw fluently. I could say hello and goodbye. Hello, how are you is *Halito! Chim Achukma.* Then we learned a little song in Choctaw, and our music teacher taught us that, but she was fullblood white. She was a *na hollo,* that is a white person. And she didn't know how to speak Choctaw either. And I can't remember who taught us that song. But she had to have help, because she didn't know any more than I did about Choctaw. I remember the song. My voice has changed considerably since then.

Mother then sang a hymn in Choctaw that she had learned, and which she sang to me during my childhood. The language was so important to her that for more than sixty years she sang the song to herself so that she would remember the Choctaw language. This assault on and resulting loss of Native languages runs as a thread through American Indian literature. Diane Glancy, for example, published a poem, "Death Cry for the Language," which contains these two lines: "On that cold morning in the boarding school / they lined up the language to be shot."[33] Currently when on hold during a phone call to Choctaw Nation, one can listen to songs sung in Choctaw. This is a part of the cultural revival movement going on in Indian country. I like it that my mother's work with the tribe helped make that revival possible, as is reflected in my mother's story.

After singing the Choctaw song, Mother started talking about the summertime and living with her mother Maud, after Maud rented an apartment that was big enough for her two girls.

MCKINNEY: But in the summer, she [Geraldine's mother, Maud] worked. She had to work all the time. And she always had a pretty nice, little apartment, close to where she worked. And my brother never did stay with us. Very seldom he stayed with us, in the summer. He always stayed out on the farm with my grandfather. And Beatrice and I stayed in Durant, and since she was older, she was in command, while Mama was gone.

BAKER: (laughing) Did she command you?

MCKINNEY: She did her best (laughs). And we did the housework and the cooking and the washing and ironing and did all the chores for Mama. We had been taught that at Goodland. And that is something I have never regretted, going to Goodland, because they did teach us how to do and what to do, and so it didn't hurt me. In fact, I have friends who had been quite a success in life, so I'm sure, Goodland, we all thought, was a wonderful school.

After Lafe ran off with the dressmaker, and many years had passed, Maud divorced Lafe. In 1928, she married John Williams, a law enforcement official in Durant, and Mother returned to live with her family, which included a new little sister and brother, the children of John Williams. Mother described her emotions at this time.

MCKINNEY: The first year I was at Goodland, I guess I cried every night I was there. And then the second year, you begin to taper off, not that you didn't want to go home or you didn't want to see your folks, but you had your friends. And the last year I went to school at Goodland, I just couldn't wait to get back. And then when I went home, the last summer, my mother told me that she thought that she and Daddy [Williams], that they had made arrangements for me to live with them. And, of course, then I cried because I couldn't go back to Goodland.

The boarding schools changed marriage patterns, as Mother describes.

MCKINNEY: There was a Winnie, who was a music teacher from Boswell, Oklahoma, and Paul, who was a cousin of my daddy's [Lafe], was a student there, and they married. And, yes, there has been just lots of students who married one another there at Goodland. And they were from different towns. And that's where they met one another.

As an adult, Mother continued to see some of her Goodland friends and made friends from other boarding schools. I asked her about the other boarding school students she knew.

MCKINNEY: I have friends living in Tuskahoma now that, in fact we visited them over Labor Day. And she works at the hospital there at Choctaw Indian Nation Hospital in Talihina. And you just run into everyone. The BIA, Bureau of Indian Affairs in Talihina, when I go up there, I don't know that any of them are still there but, several years back when I was working with Choctaw Nation, I met an awful lot of kiddos from Goodland. In fact, there's a retired teacher in Durant now, Doris Smith from Antlers, who went to school at Bacone. And then, by the way, she graduated from Northeastern.

Goodland didn't cost anything for Choctaws. My father, Lafe Hull, was on the Dawes Commission rolls; he had a roll number, and all these years I have used it. If you have your mother or daddy or your grandfather or grandmother, any relative who was on the Dawes Commission, you are eligible to use that roll number. Like you, you use my daddy's roll number.

Still, a constant was that the children at Goodland were learning the white way, good and bad as Mother had said, "So they would know how to survive." Alma Hogan Snell recounts her sister's explanation to her Grandmother Pretty Shield: "At school, they will teach her how to make a living, and when you're gone, she'll need that."[34] The Cherokees also thought that to be educated in the "white people's world" was necessary for survival. Devon A. Mihesuah writes about this:

> In 1843, there were five hundred students enrolled in the eleven schools and they were taught by two Cherokees and nine whites. That same year the National Council authorized the building of seven more common schools. Noncitizens living in Cherokee Nation were not allowed to attend Cherokee schools, but they could enroll in the mission schools. They also had their own "subscription schools."
>
> The success of many mixed blood merchants convinced Cherokees who had been reluctant to send their children to school that education could help them rise from "ignorance to intelligence" and from "obscurity to distinction." Others believed that the "white man's education" would help their children become "qualified for any business in life, whether civil or political."[35]

Mihesuah goes on, "The progressive Cherokees certainly did not believe themselves 'primitive' and were determined to prove it by making their tribe a model of white society. These progressives wanted an educational system in order to 'uplift' the entire tribe, including poor full-bloods and some mixed-bloods, whom they considered to be 'unenlightened' and uninformed.'"[36] Mihesuah notes that in 1847, "Chief Ross and the executive council selected the sites for the schools [a female and a male seminary] and contracted for the construction of both buildings. They decided to build the Female Seminary at Park Hill, two miles south of Tahlequah, and the male institution two miles to the southwest."[37] Both of the Cherokee male and female seminaries were tribal boarding schools.

While the mission and federal boarding schools were established to erase Native American identity and values, K. Tsianina Lomawaima presents interviews from students who attended the Chilocco Indian Agricultural School, a federal off-reservation boarding school, and says something very different happened:

> The fact that schools often strengthened rather than dissolved tribal identity is not the only surprise tucked within alumni reminiscence. The idealized school society envisioned in federal policy often bore little resemblance to reality. Federal practice in the schools more frequently subverted the idealism of policy than supported it.[38]

Later Lomawaima comments about the resilience of the students in much the same way that my mother, Geraldine Hull McKinney, did when she said it was different for everybody. Lomawaima says, "Yet, boarding-school students had the resilience of children, and in many cases found happiness in their surroundings. Some people hated and endured their boarding-school years; others hated and did not endure; they ran away. Some count their years away at school among the happiest and most carefree of their lives."[39]

In Lomawaima's interviews, some of the women talk about what they learned that helped them later, both in their own homes and in their public working lives. A Cherokee says, "My mother was a very ambitious sort of person and wanted us all to be educated and to learn, but we were able to learn things up there that we would not have learned in grade school, in public school."[40] Ellen, a Creek, says, "I think that Home Ec did [good], especially the sewing class. You know that's the way I make my spending money. I sew all the time, and I worked in sewing factories like [when] I lived in Los Angeles, and worked in those factories and that helped me a whole lot."[41]

My mother Geraldine was a very optimistic and humorous person, always making lemonade from the lemons life had given her as a child. Alma Hogan Snell remarks that "we never talked about it. We were too shamed. We wanted to forget it."[42] I do not believe that my mother Geraldine felt shame, but I do believe she wanted to forget, and I know that her pain at the separation from her mother colored her life. When I was two years old and my older sister six years old in 1950, Mother drove to California by herself with us to find out how her Mother Maud was faring. Maud had married for the third time and had gone with her new husband to work the fields in California. A few years after that, Maud returned to Oklahoma with her husband, first living in Calera, and then after she became a widow, she moved to Durant and lived next door to us into old age. Mother always treated her mother Maud with great care and love, trying I think to make Maud's last years more comfortable and more filled with family affection and love than her years as a young, abandoned mother had been. Maud was a wonderful grandmother, but she was always gently sad.

When Mother returned from Goodland after her seven years there as a student, she lived for several years with her mother Maud and her stepfather, John Williams. John became sheriff of Bryan County, and then on November 4, 1938, he was killed in a car accident while he was returning to Durant after transporting a prisoner to the state penitentiary. Maud was asked by the county commissioners to serve out the rest of John's term as sheriff, and she did. This allowed her to care for her own children and John Williams's two children.

My Mother Geraldine graduated from Durant High School and went to work at the Bryan County welfare office established by President Roosevelt. In No-

Geraldine McKinney and her husband, Raymond McKinney. Courtesy of Terri McKinney Baker.

vember 1941, one month before Pearl Harbor was bombed, Geraldine married Raymond McKinney, the son of the second white family to settle in McCurtain County, Oklahoma. Raymond served as a glider pilot in the European theater during World War II. Geraldine was transferred from the Bryan County welfare office to Washington, D.C., where she worked at the Pentagon. Before Raymond left for Europe, Geraldine followed Raymond to various training facilities in the United States. When the war ended, Geraldine and Raymond made their lives in Durant, in a house on West Evergreen, which had been purchased by Geraldine and Maud in the late 1930s. Geraldine and Raymond had three daughters. I am the middle daughter.

Mother and Daddy at various times owned three restaurants in Durant, the last being the White House Café on Main Street. They created middle-class lives and provided their children with the perks available to that socioeconomic class. In the 1950s, on their way to shows in Texas, Bob Wills and the Texas Playboys would stop and eat at the McKinney twenty-four-hour café in Durant, the TC Lunch Room. The front booth at the TC Lunch served as the Bryan County office for Carl Albert, the forty-sixth Speaker of the U.S. House of Representatives, when he was running for office—and the bootleggers used it, too, meeting for breakfast after they came in from their runs to Texas. Mother was determined to overcome the poverty she had known, become middle class, and enjoy the benefits of being an American. Daddy complied with her wishes to become more "respectable," finally selling the bars he owned, and in later life becoming the chairman for life of the Durant City Hospital Board.

During my childhood, I took piano, dance, and voice lessons. We camped out at Lake Texoma. Mother danced around the kitchen to country western swing music, gave bottled Coca-Cola to the city trash collectors, helped with Bluebirds and Campfire Girls, and worked with my father in the White House Café, which she co-owned. And my parents helped people, employing American Indians in their cafe and employing people abandoned by families and society as waitresses, ranch hands, handymen, bookkeepers, accountants, drivers. Such people were a part of my childhood. This, too, is a part of American Indian women's power, which includes helping the vulnerable. Their generosity included helping a basketball team whose bus broke down in Durant. The team had no money, and so spent the night on our floor and ate meals brought over from the White House Café.

During those years when I was working on graduate degrees, Mother and I lived our separate lives, and I did not fully understand her involvement with the Choctaw tribe until after her death, when I inherited her papers. What I found often left me breathless. Mother's papers tell a story of the Choctaw governmental revival, which today, as I write, brings in millions and millions of dollars that fund the Indian Health Service Hospital in Talihina, many health-care clinics, travel plazas, a technologically focused production company supplying parts to a high-tech company in Texas, a tourist industry, assisted living centers, housing, rehabilitation, food assistance, summer youth programs, and educational assistance. The extensive list of programs reflects all the elements a community needs to thrive. This financial progress began in the mid-1970s, pursuant to significant governmental reform.

In 1971, the Five Civilized Tribes—Choctaw, Cherokee, Creek, Chickasaw, Seminole—began to elect their own chiefs directly by means of a regulation established by the Bureau of Indian Affairs. Previously their chiefs were appointed by the president of the United States.

When Fred Harris was in the Senate, he introduced a bill to provide that the enrolled members of each of the Five Civilized Tribes would elect their chiefs. Only after he left the Senate was the election legislation passed.[43]

Jimmy Belvin, Mother's former house parent at Goodland, had been appointed by the president as principal chief in 1948, selected and approved by the president of the United States, and remained in office for the next twenty-seven years. During his tenure, Chief Belvin "with the help from Speaker [of the House] Carl Albert of Bugtussle, finally ended the policy of termination and inaugurated numerous programs for the tribe, including public housing, community health programs, founded an industrial park on tribal lands, renovated the Choctaw council House and grounds at Tushkahoma, procured an adult Indian Education Program through the Bureau of Indian Affairs, established a culture center and a museum, built three Indian clinics, and other things."[44]

Then in 1971, Jimmy Belvin was elected principal chief when the challenger

David Gardner was disqualified because of an age requirement. Controversy surrounded Chief Belvin's last years in office. David Gardner ran again in 1975, winning, and then Chief Gardner began an economic revival of the nation. He also
founded *Hello Choctaw*, which later became the tribal newspaper, the *Biskinik*.[45]
David Gardner died in January 1978.

My mother and I talked about her work with the Choctaws, and in 1995, I
asked her to write what she had been telling me. She did write it down. In my
mother Geraldine's papers is a handwritten note, which is then typed and dated
1996. It reads, "When Chief David Gardner died [in 1978], a group of men from
the BIA office in Talihina came to our home and asked me to serve as chairman
to bring up our enrollment of the Choctaw Nation according to the CDIB record which is in the Dawes Commission records. I was employed for three or
four months."[46]

Beginning in 1978, my mother Geraldine further developed and expanded the
Choctaw voting rolls. She was enabled in her task by her membership in organizations in the Oklahoma Federation of Women's Clubs, the Ohoyohoma Club
(Choctaw women's club), and the Democratic Federated Women's Club. She
was also a member of the First Presbyterian Church in Durant. Mother knew
many people in Oklahoma. She developed coalitions. Her friends knew other
people, and the network grew. In my mother's papers, I found a copy of the *Constitution of the Democratic Party of Oklahoma*, *The Club Woman's Handbook of
Parliamentary Law*, the Choctaw constitution, and *The Ohoyohoma Club Year-
book*. Clearly, she learned how to run a meeting and what the rules were, and she
used the books for research.

Over the next eighteen years, Mother worked or volunteered for the Choctaw Nation on the hospital board and chaired the board of trustees for the
Choctaw Hope Development Corporation. She also chaired the Choctaw Nation Senior Citizens Lunch Program. She served on the Choctaw Nation Election Board.[47]

In 1978, Mother began to work with the Choctaws as registrar, using the
Dawes Rolls to find the enrollment number of those Choctaws who came to
the Choctaw offices to register to vote. She worked for several years to enable
the Choctaw people to participate in determining their own political process.
One story demonstrates the trust in which she was held. Old Mrs. Pitchlynn
came to vote. She was blind and requested that Geraldine help her. My mother
Geraldine said to Mrs. Pitchlynn, "I will read exactly what is on the ballot and
mark it as you say to do." Mrs. Pitchlynn said, "I know you will. That is why I
asked for you." At one point Geraldine acted as the Choctaw Nation district elec-

tion chairperson for the Durant area in Bryan County, which entailed collecting the ballot box and transporting it to Tushkahoma, in the southeast corner of Oklahoma. During contentious elections, Mother drove and Daddy rode shotgun, literally, as he carried a loaded shotgun with them in the car.

Mother also believed that the Choctaws constituted a voting block and worked to encourage people to vote in all elections. Mother lived her American Indian women's responsibility, helping and empowering women, the tribe, and people outside the Choctaw tribe who had often been abandoned by their families and the larger society. She did this quietly. This is the manifestation of American Indian women's power and resilience.

American Indian women's power differs from white women's power in clear ways. One is that Native women and some men engage in activism in recovering specific traditions. Some recover tribal history and some research and teach in universities in American Indian Studies programs. Other tribal members also work to preserve the languages, to encourage healthy food preparation, to research farming habits and Indigenous food production. Some work in American Indian politics. Native people also work on knowing more about their identity. They nurture and treasure Indian identity, as in the case of boarding school students like my mother, who as adults teach their children about tribal identity.

Powerful American Indian women learn about Native American history, and they also learn how to navigate the white world to benefit tribal people. Some women also tend to become educated in the white way. The American Indian women survive the almost constant battles, partly because of a profoundly active sense of humor. Laughter is truly a force that leads them on. We have retained our identities as American Indians and will continue to retain them, not because to do so is easy, but because to do so is simply who we are. The struggle is difficult but continues. Clara Sue Kidwell makes this clear in her scholarship when she notes, "The Choctaw Nation has survived the vagaries of federal policy and some of its members have preserved the language, customs, and land that were the core of its identity in 1855. Its adaptability has and will sustain it in the future."[48] To deny our identities is just absurd. It is fundamentally important for Americans to learn about American history, which begins and continues with American Indians.

CHAPTER TWO
MY OWN STORY
TERRI MCKINNEY BAKER

With this poem, I invite you to consider the complexities of living as a powerful,
Native American woman in Indian Country.

Medicine Man Blues
—Terri M. Baker

I live in a town
Where a medicine man
Sings the blues.
He wails for us all
For pain we fear to know
     Lest it consume us.
His is the voice of
Mothers crying for
Children taken
     By crack—by alcohol, by war,
     By diabetes which
       Eats a piece at a time.
He howls our pain for the
     Friend blinded by a
Three-month lead on an
Appointment,
Tradition,
And
       A long line at Indian Health Care.
He moans for us all—
     For
       Loss of power,
       Lack of respect,

For

      Stabs of

      Discourtesy that

      Knife our souls

           Quietly and eternally.

I live in a town

Where a medicine man

Sings the blues.

Blues welling up from

    Earth

        And

        Dripping

        Ancient

        Blood.

I live in a town

Where a medicine man

    Sings the blues—

He wears a skinny brim hat

    And sparkly shoes.

I live in a town

Where a medicine man

Sings the blues—

    For me

And I am

    For a while

    Cleansed.

I live in a town

Where a medicine man

Sings the blues.

Yokoke

    Thank you.

Yo Ko Ke

    I regret.

I live in a town

Where a holy man

Sings the blues.[1]

My mother, Geraldine Hull McKinney, taught me that passing on responsibility, skills, worldview, identity awareness, network building, and coalition development is fundamental to Native American women's power. This female legacy acts to ensure tribal survival. The passing on of these behaviors and knowledge may occur within a family or among nonfamily members in a tribe. So it is that my mother Geraldine passed on to me responsibility to work for the tribe and other American Indians. Indeed, when Mother was quite elderly, she told me that she was too old to carry on and that now I must take up the work. I agreed. This chapter recounts how I lived out that agreement.

My work differed from the work of my mother. For me, the work had enlarged from working for the tribe to working for American Indian people in general. Because I "went out" (from Oklahoma) for my education, as my mother put it, my work eventually became the work of a scholar. I worked to learn about and then to educate people about American Indians.

I entered college in 1966, and in 1969 I graduated from Southeastern State College in Durant, Oklahoma. During those years as an undergraduate, I was active in a number of campus activities—theater and sorority are the ones I remember. After the first year finding the sorority too elitist and too snobbish to endure, I resigned. The civil rights movement was going on even in Durant, and I was active in spreading information about voting by posting flyers in convenience stores where African Americans were known to shop. I always knew I was a feminist because it just made so much sense to me. My mother and father were business partners, engaged in civic activity, and had encouraged me to get an education and move into the professional world. But as I recall, there was little support for feminism beyond my family, and I do not remember using the word. I do not recall any feminist activities on campus.

My family remained in Durant, Oklahoma, where I was born in 1948 and where my family owned a local restaurant. After high school graduation from Durant High School, I married unwisely. I attended Southeastern State College in Durant and graduated. Several years later, my husband demanded that I quit graduate school and my job to stay home and be a good wife. I divorced him. We had no children.

Later I learned that Wilma Mankiller had a similar experience in her first marriage, though she had two daughters. Because she lived in San Francisco, she became friends with a wide variety of American Indians. That opportunity would come to me after I began working at Northeastern State University, which drew many American Indians to its campus during the annual Symposium on the American Indian.

Like Wilma, I was interested in transforming our culture, and I went at it in ways available to me, much like Wilma went at it in ways available to her. This is an important point in how men and women pursue their goals. When I attended graduate school in Baton Rouge at Louisiana State University, my graduate group taught me that men usually act professionally, guided by their mentors, who may be professors or fathers or business associates. Women, I noticed back then, often acted in place, seizing the opportunities available to them where they lived with husbands, brothers, families. Over the years I have watched that change gradually, as more women have gained power in the American system. Women have now formed networks.

During the occupation of Alcatraz and the battle at the second Wounded Knee, I was envious of the participation of American Indians who were more activist than I, but following the instructions of my mother and Chief Jimmy Belvin, I continued to try to figure it all out. Whatever "it all" meant! *All*, I came to know, meant being American Indian in a country essentially occupied by Europeans who held all the power. Simple, direct. We live in a complicated world. For tribal people in the United States, it is an occupied world. Wilma and I talked about that briefly after she came to Seminary Hall at Northeastern State University in 2009.

Long before that, however, Wilma was important to me, and she hovered at the edge of my mind as I lived on Lake Oologa near Claremore. Beginning in 1982, I worked in Tulsa at an art museum that showcased its European art and housed its internationally known American Indian Art in a gallery on the lower level, which had been a basement. I learned a great deal. I saw American Indian artists insulted, patronized, and ignored. Once a colleague who had been recently at Harvard University asked me where all the Indians in Oklahoma were. "Well," I replied, "one of them is sitting here talking to you." He sat in silence. But I knew what he meant. American Indians are still supposed to speak broken English, wear buckskin clothes, feathers, faces with painted designs, and say "How!" A Choctaw with a PhD and a wide vocabulary creates paradigm dissonance. In 1987, I accepted a professorial position at Northeastern State University in Tahlequah, Oklahoma, and moved there with my husband and baby. There I began to create paradigm dissonance combined with lots of laughter. My life began to change, as Wilma's life had already changed.

Let me tell you how I got there. I did one year of graduate school at Oklahoma State University, and while there I joined with the few other feminists to talk and attended one consciousness-raising session, during which a man lectured us. I never returned to the consciousness-raising group, being already conscious. I also joined a protest against the war in Vietnam one night as I was studying in my graduate office. The doors slammed open, and a voice called out, "We're here to protest the war. Are you with us or against us?" I waited, heard office doors slamming all up and down the hall, and watched as lights reflected on the lawn outside went out. A man stood in my door and said again, "Are you with us or against us?" I replied, "I'm with you." So I closed my book, got up, and joined them as they marched to the ROTC building next door. Oh, we sang a song or two, stood around for a bit, and then left. I still own the first issue of *Ms. Magazine*, which I purchased at Oklahoma State University, which was a very conservative campus with very few students who were politically active at all. I had lived in Denver briefly after college graduation, had attended antiwar protests there, and had declined an invitation to join a city commune when I noticed that the women did all the work and the men sat around getting stoned and being cool. That was not for me.

After a year at Oklahoma State University, I followed my first husband to Salt Lake City, transferred to the University of Utah, and continued to work on my master's degree during 1972–1973 and the second Wounded Knee. At some point, there was a benefit pow wow on campus for Wounded Knee, and I attended alone. I had found no American Indian community at the university, and so had no connections. Some women behind me on the bleachers were laughing and talking about Oklahoma, calling it the Holy Land, I suppose because so many American Indians live there. Or the comment may have been sarcastic; American Indians can be contentious. I was moved by the calls for help for those at Wounded Knee, and I had been reading everything I could find about the movement. Later, after the pow wow, I phoned Mother and asked what I should do. She consulted our chief Jimmy Belvin and passed on the message that I was to go to graduate school and figure it out. I wasn't sure what that meant, but I did as she said.

Back in the mid-1970s, as far as I knew, there was only one school where I could study American Indian subjects, and it was out of my reach. Currently there are more opportunities to learn about American Indians in academic settings. In the 1970s, I was making it up as I went along. There were no courses in American Indian subjects in the English Department at the University of Utah, so I took Black American Literature and African Literature classes from Shelby Steele, and wrote my master's thesis and eventually my doctoral dissertation on the subject of John Milton's theological positions as expressed in his poetry. The classes with Shelby Steele taught me about the African American struggle in America. Other graduate classes taught me to focus, to read "professionally" things that were difficult to read, to consider how cultures connected or didn't connect, to research, to remember detail, to persevere. My sense of independence helped me ignore conventional approaches. Several years later, I discovered that my doctoral dissertation was written using an ethnohistorical methodology. At the time, I did not know what "ethnohistory" meant.

In 1981, when I earned a PhD in English from Louisiana State University, I was still figuring it out. There was a lot to figure out. Some of the mystery had to do with feminism, and some with American Indian identity. One of the really important things I learned is that you have to choose your battles. So many battles are offered. While at Louisiana State University I worked briefly for a group gathering data about financial credit for women. I discovered that married women could not get credit in their own names, even if they had jobs. I bought books at used bookstores in New Orleans relating to feminism, and I began to seek a community of feminists. There was no community of American Indians for me at LSU, at least not one I could find. Graduate study prepares a person for lifelong academic work. My parents had taught me that education was the way out of poverty and into the mainstream, and I was on my way to a career in the "academy," as it was so grandly called at LSU.

At LSU, my 1973 PhD reading list contained the names of nine women, including zero women who lived and wrote before 1800. Two African American writers were listed, zero American Indians, zero Hispanics, zero Asians. Yet, when asked what the general written PhD exam would cover, one of the women professors would reply grandly, "Literature." Even then, I knew they were challenged intellectually. My women friends and I called the reading list the list of "Dead White Men."

But I have to say that I understand. The professors at the university believed that Louisiana State University was "the Harvard of the South." They had been taught and did not question the notion that American culture was white. They believed without question that American history began only when Europeans invaded. For many in the South, the nobility of the Civil War was a given. There was even a fraternity on campus that, for an annual party, dressed in Confederate uniforms and escorted their antebellum-clad dates to a "ball." A graduate school associate once asked me "Terri, you are not a real Indian, are you?" I replied as a good Choctaw would, "My mother says I am." Choctaws are matrilineal.

Then, when I took my general written examination, a dust storm came in from the West. I believed it was my ancestors who had come to support me. I needed the support, because in a group of eight or nine taking the exam, I was the only woman. After completing the dissertation, I sat for the defense wearing a ribbon shirt and a feather in my long hair. I had experienced just about as much as I could take. The defense, which was supposed to last two hours, lasted about forty-five minutes. As each member questioned me, I would answer briefly and then point and say "Next." I recall being asked why I chose to study Milton. This was an invitation to a long scholarly answer. I answered, "He tells a good story. I wanted to find out what was in the minds of the English when they landed here. And boy did I find out. Next." But I passed. I think of this event as wrestling my committee to the ground and taking my PhD credential from the university.

Afterward I went to a party that lasted until four in the morning, and then I returned to Oklahoma. I had to return to Oklahoma after the defense, because I had moved back there even before finishing my dissertation. My husband, Tom Baker, had agreed to this. He really is an unusual man—secure, loving, and able to entertain himself. He once defended me when one of his colleagues, on being introduced to me by Tom, who had used his first name, said pompously "I am Dr. Smith." Without missing a beat, Tom (who also is entitled to be called "Dr."), replied, "Terri will receive her PhD in a few weeks, and then she will be Dr. McKinney." He is a keeper.

When we were living in Baton Rouge, after our marriage in 1978, I said to him one day, "We have to go back home." Tom said, "I thought we were home." "No," I replied, "Home is in Oklahoma." And so one summer, we sold everything and moved to Oklahoma. I tell my American Indian friends that I snagged Tom in Louisiana and brought him back to Oklahoma with me. Tom grew up in Florida, and in Oklahoma he had to learn to drive in the snow and ice. He slid into the yard once or twice. But just about everybody does.

As I grew up in Oklahoma, I think because of Mother's childhood experience of poverty at Christmas, she and Daddy provided a splendid Christmas celebration for us with a big natural cedar (juniper) tree with lights, decorations, and tinsel. Santa Claus came on Christmas Eve and left many presents. We left a slice of pecan pie and a coke for Santa. As I became an adult, the family celebrated with a big, rowdy party on Christmas Eve, where bootleg whiskey, tempered with maraschino cherries, was the traditional drink. Even Grandmother Maud had a glass of wine. When I took my future husband Tom home to meet my family in Oklahoma, I warned him not to take a pale cherry if somebody offered him one. But he did, and the family pronounced him acceptable and a good husband for me.

Tom loves Oklahoma storms and the vistas. We went to Choctaw meetings when visiting my family and once attended a political "speaking" in Colbert near the Red River. He seemed to be charmed. He was always very interested.

When we attended these events, I watched my mother work the room. She seemed to know everybody and assumed neutrality as much as possible. I learned from her. I also learned from Mattie, her boarding school "sister." One of the things that I have learned over the years is that geographical location is profoundly important to American Indians, even though they may not live in their historic homelands. They tend to visit tribal land areas, historic and modern. They tend to visit those areas where American Indian culture is evident. This is why I needed to return to Oklahoma, why I needed to go home. My husband Tom supported me in this.

In the beginning of our years of living in Oklahoma, in the early 1980s, Tom and I lived on Lake Oologah, west of Claremore, where Tom practiced optometry. I taught in public school, and after that I commuted to Tulsa, where I worked as a research assistant at the Philbrook Art Museum, as I mentioned earlier. I also taught part-time at Tulsa Junior College (now Tulsa Community College), and Northeastern State University in Tulsa. I was a "freeway flier."

During my three years at the Philbrook Museum, I worked in the non-Western Art department for art historian and Native American Art specialist Edwin L. Wade, and I met and worked with his wife, Carol Haralson, head of graphic design. I met Dr. Gloria Young, an ethnomusicologist. I also met Rennard Strickland after I purchased his book, *The Indians in Oklahoma*, which has an excellent bibliographic essay that helped me figure out what to do: using the sources listed by Strickland, I would research American Indians.

All these serendipitous meetings moved me along my life's path. Following my mother's example, I was building my network. Ed taught me about American Indian Art. Rennard and Ed taught me about research in American Indian subjects, and Carol taught me about nonacademic writing, editing, and publishing. They all gave me friendship and, I think, liked my willingness to learn. Ed and I often argued, and we all laughed a great deal.

I once asked Gloria Young what an ethnohistorian did. She said that ethnohistorians studied what nobody else wanted to study, as she did as an ethnomusicologist. Ethnohistorians research history and culture, as well as the events and literature and other arts that evolve from that history and culture. Gloria was correct in saying that very few people are ethnohistorians or ethnomusicologists. Such work requires a great deal of research and going "outside the box" of rigidly defined academic disciplines. So that is how I began at the Philbrook, using what I had learned about research from my work on John Milton and translating it to American Indian Studies with the help of my friends Ed, Carol, Rennard, and Gloria.

I once went on a road trip with Gloria to meet Theda Perdue, the famous historian who wrote books about Native Americans of the Southeast, at an ethnohistory conference in Bloomington, Indiana. We drove a university's forensic anthropology van, and I rested on the cadaver shelf, because I had hurt my back. We stopped at St. Louis to visit the Cahokia State Historical Site, the original ceremonial center of all the Mississippian cultures of Native Americans, including the Choctaws, and I learned about the male bias present in anthropological interpretation when we were viewing a reproduction of a "sweat lodge." When I saw the fire pit, I asked the director how he knew it was a sweat lodge, and not a menstrual hut. There are no fire pits in a sweat lodge, but there is a pit for heated rocks. There can be a fire pit in a menstrual hut. The director had no answer. The dominant male interpretation was the default position, the male authoritative position. I was not surprised. The standard is the white male standard. I had known that since I was child.

I learned a lot from working on diverse projects with good people at the Philbrook. One of these was researching the use of the masking tradition in American Indian culture, working with Ed Wade as he put together an exhibit titled "As in a Vision." I researched Korean culture for another interpretive exhibit, I researched and wrote material for a newsletter, and I wrote grants. I worked on a jewelry exhibit. I learned to recognize human connections across cultures. For a time, I worked under Ed Wade's direction on a nationally touring exhibition and his book *The Arts of the North American Indian*. My network was growing. In addition to research, I learned a good deal about the museum world.

What I also learned was that I wanted to go into full-time university teaching, because teaching students to think is so important. So I applied to Northeastern State University, and I was hired in 1987. Northeastern State University was to be my academic home for the next twenty-four years.

Seminary Hall was my office location—third floor, smelling of bat guano, full of wasps, creaking wooden floors, and windows against which a wise person did not lean. Individual air conditioners cooled the rooms—sometimes. The building, called the "Grand Old Lady" by the university president, had been remodeled about twenty or thirty years earlier, but had been ignored since then. Still, I felt privileged to be there and would sometimes put my hand to the wall in affection, as I thought about the past.

Many of my students were Cherokee, as Tahlequah is the capital of the Cherokee Nation, and Seminary Hall had been, before statehood in 1907, the second site of the National Cherokee Female Seminary, after the first seminary burned in 1887. The National Cherokee Female Seminary was founded in 1846, and

Northeastern State University's link to that seminary makes it the oldest institution of higher learning in Oklahoma and the trans-Mississippi West. After the seminary property was declared surplus during allotment and sold to the state of Oklahoma for a bargain price, fewer Cherokees attended, so that by the 1980s, American Indians were tolerated because they paid tuition, but they were not treasured. There was an American Indian Studies program that received almost no support from the administration, and there was a Native American Student Association, supported by a few American Indian staff and faculty members. In 1987, these organizations were not robust, and American Indian students had only a little campus community support from staff and faculty.

Local people whom I met and enjoyed most in Tahlequah were the funniest. Robert Conley and his wife Evelyn were friends, and I would pay Robert a bottle of Wild Turkey to speak to my class. Joshua Nelson, now at the University of Oklahoma, assisted me in my work at NSU for a time, and he met Robert Conley at my house. How we laughed that evening!

For about six months after my arrival, I kept my head down, but during that first year, a professor retired, and I inherited her American Indian Writers course. I taught the course using theories and principles that I had learned from my museum research. I included feminist ideas, links, and historical connections to literature and writing in all my classes. Over the years, along with others, I sponsored the Native American Student Association, continued to teach the Indian Writers course, published a bit of poetry, and researched material that I turned into essays, class lectures, conference papers, plays, and eventually a book, *Women Who Pioneered Oklahoma*, which I coedited with Connie Henshaw.[2]

I also participated in the university's American Indian Heritage Committee, which each year produced the National Symposium on the American Indian,[3] which drew Native Americans from all over America. A few came to burn tobacco at the grave of Chief John Ross south of town. Some came to visit a campus famous in Indian country because of its roots in the National Cherokee Female Seminary. Many came to see old friends. During those years I was there at the Mother Ship, Northeastern State University, I was constantly learning and using the knowledge.

John Trudell was one of those who came to the American Indian Symposium to visit his old friend from the Alcatraz occupation days, Wilma Mankiller, who lived near Tahlequah. He spoke during one of the sessions, and I was assigned to be his contact. One of my favorite memories of this time is of John wearing a black motorcycle jacket and sporting a mohawk haircut. I think he had been filming *Thunderheart*. I was wearing a tasteful off-white silk and linen suit. When asked by an awed student during his session, "What is your Indian name?" John replied "John Trudell." When we met again during a second symposium, John said he had a message from Wilma and him to me. Their message was, "Be careful!"

Now when John Trudell and Wilma Mankiller tell you to be careful, you should pay attention. So I took the "Free Leonard Peltier" ribbon off my car's review mirror and taped it to my office bookcase. I could think of nothing else to be careful about. I could not think of anything that I was doing that was a problem. I was only researching and sharing my findings with my students. If my scholarly research disturbed my students or other people, that was a problem for them to solve.

During those years, I met many people and enjoyed being in the American Indian community to some extent. Still, I was a part of the university—the gown. Other groups, such as the American Indian writers' group, the Wordcraft circle, met at NSU, and I heard much laughter and some snarky "gatekeeper" comments.

American Indians have many "gatekeepers," and all these gatekeepers believe that they are the "real" Indians. I am puzzled about what "real Indian" means. Maybe it is like "the Velveteen Rabbit"—when all your fur is rubbed off, you are real. Sometimes the gatekeepers are colorists, believing that the darker you are, the more "real" you are, ignoring the long history of rape, intermarriage, and hostage-taking of Indians that has occurred in Indian country, both by Europeans and by American Indians. Some gatekeepers focus on language, believing that "real" depends on tribal language fluency, discounting the long history of suppression of tribal languages during the boarding school years and the relocation years, which robbed many American Indians of tribal cultural context. Some of it focuses on geographical location—what is "real" somehow means that you live in South Dakota or Oregon, or on a reservation, or in western Oklahoma. Some of the gatekeepers are tribal, believing that their tribe is composed of "real" Indians." A lot of victim-blaming goes on. However, the Supreme Court recently found that eastern Oklahoma is still a reservation, so maybe we all are real Indians, too.

This kind of "gatekeeping" shows up in the scholarly literature, too. W. David Baird addresses this in his comments on a review of G. W. Grayson's autobiography, which he had edited. The reviewer said the book "would be better titled 'A Walk on the White Side.'" Baird responds: "Never mind that Grayson considered himself and was considered by others a Creek, lived in the Creek Nation his entire life, spoke Creek, worshipped with Creeks, was elected as a Creek by Creeks to numerous tribal offices, and was listed as a Creek on the final rolls of the Dawes Commission! To my reviewer, he did not *look* or *write* like an 'Indian' and, therefore, could not have been a *real* Indian."[4] Baird goes on to note that "the Five Tribes people, over time, have behaved differently than other Native groups. Without traditions premised upon a single metaphysical perspective, for example, they often accommodated, even embraced cultural change."[5]

I, too, sometimes wonder what writing like an "Indian" means. Dr. Amelia V. Katanski points out that the insistence on assimilation in the federal boarding schools resulted in students being required to learn and to demonstrate Standard English.[6] This was true all over; readers of the previous chapter of this book will recall that in Mother's mission boarding school, students were also required to learn Standard English.

Despite all this, or maybe because of it, this "real Indian" gatekeeping conflict stirs the pot in a number of significant ways, because so many people believe they have the right to decide what a "real Indian" is. The conflict also underlies the disunity that exists among Native Americans. In his valuable 2000 book, David LaVere explores how this conflict developed in Oklahoma:

> The Southern Plains Indians and Southeastern Indians existed as two wholly
> different peoples. They had completely different cultures, had different ways
> of life, and looked at the world in very different ways, despite being grouped
> together into one "Indian" racial category by white Americans. Once they
> were forced to become neighbors in Indian Territory during the nineteenth
> century, instead of creating a middle ground of cooperation and unity, they
> remained different, suspicious, and separate. Their interactions and relations
> in Indian Territory, always complex, ranged from raids and counterraids to
> diplomatic councils and trade connections but did little to bring about any
> melding of these two types of peoples. If anything, their differences became
> only deeper and wider, more exacerbated, and the turn of the twentieth
> saw them no closer than at the turn of the nineteenth century. And in many
> ways their traditional culture and their history keep them separate at the
> turn of the twenty-first century.[7]

I invite non-Indians and some American Indians who believe it is their right to decide who is a "real Indian" to know that only the individual tribes have the power to decide legally who is a member of their tribe.

Over the years, some of Northeastern State University's National Symposium on the American Indian topics dealt with the "real Indian" controversy, both directly and indirectly. The Annual Symposium meetings drew scholars—American Indians and non-Indians—from across the nation, from many different tribes and cultures. Their presentations offered information about culture, history, art, literature, law, and so on. However, the symposium also offered fascinating experiences that were not enjoyed, generally, by the non-Indian faculty and their students. Usually only two or three non-Indian faculty members attended the events and encouraged their students to attend these sessions, even though world-famous Native American speakers appeared, such as Lieutenant Commander John B. Herrington (Chickasaw), NASA astronaut mission specialist; Simon Ortiz (Acoma Pueblo), poet, short story writer, essayist, and author of children's books; N. Scott Momaday (Kiowa), Pulitzer Prize–winning author; and Joy Harjo (Mvskoke/Creek), poet laureate of the United States. Joy Harjo read her poetry, played the saxophone, and danced with some of the students. In addition, lectures were presented by leading American Indian actors, such as Wes Studi and Steve Reeves. One symposium hosted American Indian Movement speakers. (We all played "spot the FBI agents" that year.) Renowned Indian educators appeared, such as Dr. Henrietta Mann (formerly Whiteman).

But the non-Indian faculty stayed away for the most part, unless they were presenting a paper. Few non-Indian students attended independently, because even if they were interested, they lacked the support of their teachers. Perhaps they were afraid to attend. This lack of interest, or support, or fear results partly from the continuing invisibility of American Indians.

At the same time—though in my opinion Native students were not treasured by the university administration in the 1980s and 1990s—the university was deemed "Indian friendly," hosting students from many tribes and providing them with educational opportunities. I suspect that is partly because Jake Chanate participated in pow wows in many places in the United States and recruited Native American students he met. Jake was a Kiowa storyteller and Vietnam veteran who talked with my classes and with whom I worked for many years in the Native American Student Association. Jake was in the habit of calling me on the telephone to alert me when "Indian hunters" were on campus. There were a number of those—people who came to learn from Indians some mystical knowledge which only we hold somehow—which is a puzzle to me. We were all kind to such seekers. Jake also taught me about pow wows. Choctaws did not pow wow when I was growing up. However, his activities were not valued by the administration; his funeral was attended by only one Northeastern State University administrator as far as I could tell. Nonetheless, Jake Chanate was valued in Indian country. During his funeral, the singing in Kiowa and Cherokee comforted many mourners.

It seems to me that all the American Indians at NSU during those years were living within American Indian power. Ken, a Tohono O'odham worked at the office of traffic and parking, and sat at the drum. He helped sponsor the Native American Student Association. He would give me the peace sign in greeting. He was a fierce handball player. We all worked to help our students thrive and worked to provide them with a university community in Tahlequah. Often I would introduce students to symposium speakers. I recall offering to introduce students to Wilma Mankiller at the symposium, only to be told by one, "Oh, that's OK. She's my cousin."

The Native American students at NSU learned to work a room at receptions during the symposium. They learned to run a meeting using Robert's Rules of Order. When they came to my house to make stickball sticks, to honor them I brought out my best china, silver, and crystal for dinner. They were so polite, and they left my kitchen cleaner than it had been before dinner. With nostalgia, I remember watching older students showing new students how to load my dishwasher. The older students would bring newer students to my house in the Illinois River Valley and introduce them to our German shepherd dogs. I was always aware that these students might well become tribal leaders, and many of them have done just that. Many work in tribal offices, and some work for the Bureau of Indian Affairs. Some work as educators, some as social workers, tribal media directors, and tribal public health workers. They work in positive ways for American Indian people.

My work for the students—that is, helping to create an American Indian community for them—was partly motivated by an experience I had at age fourteen. At a summer camp, I overheard a preacher telling a youth leader that that American Indians peaked at age fifteen, and from that age, their intellectual and physical abilities declined. So, in the months leading up to my fifteenth birthday, I worried. When I woke up on my birthday, I reached for a book and was relieved that I could still read and understand the words. From that day on, I have known to question authoritative pronouncements about abilities. I believe my mother. We are all different.

Working for the good of American Indian people is a marker of Native American women's power. Following my mother's example, I also believe that learning to survive and even thrive in the "white world" is necessary. It is also necessary for women to survive and thrive in a world dominated by males.

During my years at Northeastern State University, three of my students died tragically. And there were those students who left to travel home and never returned, because their families needed them. Jake would take up a collection for gas money and of course I contributed.

There were odd moments of conflict at NSU, as when a "New Age-y" dean in my college decided during the summer when the campus was empty to invite a white artist to deposit a statue on campus. It is there now, an unfortunate appropriation of American Indian symbols and suffering. The artist came to a meeting of the Native American Student Association, seeking their blessing for the statue which, she said, was about forgiveness. The American Indian Movement representative at the back of the room stood up and said, "There are some things I am not ready to forgive yet!" So this is another example of non-Indians thinking that they can appropriate, in this case American Indian tragedy, and decide for Native Americans to forgive! Recently the controversy about the statue has resurfaced among "some students, faculty, and area residents who say it is demeaning to Indigenous people."[8]

Over the years, there seemed to be some opportunities to educate the university's administrators. One fairly new Vice President for Academic Affairs asked me why American Indians were so patriotic. I replied, "We have been protecting the homeland since 1492." He did not laugh. I told him briefly that we had fought in all the wars of the United States. And I mentioned the Navajo code talkers of World War II fame. He seemed puzzled. I have never known if such discussions make much difference. To make a big difference in education would require a huge investment in researching, teaching, and changing the idea that the history of the United States is white. Real change would require systemic overhaul. Textbooks would have to change, from grade school on up. As Martin Luther King Jr. said in *Strength to Love*, "Nothing pains some people more than having to think."[9]

Then there was the Northeastern State University fraternity that wanted to hang and burn an Indian in effigy on their homecoming float when we were playing the Savages from Southeastern Oklahoma State University. Southeastern later changed their team's name, as did many other universities with Indian mascots. The fraternity guy said that he was a tribal member and asked the Native American Student Association if they would mind the effigy burning. The Native American Student Association president said, "Yes, we would mind." He did not smile. There was no effigy burning.

Perhaps one of the most instructive events during my NSU years concerns the utter ignorance with which a famous mural was viewed. It was and is a WPA mural painted by Stephen Mopope, one of the group of famous early twentieth-century Native American artists known as "the Kiowa Five," or "the Kiowa Six," if you include Lois Smokey, which you should. When Seminary Hall was being renovated in the mid-1990s, one of the food service staff members overheard the architects talking about knocking a hole in the mural to create a curved door into a conference room. This would have destroyed one of the few remaining WPA murals in a public building in Oklahoma. The architects thought that an artist could create a poster of the mural they wanted to destroy. Fortunately, the food service staff worker who overheard the conversation was the mother of the president of the Native American Student Association. Much consternation ensued.

I got in touch with Rennard Strickland, who was in Tulsa for a meeting—so I called Rick West, the executive director of the National Museum of the American Indian. The person who answered the phone at the National Museum of the American Indian called out, "Get a load of this. It's Terri Baker from NSU in Oklahoma, and the administration is threatening to destroy the Kiowa Five Mural in Seminary Hall." I could hear people laughing and commenting in the D.C. office.

Other NSU people made phone calls. The students were threatening to have a sit-in. American Indian faculty and staff called in all their chips. Finally, the president of the university reached the conclusion that the mural was not just an old Indian painting, and it was saved. We let the president take all the credit for saving the mural. Then we raised the money to have it restored, and in the next few years students paid for a protective rail.

The point of these stories is that the American Indian community at Northeastern State University worked together to support the students by welcoming them and providing an American Indian community on campus for them. The university's American Indian community in many ways worked to stand in solidarity for the good of tribal people. Many of these people were women. They exhibited American Indian women's power working in the lives of the people. This is not to say that we were always unified because there were moments of conflict. Among American Indians, there are always moments of conflict, just as with other groups. We also suffer from intergenerational trauma, as do many groups in the world. Some of the Northeastern State University's American Indian community were men, some were women, but generally, we were all working together to provide a community for our Native students and working to educate mainstream people about American Indians.

In addition to Northeastern State University, the broader national community was also a part of my professional life. In 1994, as a result of my meeting Theda Perdue in Bloomington through the effort of Gloria Young, I applied for and was accepted as one of twelve Fellows for the National Endowment for the Humanities Summer Seminar for College Teachers on the Ethnohistory of Southeastern

Indians. Theda and her husband Mike Green directed the seminar, which took place at the University of Kentucky. This seminar changed my life. I would not have known about the Summer Seminars had it not been for Gloria Young. In Kentucky I read, argued, learned about ethnohistory, and developed friendships with scholars which have lasted until this day. Carolyn Johnston, my coauthor of this book, is one of those friends—on a fieldtrip we were roommates, and she has introduced me to her circle of friends and scholars. My network grew.

That, too, is women using their power by helping other women to live rich productive lives. Women help women, women advocate for women, and tribal women help their tribal members—members of all Native American tribes as they walk their paths. My Kentucky friends push forward the search for truth in the history of America and in the world, and they help me in my search for truth. These scholars I met in Kentucky challenge Gloria's old comment that ethnohistory is history that nobody else wants to study. More and more scholars are making connections, and more and more publications by university presses are reaching the public.[10]

Another part of my broader community included friends and associates in the American Association of University Professors, in which I was active for a number of years. The years I spent working with the AAUP were not always peaceful, but the work was interesting and supportive, as I met with university administrators and professors to solve problems. Sometimes we won. It seems to me that mostly we lost. A current manifestation of the losses is the corporatization of the academy that is now occurring in the United States. Still, it started many years ago. Corporate universities place little value on the humanities. That is unfortunate.

One major thing I discovered along my slow, turtle way is the astonishing ignorance that exists about American Indians. Some mainstream people think that American Indians are extinct. Some non-Indians as well as American Indians believe that they have the right to decide who is and is not a "real" Indian. My students would tell very funny stories about helping tourists at an American Indian family–owned convenience store. Surrounded by American Indians, the tourists would ask where they could find Indians. Usually, those tourists would be directed to the center south of Tahlequah, which includes an ancient village in which a number of my students worked during the summer months. One tourist asked one of the students who worked in the Ancient Village what it was like to live there, not understanding that the student worked there while living in a conventional brick three bedroom, carpeted, climate-controlled house some miles down the road.

So I have struggled with mainstream ignorance, as well as beliefs about American Indians that perhaps may come from seeing too many John Wayne movies. I do know that often people are surprised that Oklahoma has many lakes and that I live in a river valley in northeastern Oklahoma. Perhaps such notions come from seeing all those movies filmed in Monument Valley.

Some Indians attend Christian churches and American Indian ceremonials. Some belong to the American Indian church, some pow wow, some do none of those things. We attend white Christian funerals, and afterward in private, we may burn cedar for the dead, but not all do that. As my mother taught me, being an American Indian is different for everyone.

Some American Indians are urban Indians, some are rural Indians. We all live in Indian country, and most of us know what that means. About a third are urban Indians, a third reservation Indians, and a third Indians living off the reservation in land areas possessing heavy populations of American Indians. Of course, currently the numbers living on reservations may be changing because of the recent Supreme Court decision saying that, because reservations had not been disestablished, the eastern part of Oklahoma is still a reservation.

Many years ago a Vice President for Academic Affairs at NSC was pressing me during a meeting in his office about the need to recruit students. In the process, he engaged in the "eternal insult," though I have learned that such comments are now called "microaggressions." As I gave programs in area schools, mostly about American Indian subjects, I assured him that I did recruit. "But look who you recruit," he said with some disgust. "They are my natural audience," I replied. "I often present programs to schools with high numbers of American Indian students." He did not answer, but cleared his throat and changed the subject.

When I first began at Northeastern State University in the mid-1980s, I attended a party given by the local arts organization, and I met a woman whose daughter had just become a student at the university. She wanted to know what I taught and I said, "American Indian Literature." She stepped back and said, "Oh no, I want her to study something worthwhile." I assured her that my subject was worthwhile as she fled. A professor or two complained to me that Cherokee County had no culture, apparently unaware of being surrounded by American Indian culture. Students in my courses would sometimes ask with hushed voices if I were a feminist. They clearly associated feminism with some kind of evil. I would reply with a smile, "Oh, yes." After a time, such insults pile up. The students have to learn how to manage. Many years ago an American Indian student in some distress came into my office and asked, "How do you deal with this stuff?" I replied, "Well, Jake (Kiowa) drums and pow wows, Joseph (Lakota) prays, and I (Choctaw) laugh because so much of this 'stuff' is so absurd."

The mainstream wants our medicine (which the mainstream thinks of as talent, I think), but they feel it their right to simply enjoy and to take anything else—like land and natural resources, including oil. The actions of the mainstream say, "Don't bring along your real identity as Native American—your beliefs, traditions, behavior patterns, worldview—because your identity is not valuable to us unless we can use it. Besides, American Indians make us uncomfortable." Consider the many musicians who are tribal people, documented and undocumented. Their medicine, or talent, is enjoyed by millions, but their Native American identity is largely invisible. Rock music owes these musicians big time.

This same sort of invisibility is present in universities. In Tulsa, I once attended a university-sponsored lecture whose subject was billed as "American Indian Literature." The university professor talked about the federal reports of military actions against American Indian communities, with some comments about Walt Whitman. The presenter knew nothing about the richness of American Indian literature. American Indian Studies requires learning history and gaining cultural knowledge, studying federal Indian law, as well as learning about American Indian music, dance, literature, economics, medicine, politics—all the things that make up a society. American Indian studies also requires researching women's power and how women exercised power and still exercise power in tribal societies.

As an ethnohistorian, I had to swim in a vast informational sea and connect details of history, culture, law, music, and so on to literature. At times I have needed a life jacket to keep swimming. Making the connections took years. I am still learning. I think that a love of learning and reading is my medicine—that, and laughing at my weaknesses. You have to exercise your memory. And still no matter how much you learn, often you are invisible, because you are not identifiable by color or buckskin or feathers or accent. Maybe you just have to depend on your intellectual muscles and balance.

This idea of balance is important to many tribes. Here I will give you as a gift a Choctaw story about balance. The old Choctaws believed that immediately after death, the spirit of a person found herself or himself on a peeled log bridge over a chasm. The bridge was slippery, and howls of suffering and lamentation came from the rocks and rushing water far below. From the other side, which was the afterlife, came sounds of song, laughter, and happy greetings. Good cooking smells wafted from the other side, and the spirits who had gone before waved the spirit to cross over. The only problem was that everything the spirit had done in life also waited on the other side, including the evil things. The evil that the person had done in life threw rocks at the crossing spirit. Some rocks were large, some small, some made up of clouds of sand. And so the spirit moved across balancing on the log. If the spirit fell into the chasm, the spirit was doomed to be forever exiled from family and good things. If the spirit crossed, the spirit was reunited with loved ones. There was no forgiveness. There was just what the person did in life.

Balance supports. So it is that I must balance—my knowledge and reactions to knowledge, my activities, and my responsibilities. That is why I try to be kind to those who know so little about American history, to professional historians who believe that American history is white history, and who further believe that they somehow own history. Such attitudes are changing, slowly. Presses, especially university presses, publish many books each year focused on American Indian subjects, because scholarship is the search for truth and supports learning.

One of the things I have learned is to look for patterns, because so much knowledge has been destroyed or hidden. Cultural patterns and lifeways are sometimes subtle and hard to recognize. Now I do not claim that the tribal cultural patterns have survived intact. They have not. Still cultural remnants endure. Native Americans possess a complex story. One of the things I have noted over the years is that tribal people do not wait for help from the mainstream. That is, tribal people are helping themselves. One example is a concert, which occurred in Santa Fe in October 2019 and featured Buffy Sainte-Marie, held as a benefit for Indigenous Solutions. The nonprofits supported by the October concert included Indigenous Solutions/Indigenous Ways, The Friendship Club of Santa Fe, and Tewa Women United. These groups work for the good of tribal people. These women are not waiting for outside "superman" help to arrive. The concert itself emphasized support for "efforts related to Missing and Murdered Indigenous Women." This is certainly women's power in action.

Economic growth as self-help has also been activated by gaming for many tribes. Consider the example of the Choctaw Nation of Oklahoma. For the Choctaws in Oklahoma the casino income helps by providing jobs as well as revenue used for tribal services and for matching funds for grants. Some examples exist in the 2019 *Choctaw Nation of Oklahoma State of the Nation* publication mailed to tribal members. Pages four and five of this publication contain graphs. One graph is titled "Where the Money Comes From." According to the report, 54 percent comes from Business Operating Income (net). Thirty percent comes from federal and state grants. Thirteen percent comes from Medicare and third-party insurance. Two percent comes from general governmental revenue. One percent comes from housing. Page 5 of this publication shows by graph, "Where the Money Goes." Seventy-nine percent goes to member services. Seventeen percent goes to Investments/Sustainability. Four percent goes to capital projects.[11] The total health budget for 2019 was $247,475,922. This includes patient care, prescriptions, senior nutrition, wellness centers, eyeglasses, dentures or partials, and hearing aids, among other health-care items.[12] In addition, tribal members pay taxes, purchase clothes, food, cars, gasoline, and entertainment, just as mainstream American citizens do. We contribute to the overall state and national economy.

From time to time, I have had conversations with non-Indians whose complaint is "Why should Indians get free health care when I don't." My reply is "We paid at the gate." Our treaties and years of litigation have included health-care clauses. When American Indians began operating casinos, the income was used to benefit tribal people. That is income earned by the tribe. Once a man said to me in some disgust, "Indians don't deserve this [income]." He seemed to think it was a matter of work ethic or moral merit, and that we were lacking in those areas. Maybe he just didn't like American Indians. I explained that the income is payment for theft of land and resources. It is like owning shares in a stock that, with luck, will provide income. In the case of American Indians, the shares are tribal membership. He was quiet, and I do not know if he understood or not.

But I want you to understand it. If one is a tribal member, tribal services are available. Some casino tribes share the income with tribal members via cash payments. Some do not. Some tribes do not have casinos. But being a tribal member is somewhat like owning stock in a company. Tribal membership is historical ownership of stock or identity. If one is undocumented and seeks no profit from American Indian heritage, but knows family lore, that is fine. We all need to know who we are. The undocumented, however, should not seek to profit from stories of descent without evidence.

All people benefit from increased American Indian prosperity. In Oklahoma as in other states, American Indian tribes compact with the state to build roads, where before, only dirt, gravel, and tracks existed. All people use the roads—no passport required. Many people, tribal and nontribal, work in the offices and health-care centers where tribal services are provided. Economics are important in Indian country, because Indian land areas tend to be among the poorest areas in the nation. That is a consequence of historical mainstream behaviors. Some of that is changing slowly as many tribes have pulled themselves into financial prosperity.

Another important thing is the American Indian concern for the earth, Mother Earth. Many tribes identify as people who emerged from the earth as Mother. They know that we need clean water, clean air, and healthy food. They know that we cannot drink oil. So American Indians attempt to protect the earth as at Standing Rock. That is why American Indians, along with their white neighbors in Cherokee County, Oklahoma, are attempting to take care of Clear Creek and the Scenic Illinois River. Coalitions are built.

Comments that I have heard about the earth from mainstream people largely seem to be along the lines of, "Well, we had our use of it." I see little concern for the future, but I hope concern for the future is growing. Such concern seems to be present with the younger generation. Understanding that there is a future is why American Indians pray for the seventh generation.

American Indian women's power is profoundly linked to activism. That is, we teach, we protest, we provide services to people who need them. For American Indians, the United States is an occupied country. So it seems to me that our choices are direct: violence, despair, or education. I chose education long ago. My mother and father believed that education was the way out of hard times. And so it has proved to be for me.

What is good for American Indians is also good for mainstream Americans. Reading N. Scott Momaday's *The Way to Rainy Mountain* is a marvelous experience for all readers, not just American Indians. Education for all is necessary for a democracy, not just for American Indians. During the course of researching for this book, Carolyn and I interviewed a number of people. Their stories weave patterns of activism, tradition, history, creative work, politics, and education.

When American Indians meet, we play "Who is your mama?" as we establish identities, family locations, tribal affiliations, our place in the web of life, and we laugh to survive. My mama was Geraldine Hull McKinney, daughter of Maud and Lafe Hull, granddaughter of Lena and Old Man Hull, great-great-granddaughter of the one who walked the Trail of Tears to Indian Territory, five times the great-granddaughter of the one who came from Sixtowns in the old country in what is now the southeastern United States. To them I say, *Yakoke* (Thank you). To them I say, *Ya ko kee* (much more slowly) to indicate regret that I do not know more and that I have forgotten so much.

Now, after about forty years in education, working in tense environments, and weaving in and out of the reach of bullies, I have retired to my river valley near Tahlequah, Oklahoma, where I exercise to put off total dependence, read, write, and cook to nurture harmony within my heart and mind. About 70 to 80 percent of the time, I find that harmony—popcorn helps. I had quite a ride with my professional career. Because of my home university, I met lots of interesting people. I also learned to dodge and weave by engaging in fairly constant battles, many of which I lost. What I learned may be helpful to those somewhere along the path of decolonization.

All Americans need to learn about the significant participation of American Indians in the life of the United States. I could provide a long discussion here about people such as William Apess, Metacom, Powhatan, Sarah Winnemucca, Nancy Ward, Chief Joseph, Geronimo, Ada Deer, and many others. The discussion could be filled with exploits of the code talkers (Choctaws were the early code talkers during World War I). Or I could mention the scholar Vine Deloria Jr. and his son Philip Deloria, writers like Louise Erdrich, the Cherokee potter Jane Osti, the famous chief Wilma Mankiller, the famous American Indian ballerinas. I could note that Elouise Cobell filed a class action lawsuit focused on the mishandling of Native American funds, and the federal government eventually paid $3.4 billion to affected tribes. But change is slow. This is why my casual friendship with Wilma Mankiller was important. We could huddle together for a moment in her office and then go on. I know that Wilma always said that she prayed to be a good person. I have taken to doing that, if for no other reason than to remind myself to retain my balance lest I fall into the abyss.

The thought of prayer takes me to religion. Religion is another reason that Indigenous people and their place in U.S. history is not robust. Lions and tigers and bears are not so terrifying as religion. Very early in Euro-American history, one finds documentation for those who would profit from a belief in "manifest destiny." The oppressive behavior started early, before European contact with North America.

Consider William Bradford of *Mayflower* fame who lived from 1590 until 1657. A civic-minded fellow and most influential in the history of the United States, he authored *Of Plymouth Plantation* over the years between 1630 and 1650. It was published in 1856, and because the document's creation is so early in European colonization, in the nineteenth century it found a ready audience that needed justification, if they were seeking justification, for taking the land, the lifeways, and often the lives of the original inhabitants of North America. In chapter 9, "Of Their Voyage and How They Passed the Sea; and of Their Safe Arrival at Cape Cod," Bradford writes: "Being thus arrived in a good harbor, and brought safe to land, they fell upon their knees and blessed the God of Heaven who had brought them over the vast and furious ocean, and delivered them from all the perils and miseries thereof, again to set their feet on the firm and stable earth, their proper element."[13] God brings them to North America. The "stable earth" means North America and it is "their proper element." This is an early statement of "manifest destiny." Those people believed that God brought them to North America and it is their proper place.

Later in chapter 10, Bradford's men are scouting around for food and a place to live. They find a clearing with a garden and some graves. Looking around, they find a place where the sand has been disturbed and they dig. They find "Indian baskets filled with corn, . . . So their time limited them being expired, they returned to the ship lest they should be in fear of their safety; and took with them part of the corn and buried up the rest."[14] Please know that they are aware that they are stealing food and seed corn that belongs to someone else, because they are in fear of their safety. The people to whom the seed corn belongs will probably starve. When I bring up this incident, some historians usually say, "but they left some corn." Bradford's men were thieves. Their first act upon exploring their surroundings was to steal property belonging to someone else, and they knew what they were doing.

The English Puritans acted in such a way because they believed with all their faith that they had the right to do so. They believed that their Christian God gave them this right. Never mind the commandment about not stealing. Somehow, taking things from American Indians is not stealing. *Things* include land. They did it because they could.[15] Then time passed, a revolution took place, and the United States was formed. Roxanne Dunbar-Ortiz reports that "from the mid-fifteenth century to the mid-twentieth century, most of the non-European world was colonized under the Doctrine of Discovery, one of the first principles of international law Christian European monarchies promulgated to legitimize investigating, mapping and claiming lands belonging to peoples outside Europe." Dunbar-Ortiz points out that "in 1792, not long after the US founding, Secretary of State Thomas Jefferson claimed that the Doctrine of Discovery developed by European states was international law applicable to the new US government as well." To Jefferson this justified the theft of property from Indigenous inhabitants. So it was that the doctrine of discovery transformed into manifest destiny and thereby justified genocide.[16]

I suggest that mainstream white America from its earliest days existed in a state of double consciousness—perhaps multi consciousnesses—for they had to work to reconcile their belief that they were Christians with their contradictory actions of stealing from, killing, enslaving, and generally oppressing people whom they encountered or brought to North America. They did this by dehumanizing people different from them from the beginning and lived with their actions by believing in their own European notions of supremacy. Clara Sue Kidwell recently published a most instructive essay, "How America's Destiny Became Manifest," focusing on the significance of the building of railroads in North America. Kidwell points out that "a major impediment to western railroad expansion was the existence of Indian Territory in the west."[17] Indeed, treaties were broken, railroads were built, and manifest destiny played its tune.

Early on during the European contact era, the stage is set for all that is to come in American history. I hear scholars of African American history refer to slavery as "America's original sin." While African slavery is an abomination, it is not the original sin of America. When writing about the number of deaths among Indigenous people, Andres Resendez notes that "between 1492 and 1550, a nexus of slavery, overwork, and famine killed more Indians in the Caribbean than smallpox, influenza, and malaria. And among those human factors, slavery has emerged as a major killer," Europeans enslaved the Indigenous people in the "new world" upon contact.[18] Bradford simply records the continuation of this life of sin in *Of Plymouth Plantation*.

Thus, this notion or faith in supremacy, or emotionalism, or simply destructive self-love, is fundamental to America. It resulted in five hundred years of conflict, suffering, wars against the original inhabitants, oppression of people of color, and a strange schizophrenia in American identity. A strange but understandable reason that Indigenous people in U.S. history are invisible rests with historians educated by the winners. You see, education has to do with colonization and the construction of our U.S. history. Construction means how we as Americans construe our world reality.

Wilma Mankiller and I talked about such things in short bursts at lunch, just before we shared our brownie, after she became the Sequoyah Fellow at Northeastern in Tahlequah. Most American Indians and non-Indian scholars whom I know talk about this. We possess shared knowledge and exchange sources. Sometimes, say at 3 a.m., I wish I did not know all this. But once known, a person cannot unknow it.

Consider odd moments that came my way. My friend Wanda, a social worker, and I used to go to sweat lodge together, and one time when we arrived, we discovered that some teenyboppers from Tulsa had somehow found the location and had come to "recharge" their crystals. I don't know what that means. Later after we had crawled out of the sweat lodge and had thrown ourselves face-down into a snowbank, Wanda snarled, "They don't respect our traditions!" I replied, "Ya, but they got real hot."[19] "Oh, well," as Wanda would say. Social workers are good to know. In fact, in bad weather, I used to try to park on the east side of Seminary Hall because the windows of the social work faculty looked out over the parking lot. Once when a lot of ice covered the parking lot, I got out of my car, got out my walker, and began to walk toward the building. Somehow I got stuck and found myself surrounded by ice. A social worker looked out her window, saw me, and walked down three flights to come rescue me. I am working on a balance theme here.

Many Native Americans share knowledge about Andrew Jackson and broken treaties. When I was in school, this knowledge was not usually included in any curriculum in k–12, university, or graduate school that I attended. So my generation had to create our own course of study. We buy books, give books to friends, loan books, check out books from libraries, watch documentaries, and today, research around the internet. We increasingly interview our family members and listen carefully to the stories of elders. Once some time ago, I asked Clara Sue Kidwell something like, "Did you learn any of this in college?" Without the phone, I could hear her laughing all the way from Norman, where she was serving time as director of American Indian Studies. I taught my classes and incorporated this knowledge into my coursework. Some of the students understood. Some rejected it. The artists—visual, musical, dramatic, and wordcrafters—use their skills and pass on their skills to please us aesthetically and to teach us. They make lives better. Wilma Mankiller used her knowledge internationally to make the lives of American Indians better. She was a social worker. On a local level, I used my knowledge to create teachers, networks, and pathways. On a national and international level, Clara Sue Kidwell used her knowledge to create more scholars and networks.

All of this is better than killing people. If you kill people, you just end up with a lot of dead people. Wilma and I never talked about our disabilities; we just knew that they existed and that we had to live with them. Once I waved to a professor, and the professor very publicly snubbed me. I said to Wilma, "Oh, I forgot, she does not talk to me now." Wilma said, "I have people who won't talk to me too." Wilma and I did not talk specifically about all of this, but we knew things. I remember we talked lovingly about opera and *Madame Butterfly* and where we had learned to love opera. She learned in San Francisco; I learned in Santa Fe. American Indians enjoy cultural knowledge from many cultures. We can hold more than one idea in our heads. From time to time, American Indian scholars exchange long looks, then go on about our business. My business was in the university system. My heart was with my people.

CHAPTER THREE

WILMA MANKILLER'S STORY
LEADING WITH INDIGENOUS WOMEN'S POWER

Wilma Mankiller lived feminism and Cherokee values throughout her difficult yet highly effective life of struggle for her people and for all women. One of those moments occurred when she served as the chief of the Cherokee Nation and attended a meeting of the Five Civilized Tribes at Stilwell. Much to her surprise, there was not a chair for her at the table. The other chiefs, all men, sat there as though nothing was out of order, so she went and got her own chair, joined them, and began discussing mutual concerns like the reunion of the Eastern Band of Cherokees and the Cherokee Nation of Oklahoma. Initially upon her election as the first female chief of the Cherokees in 1995, she experienced death threats, slashed tires, and phone harassment. Despite this, she earned the trust of the people, governed 140,000 Cherokees, and oversaw a budget of over $75 million.[1] Wilma championed tribal sovereignty and lived the power of Cherokee women, rooted in her tradition's stories, like those of Selu, Kanati, and other female deities.

Tahlequah, Oklahoma, where Wilma was born in 1945, was a small town. It still is, though today Cherokee County prospers from Indian gaming and offers health care in a newly enlarged Indian health-care facility. The increase in Indian health care has created a dynamic that results in an increase in health-care availability for non-Indians, also. "Indian friendly," Tahlequah is called a "Rez town" by some, and it enjoys an integrated population. Staff of the city hospital includes tribal members. African Americans, some of them descendants of freedmen, are active in the community. American Indians of diverse nations are business owners, artists, bankers, attorneys, university professors, public school teachers, and pastors—all the elements of an American town, including, of course, some of the problems.

Wilma grew up in Mankiller Flats, which still exists today near Stilwell, Oklahoma, east of Tahlequah. Her ashes were scattered there. As part of the federal policy of relocating American Indians to urban areas in the 1950s,[2] Mankiller's family moved from Mankiller Flats to San Francisco in 1956, when she was eleven years old. The policy's goal was to sever Native people's ties to their land and cultures by providing economic opportunities away from tribal homes. Her father became a shop steward and labor organizer. When Wilma arrived in California, she had a troubled adjustment and ran away from her home in Daly City to her grandmother's house in Riverbank, in the Central Valley's Modesto County. She felt alienated in school and suffered from lack of self-esteem.[3]

After high school, Mankiller attended Skyline College and then San Francisco State University. There she met and married fellow SFSU student Hector Hugo Olaya de Bardi, a native of Ecuador, on November 13, 1963, when she was seventeen years old. Their first child, Felicia, was born on August 11, 1964. Gina, their second daughter, was born in June 1966. Hugo wanted her to stay at home and enact his patriarchal view of marriage, but Mankiller had no wish to be a subservient wife. The year 1968 was the high mark of the women's movement, which ushered in a new era of women's power and was transforming American culture.[4]

In her autobiography, Wilma describes the powerful impact of her time with a group of friends who met weekly in Lou Trudell's kitchen during the San Francisco years. The core group—including Wilma; Lou (Fenicia Ordonez) and Linda Aaronaydo, a Creek and Filipina; Susie Steele Regimbal; and Gustine Moppin, a Klamath woman and an incredibly optimistic person—was constant, even though the larger group was constantly changing. They shared their thoughts through conversation. They found that "the personal was political," and that they shared many of the same constraints stemming from sexism. Wilma recalled, "I suppose in a way together we spoke our songs of independence, rather than sang them."[5]

Part of Wilma's ability to inspire centered on her activism. Because Wilma was an unapologetic feminist, sometimes people ask us about the difference between activism and feminism. There may not be much difference for American Indian women who identify as feminist. They work for the survival of tribal identity and sovereignty. They work to educate all people about American Indians and their place in American history. Some people say that is activism. However, the first activist group that Wilma Mankiller truly identified with was the Black Panther Party. In addition, she recalled: "My spirits were buoyed in the 1960s [by the] National Farm Workers Association led by Cesar Chavez." Later she became acquainted with Delores Huerta.[6] "Whenever I do pause to reflect, I find many of my hopes and aspirations were formed during those wonderfully sad and crazy years of the 1960s in San Francisco. The Vietnam War was in full swing, the civil rights movement, peace demonstrations, and the seeds of the Native-rights movement—[all of these] had a lasting influence on me."[7]

When Wilma Mankiller began to feel the constraints of her situation, she tried to find peace. She recalled, "As many people tend to do when oppressed in some way, I found methods of escape, harmless ways to rise above my current circumstances; men take wing and fly away. For me it was an easy thing to do—I simply turned on the radio, closed the door to the rest of the house, and sang along with the radio. Soon I had the sense of freedom and joy that only hearing music and singing could provide me."[8] Mankiller grew up with a lot of Cherokee songs, stories, and music. Traditionally, American Indian women sang to plants to make them grow, sang to children to care for them and sustain life, and sang to sustain themselves so they could continue to bring and nurture life. She and her friends had long talks:

> We talked about our children, the emerging women's movement, the role of women in the Indian rights movement, indigenous rights, the environment, and Bay Area Indian politics and life. Though we spoke about men, we spoke to one another about things we would never share with a man. We told our stories and spoke about our anger, fears, vulnerabilities, and dreams—we spoke a lot about our dreams, secret dreams shared only [in] Lou's kitchen. Occasionally we would go on picnics, to meetings, to a raunchy bar in east Oakland or to a pow wow, but mostly we just talked, sang, and danced our way into our future uncertain where we were headed, but sure we couldn't turn back, because the foundations of our lives were already crumbling and we had to move on.

Wilma had a difficult time adjusting to urban life and found refuge in the Indian Center in San Francisco. There she met Indians from many different tribes who faced the same challenges. When the Indian Center burned down one night, the whole Indian community in San Francisco was devastated.[9] Mankiller described how this burning of the Indian Center led to intense activism for Indian rights and the occupation of Alcatraz and its history.

A new era of activist militancy began with the American Indian Movement, AIM,[10] and Wilma Mankiller's "awakening" occurred in San Francisco. On November 9, 1969, Indians of twenty tribes seized the island of Alcatraz, the former site of a maximum-security prison in San Francisco Bay, citing a treaty clause that said unused federal lands must revert to Indian use.

The occupation of Alcatraz changed Wilma forever. She says in her autobiography: "It was on Alcatraz, that irregular oblong hump of barren sandstone stuck in the bay waters between San Francisco and Sausalito, where at long last some Native Americans, including me, truly began to regain our balance." Her narrative goes on to point out that the U.S. Army had turned it into "a military

prison and disciplinary barracks . . . not just for Confederate captives and con-
vict soldiers, but for the native people whom the whites enslaved." Mankiller
briefly relates the history of Alcatraz and remarks that Native people could relate
to that history.[11]

The AIM occupiers held "the Rock" for nineteen months. Four of Wilma's
brothers and sisters as well as her children joined the band of Native Americans
on the island. Mankiller's sister Linda stayed longest of all of them, until June
1971. John and Lou Trudell came up with their daughters, Maurie and Tara, to
join the "Indians of All Tribes." Their son Wovoka was born on Alcatraz. Wilma
said the many people she met there changed how she perceived herself, as a
woman and as a Cherokee: "Alcatraz, which had been a prison, ironically was extremely liberating for me." Many dramatic events marked this period in her life.
Her father died in February 1971. Her marriage began to fall apart. Hugo was not
in favor of her involvement in Alcatraz or any of her other projects throughout
the Bay Area. He didn't want her to have a car, and so she went out and bought a
red Mazda, against his wishes.[12] There was no turning back.

The Bay Area in the 1960s and 1970s was the home of every major movement
of the sixties: the free speech movement at UC Berkeley, the anti–Vietnam War
movement, the farmworkers movement, the feminist movement, the environmental movement, the LGBTQ movement, and many other movements across
the political spectrum. Mankiller became a volunteer for the Pitt River people,
who were in a battle with Pacific Gas and Electric over their right to millions of
acres of the tribe's northern California land. She was associated with the tribe
for almost five years in the mid-1970s. She organized a legal defense fund and
often visited traditional leaders on their land. She learned about treaty rights
and international law. Her friend Richard Oakes, who was a major leader of
the Alcatraz occupation, also helped the Pitt River Indians and influenced
Mankiller greatly.[13]

Locations have historically formed the basis for a life's trajectory, provide the
dynamic for growth, a widening or restricting of horizons. The Bay Area was an
energizing force for Wilma Mankiller, for feminists, for many young people, and
the dynamic begat a movement that spread all over the world, certainly all over
Indian country. In the Bay Area Wilma trained to become chief of the Cherokee
Nation. Young Indians were in college in large numbers at Berkeley, San Francisco State, UCLA, and many other institutions in the area. They read Karl Marx,
Frantz Fanon, Paolo Freire, Herbert Marcuse, many existentialists, Betty Friedan, Simone de Beauvoir, and Mao, and they also learned more about their tribal
histories. Learning about tribal histories and cultural behaviors is fundamental

to activism, because such information has been left out of educational textbooks. The young American Indians' radicalization stemmed from their intellectual and experiential lives. For many of these young Indians, activism became a return to community; their families had moved to the cities, and there they had been isolated. The Indian Center in San Francisco drew together Indians of many different tribes and helped develop pan-tribal friendships and political alliances. Alcatraz was the crucible for many dramatic actions which followed: The Trail of Broken Treaties March to Washington, D.C.; the occupation by AIM activists of the Bureau of Indian Affairs Office in Washington, D.C.; the Wounded Knee Occupation; the Fish-In movement in Washington State; and many other less well-known actions by Indian militants.

In California, Wilma Mankiller became a self-identified Indigenous feminist who saw feminism as essential to tribal sovereignty, part of the human flourishing of the Cherokee communities, and a means to return to traditional Cherokee balance of gender roles. She came to a feminist consciousness in San Francisco, and when she supported the occupation of Alcatraz Island in 1969–1970, she became radicalized and empowered by participating in nonviolent action. Her decision to seek a divorce stemmed from her husband's disapproval of her activism and his desire for a patriarchal family within which she would be a traditional wife.

Students have asked the authors how one becomes feminist. We think it is a process of events, awakenings, and the slow kindling of what will become a warming fire. We don't know people who wake up one morning and say, "I am now a feminist"—though often a single occurrence will bring together all the things that have been waiting. White men, possibly, grow into an awareness of male authority and possibilities as they take their places as class officers, baseball players, firemen, policemen, and then later as managers, CEOs, and so on. They find themselves in active roles that prepare them for future leadership. Many fewer women enjoy such opportunities, though that is changing. Men and women develop assumptions about their place in society. And it is difficult to go against the status quo. To become a feminist, one must act in ways called "outside the box of convention." One has to awaken, as Wilma Mankiller awakened in San Francisco.

Wilma Mankiller filed for divorce in the mid-1970s, shortly before she went back to her home in Oklahoma with her two daughters. She sought to reconnect there with the Cherokee traditions and people. One of those Cherokee traditions (and a tradition in most American Indian tribes) is self-help, which Wilma would pursue throughout her work with Cherokees.

The Cherokee Orphan Asylum, founded in 1871, six years after the end of

America's Civil War, provides a useful example of their self-help tradition and how the details changed with circumstances. "In 1865 the Indian Territory was a region of desolation. No great armies had operated there, and no battles that were broadly decisive had been fought within the area; but the entire population had been involved, and the destruction of homes, public buildings, crops and fences, livestock, tools and implements had been almost complete."[14] Moreover, "More than one-third of adult Cherokee women were widows at the close of the Civil War, and one-quarter of Cherokee children (1,200) were orphans."[15] The Cherokee Orphanage replaced the clan and family system of orphan care among the Cherokees through necessity. "Years of adapting to white cultural patterns while still in the southeast, then forced removal from traditional homelands, and finally the American Civil War all created conditions under which there were not only more true orphans among the Cherokee but a willingness to incorporate white institutions into tribal life."[16] Self-help and the incorporation of "white institutions into tribal life" was necessary for tribal survival. This self-help tradition and the strategy of using white institutions manifested in the famous Bell Water Project. But before she could lead the Bell Water Project, Wilma had to fight her way back to life.

Not long after Wilma returned to Oklahoma, she had a life-threatening automobile accident, one that killed Sherry Morris, her closest friend, who was driving the other car. Mankiller had multiple injuries and was near death. Her face was crushed, and her ribs and legs were broken. She was in the hospital for eight weeks and endured many surgeries. The accident changed her life dramatically. As she described her experience, "I had experienced death, felt its presence, touched it, and then let it go."[17]

Mankiller recovered from the automobile accident, and soon thereafter got a job with Ross Swimmer, who was then chief of the Cherokee Nation.[18] In 1979, she received his approval to work on community renewal. The town of Bell is in a rural area of eastern Oklahoma with around three hundred mostly Cherokee families. In 1979 the residents were desperately poor, had little education, and lacked indoor plumbing. She thought Bell was a wonderful choice for her to start a project in community empowerment. At first when she tried to get the people to attend a meeting, no one came. She persevered, assured by her community organizing experience in California that by laying the groundwork of trust, she could lead the people in identifying what they themselves cared about the most, and together they could work from there.

Gloria Steinem described the beginnings of the Bell Project as Wilma's listening to members of the community about how to meet their greatest needs:

Wilma Mankiller (*left*) and Gloria Steinem, a notable American feminist leader. Courtesy of the Western History Collection, Norman, Oklahoma, University of Oklahoma.

When she [Wilma] got a few to meet, they responded to the question: "What single thing would change this community the most?" They replied that it was a water supply, which would be connected to everyone's house with indoor plumbing. They explained that the water supply would not only make the people healthier but also cut down on their children's dropping out of school. Having no indoor plumbing meant they could not bathe regularly at home and suffered ridicule as a result at school. Then came the hard part!!! She told them that she would secure the supplies, federal support, engineers, and they the people would build it and help in the fundraising. The Bell Water and Housing Project thus began. She enlisted the elder women to get the project going. Men and women became involved in the construction tasks. The project grew from only having twelve families in the beginning to almost every family in the community. After fourteen months the community completed the project. They dedicated to continuing their work and focused on their next project, which was housing. As the members of the community bonded, they decided to hold fundraisers so the five or six families in Bell who were not Cherokee could also benefit.[19]

Steinem went on to summarize the impact of the Bell Program:

> Since renovating Bell's housing, members of the steering committee have
> overseen a senior citizen education project, an annual "fund-raising pow-
> wow," a speakers' bureau that carries Bell's lessons to other rural commu-
> nities, and a bilingual education program to help preserve the Cherokee
> language and culture. The school dropout rate has fallen, and other nearby
> communities like Burnt Cabin and Cherry Tree have begun water and
> housing projects, too. Those who were once ashamed of living in Bell had
> become proud.[20]

The Ford Foundation and First Nations Development Institute funded a two-
year project that aimed to transform the tribal-service organization. Stimulated
by this experience, Wilma Mankiller and activist Kyle Smith organized the One
Fire Corporation to continue the sorts of projects that she pioneered in Bell,
Oklahoma. Other goals include improving the institutional development and
administration processes of tribal governments by combining effective management practices with Native values and traditions.[21]

Living Indigenous women's power meant listening to the needs of others and
not trying to manipulate or dominate them, and in the process, empowering
both men and women of the community. Once when speaking to Terri Baker's
class, Wilma was asked what she considered her most important achievement.
She said it was the Bell Water project, which through community work brought
piped water to Bell, Oklahoma, so that indoor plumbing was possible.

Wilma's success with the Bell Water Project lived on in 2021 as the water projects expanded across Cherokee country. Principal Chief Chuck Hoskin Jr. announced plans and annual financial support of $2 million to "improving access to
clean water across the reservation." In line with incorporating support from white
institutions, Chief Hoskin said, "Additionally, I'm fighting for increased federal
funding to ensure that our water infrastructure needs are addressed."[22]

The Bell Project included personal changes as well: Wilma met Charlie Soap
when she worked on the Bell Project. Her face brightened when she spoke of
him. She said he was tall and handsome and was an accomplished Plains style
dancer. He had learned many dances while in college. "He is not threatened by
strong women. He is supportive of women, of women's causes, and of me and
my work." Wilma Mankiller married Charlie Soap in 1986.[23]

Yet not all the members of the nation were supportive of women in positions of power. As the first woman chief of the Cherokee Nation of Oklahoma,
Mankiller said she encountered more opposition because she was a woman than

Wilma Mankiller, chief of the Cherokee Nation, addressing
Cherokee people. Courtesy of the Western History Collection,
Norman, Oklahoma, University of Oklahoma.

because of any other reason. Mankiller became the deputy chief of the Cherokee
Nation in 1983, and then in 1985 was named the tribe's principal chief. She served
two terms after winning in 1987 and again in 1991. Because of health crises, she
did not seek another term in 1995.

Chief Mankiller embraced a maternal feminism that resembled the social program of Jane Addams and others at the turn of the twentieth century. Mankiller
drew on her Cherokee identity and history because she knew that before European contact the Cherokee women and men enjoyed equality. She formed the
Cherokee Nation Community Development Department, and under her leadership, the tribe grew from 55,000 citizens to 156,000. During her term, she helped
tribal businesses get started in horticulture as well as manufacturing plants with
defense contracts. She oversaw the building of a hydroelectric facility, and she
strengthened the infrastructure of Cherokee communities, like the water system
in Bell.[24]

Indigenous women's power is embedded in the traditional maternal role and
dedication to children and the community.[25] Scholars like Devon Mihesuah and
Renya Ramirez have contended that cultural survival and feminism are insep-
arable for Indigenous women. Vivette Jeffries-Logan (Occaneechi) explained

that the feminine role for Native women is not based on inequality of men and women. In an interview, she elaborated:

> Well traditionally . . . there is no gender inequality, because we are the ones that bring life, and because generally women have the best interest of the entire people . . . instead of just, all about me. . . . Because we raise children, and it is just like I said, I understand that what impacts me negatively or positively impacts my people . . . . and like, understanding that everything I say and do negatively will have a reflection, and it reflects upon my people. We are the wisdom keepers; we're the storytellers. The fact that I'm the fire carrier, that carries, that's responsibility. It's not me sitting up on a pedestal thinking, oh, you know everybody should be bowing at my feet. It's like, no, I have work to do. This is a responsibility, and it's an honor that I have this. I mean we have our work, women have our work, and I think, like you said everyone has their gifts, and the approaches that women have differ from men, but it's not saying that one is superior or inferior.[26]

Wilma Mankiller supported this sentiment and was a member of the Four Mothers Society, originally established to oppose allotment in the nineteenth century. During her lifetime, the society promoted traditional ceremonies, stomp dances and stickball games, and maintained ceremonial grounds.[27] She shared a similar approach to community empowerment as LaDonna Harris.[28] Mankiller wrote to Harris on June 5, 1992, about a program, planned by the Cherokee Nation to join with Eastern Band and other tribes in supporting efforts, which resembled LaDonna Harris's Americans for Indian Opportunity. As the chief, she wrote, "One thing I never tried to become as Chief was 'one of the boys,' nor am I a 'good o' gal.' I never will be."[29]

When asked by Bruce Weichert about her work, she replied to his letter: "In answering your question about my accomplishments and rewards that are most memorable, I would probably have to say all the community organizing work that I have done in our rural communities. Women's rights and tribal sovereignty are areas that I feel I have developed during my years as Chief of the Cherokee Nation."[30] The Seventh Generation organization, which Mankiller also supported, focused on the renewal of Native American communities, research, and publications, as well as the dissemination of findings to Native Americans and ideas to broaden their world. Mankiller was skillful at getting federal grants for communities and oversaw a nutrition program for women, infants, and children, as well as a food distribution program.[31]

Under Wilma's leadership in the 1980s, the residents of Bell, Oklahoma, and other Cherokee communities accomplished many things that improved their lives. She was named the first director of the Cherokee Nation Community Development Department in 1981.[32] She went on to bring new businesses to eastern Oklahoma, and sponsored $20 million in construction projects, new clinics, projects to help Cherokee women on welfare develop microenterprises, and a Job Corps Training Center, in which the tribe invested $8 million. She oversaw services for children, a new tribal tax commission, and an energy consulting firm, and she authored an agreement with the Environmental Protection Agency.

The Bell Project's enormous success launched Wilma Mankiller's political career. Ross Swimmer saw how talented she was and asked her to run as his deputy chief. Then when he was offered the position of the head of the Bureau for Indian Affairs, he asked her to step in as the chief, and then, as mentioned previously, she ran as the chief and was elected twice. At the same time, Mankiller was in close touch with the national leaders of the feminist movement in the United States, especially through her role as a member of the board of the *Ms.* Foundation.[33]

Only ten months after her devastating automobile accident, Wilma Mankiller was diagnosed with myasthenia gravis, a serious muscle disease. The chapter in her autobiography, "Dancing along the Edge of the Roof," describes her many encounters with death, but also her daring embrace of life and her profound reliance on her Cherokee traditions and values. The image of dancing captures the joy and danger of the many transformations she experienced in San Francisco, and upon her return to Oklahoma. This is who she was. This is how she led her life and the Cherokee Nation with Indigenous women's power.

Remembering Wilma Mankiller   —*by Terri Baker*

Wilma Mankiller moved into my mind long before I ever met her. She appeared in the form of a paper flyer posted on a telephone pole in Claremore, Oklahoma, in 1983. She was running for deputy chief of the Cherokee Nation, and she won. That was how campaigning was done back then—paper flyers posted in the seventeen counties that make up the Cherokee Nation. I read one or two articles about the race and noted the opposition to a woman running for a major office in the Cherokee Nation.

Because I was a feminist and trying to find my way to a professional life in northeastern Oklahoma, Wilma's activity interested me. You see, back then in Oklahoma, as in many places, women were still walled out of most professional opportunities, and I was looking for a crack in that wall. I often thought that while some had a jackhammer, I was working with a penknife, but still I persevered.

Wilma inspired many of us. I was one of those inspired by her courage and leadership power as a Native American woman, even though in 1983 I did not know her. I read about her in newspaper articles, as I suspect many women did. Wilma was three years older than I was and, like me, of mixed race. I liked that. At that time, and still today in many parts of the country, Indian stereotypes encouraged mainstream Americans to think of Native Americans as identifiable only by dark brown skin, downcast eyes, shambling gaits, and ignorance. I knew, however, that Indians were lawyers, doctors, professors, business owners, bankers, and—of course—could be Indian chiefs. I had grown up with that knowledge as I deposited money for my family in a Choctaw family friend's bank, and as I studied under a Choctaw teacher in public school and a Choctaw professor in college. I knew my Choctaw mother owned a business along with my father in Durant, where they employed a white and American Indian staff. A Choctaw lawyer lived next door to a family friend. Wilma had Cherokee physical characteristics and wore business clothes in the few images of her I saw.

Like Wilma, I belonged to the second-wave feminist movement of the 1960s and 1970s, and I knew that some American Indian women distanced themselves from feminism, because they believed the movement opposed marriage and family, or was hostile to men. Wilma and I came to feminism in different ways, but both of our paths were guided by conversations. Some were conversations with friends, like those described by Wilma that took place around Lou Trudell's kitchen table. Some came from listening to conversations by men. I remember attending meetings during the 1970s and 1980s during which women were lectured by men on the necessity of throwing off the oppressor's yoke or women were encouraged to accept blame for physical abuse. I made one man sit down and be quiet about the blame game, and simply never attended another consciousness-raising session, my consciousness having been raised at an early age. While I knew other feminists, they were generally not close friends like those that Wilma enjoyed. That would come later for me because of where I lived. However, my mother and father taught me that I could be powerful through education. That became my path.

Like Mankiller, I was aware of the diversity of feminist groups and theoretical positions. She found her traditional Indian values compatible with feminism, and she believed that such issues as reproductive control of women's bodies, fighting domestic violence and preventing rape, supporting childcare and family leave, and health care for all citizens were urgent issues for all Native people. Taught by my mother, Geraldine, I believed those things too. Just as no single feminist theory or activism could embody the diversity of those in the mainstream feminist movement, the same was true of Native feminisms. Mankiller's feminism embodied her Cherokee traditions and was influenced by major transformations in her family's life because of changing federal policies of removal and relocation. My feminism was grounded in Choctaw traditions and my mother's background as a boarding school student, but we were not affected by relocation. My views developed in Oklahoma from observing my mother, listening to her stories, and being encouraged by her and my father to achieve my goals.

During the years when Wilma acted as the elected principal chief of the Cherokee,[34] I worked as an assistant professor in the English Department and also taught American Indian literature, which was called "American Indian Writers," in the American Indian Studies program. I suspect that to call the published work of American Indians *literature* was just too much equality for the folks at NSU. For the first year, I described my negotiations with the faculty and administration as a "dance." During the second year, I came to know that what I was involved in was a war. Much later, in late 2009, I told Wilma about my change of terms from *dance* to *war*. She nodded her head, and said, "I have realized how isolated you have been."

Our paths had begun to cross during my first year in Tahlequah at Northeastern State University. At first, we saw each other as most people do in a small town—at the grocery store, at Walmart. While she lived east of Tahlequah, Wilma worked at Cherokee Nation headquarters in Tahlequah, so as a convenience, she sometimes shopped there. When she published a cookbook, I went to the bookstore downtown to get her to sign a copy for me, and another for my mother, who admired Wilma greatly.

Wilma asked me to present an overview of American Indian literature at the upcoming conference focused on Women's History Month, and she asked me to make it positive. I assured her that I would be honored to present such a lecture. One of the things I learned from Wilma was to focus on the positive in communications such as public lectures. Knowing about depredations leads to anger, and I had to work on that. That conference brought women from all over the United States (some of them no doubt thinking that they were traveling back in time) to the Sequoyah State Lodge on Fort Gibson Lake, a scenically breathtaking place. The decor was very 1950s, and I suspected that Spin and Marty were just around the corner flirting with Annette.[35] I arrived at the front door of the resort in Pat Synar's old pickup truck, from which a passenger can enjoy a view of the pavement through a hole in the floor. My car had broken down on the way back from Tulsa, and I had managed to roll into a convenience store that sported various stuffed animals—and there I found Pat, who laughed and agreed to take me to the lodge.

That conference in the early 1990s was the beginning of my casual friendship with Wilma Mankiller. She worked at Cherokee Nation headquarters south of town, and I worked at NSU on the north edge of town. I even had an office in Seminary Hall, which had once been the National Female Cherokee Seminary. The seminary was declared surplus during allotment and sold to the state for a knockdown price. Cherokees still resent that, and for a good reason—check the treaties. I have always called Park Hill, which is south of Tahlequah, "Checkpoint Cherokee."

I have been asked why I think Wilma left California and returned to Oklahoma. I think that she, like many American Indians, yearned to return to her community, her people, where she could participate in specific tribal activities, hear the language, engage in the humor, be at rest in the landscape. Many also feel a calling—as I believe Wilma did—to make the lives of their people just a bit better. Not all return permanently—some visit, or return for festivals and reunions. But they return.

Mainstream people often see in American Indian communities only poverty, unemployment, sometimes despair, but there is so much more. I also suspect that many mainstream white people are a little uncomfortable around American Indians. Tribal culture is everywhere in Oklahoma. There is opportunity to work for tribal survival. Wilma knew she could do good work. And, indeed, she did good work. Good work includes educating mainstream Americans about their history.

Some time ago, my friend Mark asked me over a cup of coffee at the local coffee shop in Tahlequah, "Are you bitter?" Now he was genuinely curious, because we are both fairly recently retired, and, frankly, I had just barely escaped the administrative posse. Mark said with a long look, "I'm bitter." So I had to pause and consider just a moment. The battles had been almost constant, and after I left in 2010, I sat on the deck at my home for over three years, contemplating the seasons so as to calm my spirit. "Was I bitter?" I started laughing. "No. I had experiences here that could have happened no other place in the world. Once when I was with the Native American Student Association, blessing the pow wow arena, I watched a grass dancer as he danced to taped pow wow music, and when he finished the dance, he went on to dance the Charleston, the moonwalk, a jitterbug—all to the beat of pow wow music."

And I went on to exclaim, "I mean where else could I have been teaching in the same building that housed Wilma Mankiller my last full semester?" I recalled that as Wilma and I walked back to Seminary Hall and approached the west entrance, she asked, "If you fall down, can you get up?" "Nope," I replied. "Turtle on my back. Cute little shoes waving in the air. You?" "Me neither," she said, and we both broke out into big smiles.

No one was around us, and we were both seeing our situation, which was isolated both physically and metaphorically. She asked me where I got my shoes, and said she had to wear shoes she considered ugly. "Well, big whoop," I said, "you can still walk." Then I helped her up the two steps to the door. The disabled helping the handicapped. Yes, Wilma and I were both handicapped; I think the term now is *mobility impaired*.

Let me tell you about the NSU campus and accessibility—which the administration views with puzzlement and some distress. Accessibility is expensive. Once in the early morning, right after an ice storm, I staged a one-woman protest, sitting on my walker and gazing wistfully at Seminary Hall, which housed my classrooms, my office, and heat. Even in my boots and two pairs of socks, my toes were a wee bit chilly in the seventeen-degree weather. The ramps, hidden from street view, had not been cleared of ice. They never were. I began to use my mobile phone. I asked the college secretary to inform my students that they should wait a bit, and if I failed to arrive, to go to the library and study the assignment. The students probably immediately slid over to the coffee shop.

A student rolled by in a wheelchair and motioned at the ice, "Dr. Baker, look at this!" I replied, "I'm on it. You get to class. Go on. I've got this." After about fifteen minutes the president's assistant showed up. "Dr. Baker, come on over to the president's office and have some coffee." "Oh, thanks. I'm fine here. I'll go in when the ramps are clear. But thanks again—very kind." I was always polite.

The president's assistant left, and then the campus police showed up. Two of the campus police ventured very gingerly out on the large ice pool that forms from poor drainage just north of the door to the building. They were so apologetic. "We are sorry, but we can't help you in, because if you fall, we will be liable." I replied, "Ah, yes. Liability. I know it is not your fault. I'm OK." They walked off helplessly and looking distressed. They were really very nice.

After the campus police, the plant manager appeared, wearing a down coat and a cap with earmuffs. He is not an evil man. Kind of slow maybe, but not evil. "What do you want?" he asked. "I want to go in." I said. He turned and left. He never talked much. I felt—as I had felt before—like I was in an absurdist drama. Maybe an open-air *No Exit*. Well, *No Entrance*.

Then I saw a man from the Human Resources coming my way. No doubt coming to have a little chat with one of the university's human resources. We chatted. He left. I may have mentioned something about ADA. I had a thick ADA file in my office. Used to enjoy slapping that file down on the president's desk.

The president's assistant came again, assured me that the ramps were about to be cleared. He was a nice young man—not what advertisements call a self-starter, but nice. I waited until the maintenance people cleared most of the ramp and the sidewalk to the door. Only then did I agree to accompany the nice young assistant to the president's office and hot coffee. Three hours out there. Seventeen degrees. I told the president that I hoped I would not have to do this again, because it was really cold. He agreed that it was cold, and then mumbled some more, as he was wont to do in my presence. The problem still exists.[36]

Now this is the reason why Wilma Mankiller—Chief Wilma Mankiller (love that word *chief*)—asked me to sit and chat with her at a reception at the Cherokee Heritage Center a week or two before classes started in the 2009 fall semester. She was about to become the first Sequoyah Fellow at the university. On the day the fellowship was announced, I had tried to hide in the back of the room, but friends kept kind of pushing me forward and laughing about my height, until I ended up in the front row. Wilma shook everybody's hand and then hugged me. I thought, "I'm doomed. She's blown my cover. Now the administration knows that she knows me. Doom."

A short time earlier, Wilma had joined me on a bench at a Cherokee Heritage Center reception. "Where are the handicapped parking spaces on campus?" she began. "I know that you know." I replied, "Well, the ones that most people don't know about are east and north of the education building. You can almost always get a space there. But not always on the first day." Wilma asked, "Which building is the education building?" I said, "OK, call Ken. You know Ken? This is his number." I wrote it down for her. "Ken will get a golf cart and take you around the campus and show you the handicapped spaces." Sure enough, a few days later, Ken and Wilma zoomed by on campus in a golf cart, waving at me and laughing.

That's a good memory, as is having Wilma not only as my lunch buddy but also as my water aerobics buddy, briefly. Of course, it was January, and you get so wet in a swimming pool. Paddling around, she looked at me once, and said, "I used to think that water aerobics were only for little old ladies." I looked at her, tilted my head, and began to smile. "We are little old ladies, aren't we?" Wilma said, and again, we were both laughing. We had known each other for many years by then, she in the Cherokee Administrative Offices, and I on campus hill. Not a profound friendship, certainly, but an old association that grows more dear in my heart. There were so many other wonderful moments that temper the memories that would otherwise embitter me. I suppose that is how memories work. I wanted Wilma to be safe in the building, and I warned her not to go into the hall when students were changing classes, because they might accidently knock her over. Generally speaking, you see, in Tahlequah, Wilma was not recognized particularly.

Wilma needed resilience—and she worked hard for it. She faced inherited polycystic kidney disease, and her brother Don donated a kidney to prolong her life. She would also experience breast cancer and pancreatic cancer. During my retirement reception in 2010, Wilma confided to me that her recent test had shown that the cancer was gone. Where we were sitting, we celebrated. But the cancer returned, and Wilma died a few weeks later. I recall that I had a flower shop take pink tulips to her service, which I was unable to attend because of a recent surgery. Pink was her favorite color.

Remarkably, she was extremely balanced and resisted the temptation of depression, clinging to her spirituality, and maintaining a "good mind." She related a prophecy: "There is an old Cherokee prophecy which instructs us that as long as the Cherokees continue traditional dances, the world will remain as it is, but when the dances stop, the world will come to an end. Everyone should hope that the Cherokees will continue to dance."[37] While she was adept at governing the Cherokee Nation with superb administrative abilities, she also embodied and lived Cherokee traditional values. Often Wilma strove to combine the two worlds. And she prayed to be a good person. She lived a life "along the edge of the roof" every day, and she was of a "good mind."

Both as chief of the Cherokee Nation, and before and after her tenure in office, Wilma Mankiller drew on her deep knowledge of Cherokee history and her understanding of colonialism and sexism as inextricably connected. She epitomized Indigenous women's power, and she lived her feminism. For her, living women's power meant recovering the Cherokee values of gender balance and equality and drawing on women's unique nature as mothers.

Gloria Steinem was with Wilma Mankiller for the last week of her life in 2010. She said that when Wilma died, "signal fires were lit in twenty-three countries to light the way for her final journey."[38] Personally, I burned cedar for Wilma. And today, I continue to work to be of a "good mind." This is how she sustained her Cherokee woman's power. As a Choctaw woman, I strive to do the same.

CHAPTER FOUR

COMANCHE FEMINIST POWER
LADONNA HARRIS'S STORY

By living her most basic identity as a Comanche woman, LaDonna Harris has served as an international leader in improving the lives of all American Indians and all women. For her, relationships are everything: "Being a good relative [means] basing the entire functioning of the community on inclusive relational webs of mutual reciprocal exchange obligations and on kinship principles. Relationships delineate one's possible roles, and therefore, the responsibilities attached to them."[1] Harris embodies the four principal Comanche values: relationships, responsibility, reciprocity, and redistribution. These core values express the understanding that all humans are related to one another and all things, and thus, we have a duty to care for our relatives. These Comanche values guide her life and her Indigenous feminism. She always sang Comanche songs when she was growing up, and today she has a tape of them in her car with which she sings along. Wilma Mankiller and LaDonna Harris followed similar trajectories in coming to a feminist consciousness, even though they had been living feminism before that point. Both were affected deeply by the movements of the 1960s, Mankiller by the occupation of Alcatraz and Lou Trudell's kitchen conversations, and Harris by the struggles of the civil rights movement and later her work with feminist leaders in Washington, D.C.

LaDonna Vita Crawford was born during the Great Depression on February 21, 1931, and she grew up on her grandfather's allotment in Cotton County, Oklahoma, near Cache Creek and the little town of Walters. Her mother worked in Indian Services and had to live in a dormitory in Lawton at that time, so LaDonna was raised on the farm. When asked how she became a feminist, she said,[2]

> Because of my grandmother and great-grandmother, who was the matriarch of the family. I guess I became a feminist because of how strong my grandmother and great-grandmother were. They both were. I always thought of my great-grandmother as regal. She'd sit in this great big old chair when we'd come to visit. There were kids all over the place. She had her cane. There were a bunch of us; we'd be around. I always wanted to listen, so I'd

sit right by her. If she needed something she'd punch you with her cane and say, "I need a drink of water," or "Go take care of those kids," or "Make those kids be quiet." I'd sit near her because I liked to hear her stories. I'd learned at a very early age, if I would be quiet around the older women, I could sit and listen to their stories, listen to them talk at church meetings, whatever the gathering was about, whatever they were doing, canning or something. They'd gossip a little bit. If I talked or asked questions, they would tell me to go play, so I learned not to do that. My father and his mother went to work in California during the Great Depression, but he never came back, so I didn't know him. But Mom wrote nice and interesting letters and asked about me.[3]

Harris recalled wearing her Comanche clothes to town, and how the older women would call her "little granddaughter." When she asked her grandmother how she was related to them, she told her they weren't really related. However, they gave her a sense of belonging. She grew up surrounded by many strong women.

Harris's grandmother was one of the first Comanches to be baptized, and she helped start the Deyo Church and the Brown Church, and then she started others like the First Indian Baptist Church of Walters. Her grandfather kept his own Eagle medicine and peyote ways, but he drove them to church and respected her grandmother's beliefs. LaDonna's grandparents respected each other's religious views, and her grandfather told her never to try to take away another person's religion, because it would hurt that person and her also.

When Harris went to high school, she met the love of her life, Fred Harris. They married in 1949 and spent three decades together, becoming a nationally powerful political couple. Fred was not a Comanche, but he learned the Comanche language and knew more about Comanches than many Comanches did. He continued working and going to college. LaDonna did not attend college, but Fred discussed his courses with her. Fred and his friends all studied at the Harris's house. LaDonna worked to support the family when Fred went to college and then law school at the University of Oklahoma (OU). When Fred graduated from law school in 1954, they went home to Lawton and decided to join the Junior Chamber of Commerce and the Historical Society, which was their greatest joy. Friends described their marriage as a full partnership.[4]

LaDonna and Fred began their activism for civil rights in Lawton, Oklahoma in 1963. They worked with a group of thirteen to integrate the town's restaurants, and they were successful. Harris said that integrating Lawton was a big thing for them: "We did it as a group activity. Women started it. We recognized that we were more than babysitters. We made it personal and got together for a very complicated first meeting. The first time we all brought dishes, and [then we] decided that was too much trouble, and then we would each take responsibility for hosting it."

In 1956, Fred Harris ran and was elected to the Oklahoma State Senate. During the campaign Fred would have LaDonna come on after he made a campaign speech, and he would often say "My wife and I . . ." She recalled:

> Another thing we changed about Oklahoma politics, not only in Lawton, [involved] bootleggers and prohibition—how they would pay people, particularly in the Indian community, the men who controlled the votes. And we figured out through our friendships and integration and relationships that system didn't work anymore.
>
> Going to OU was such an interesting thing. We went to OU and we were talking about discrimination and integration of African Americans, and labor laws and disputes and I said, "What about Native Americans?" They said, "The BIA takes care of Native Americans," and I burst out into tears, because I was so frustrated. So after that, they decided to form committees and visit the BIA, and people from other states. A group went to Oklahoma City and Anadarko BIA offices. Social workers said, "'We don't have to take care of Indians; they take care of their own. They have dens down there where they smoke peyote and do drugs.'" Two different perspectives, that overwhelmed them.
>
> But it hurt my feelings; here were the intellectuals in Oklahoma who knew nothing about Native Americans; here we have Oklahoma history in school, and they knew about the Five Tribes and that was about it. In Oklahoma they knew nothing about Native Americans.[5]

When Fred Harris became state senator, he often asked LaDonna to join him on the Senate floor to sit and watch. He was verbal, and she was visual, so he depended on her observations of people and wanted to hear them. As the senator's wife, she also played the traditional role of hostess, including for visiting state senators. Yet she also challenged the gender expectations by actively campaigning for him and working for policy initiatives. She wrote in her autobiography that she always wanted to be a wife and mother and was not particularly interested in being a professional person. Over the course of her life, however, she has become all those things, and she has found her own voice.[6]

Fred and LaDonna Harris became a powerful couple, and sometimes Fred

LaDonna Harris, who was named "Indian of the Year," riding in a parade. Courtesy of LaDonna Harris.

asked her to go to various engagements for state committees and organizations. One such event was a weeklong seminar on civil rights at the Southwest Center for Human Relations Studies at the University of Oklahoma. This seminar was transformative for LaDonna and helped set her agenda for change for decades to come, as she learned how dismissive so many policymakers were to Indian needs.

When Fred Harris was elected to the U.S. Senate, the couple moved to Washington, D.C., and LaDonna Harris met Ethel and Robert Kennedy, who lived near them. They also met Lyndon Johnson and Hubert Humphrey, among other powerful leaders. She and Fred started a new organization, Oklahomans for Indian Opportunity, and secured funding from the Office of Economic Opportunity (OEO). The goals of the organization were both to preserve culture and to improve social and economic opportunities for Native Oklahomans and other American Indians. Sixty tribes came together in this venture.[7]

LaDonna's reputation as a leader on Indian issues grew immensely during those years. She was the first senator's wife to testify before Congress. For example, she testified on July 13, 1967, before the Education and Labor Commission of the U.S. House of Representatives on the effectiveness of the OEO in Oklahoma. Along with her husband, Senator Fred Harris, she later fought for the Indian Self-Determination and Education Act, and she assisted Ada Deer in regaining the Menominee tribe's federal recognition in 1973.

LaDonna Harris went from being a rather insecure young woman with dys lexia to an eloquent and confident spokeswoman. Rather than challenging traditional notions about women's appropriate roles, Harris expanded her traditional role as a Comanche woman. Implicit in her activism was the necessity of protecting her family and children by working for policy changes. She focused on education, poverty, and health care, which were viewed as women's issues. She utilized community action programs that were open to women's involvement. Harris expressed her view that "women were better qualified to deal with certain issues because of their gender." Moreover, she wrote in an article for *Playboy* magazine, "It's easier for women to cross racial and political lines. We tend to see the woman first, then her color, and then her party."[8] Having this appear in *Playboy* was of course quite ironic, but it was an effective way to get out her inclusive vision of women's power.

Through her work in President Johnson's War on Poverty, Harris moved into addressing more women's issues in the national sphere.[9] Her appointment to the National Council on Indian Opportunity and her chairing of the National Advisory Council on the War on Poverty gave her a much broader platform to seek meaningful changes. On April 12, 1969, the council sent her to San Francisco to gather information about the urban Indian experiences. She met with Richard Oakes and Mary Justice, and together they toured the Mission District and the Indian center. Then they went with a young Alaskan Native woman to a nearby bar. Oakes announced that LaDonna Harris was there, a Comanche whose husband was a U.S. senator. Suddenly Oakes was confronted by six Samoan men with knives. The organizers grabbed Harris and rushed her to the exit at the back of the bar, only to find it locked. A fight broke out, and World War II veteran and Native activist Walter Johns helped Richard to fight them, clearing a path for Harris to escape, and then pulling Richard to safety. It was a fearful moment for LaDonna, which she later used to persuade Mayor Joseph Alioto to attend to police conditions and other concerns of Native people in the city. Months later, Richard Oakes would lead the occupation of Alcatraz Island, in which Wilma Mankiller actively participated.[10]

During the 1970s, Harris continued to be an unapologetic feminist, while growing less comfortable with traditional restrictions of gender. In 1971, she joined Betty Friedan, whom she knew socially, as well as Gloria Steinem, Fannie Lou Hamer, Shirley Chisholm, and Bella Abzug to form the National Women's Political Caucus, which they dedicated to encouraging women to run for elective office and to support their election. Harris recalled, "I was there with Gloria and Bella, all of those great women, and I knew Dorothy Height [president of the National Council of Negro Women] before I even thought of being an activist."[11]

Harris's activism for women's rights and for Indigenous rights were always interconnected. She marched to the White House for Women's Equal Pay, because she passionately believed that women's rights are both human rights and Indigenous rights. Another aspect of LaDonna Harris's role in the early movement is illustrated by the time Bella Abzug, and the other leaders of the Women's Political Caucus were blocked from entering the U.S. Capitol. LaDonna called Senator Fred Harris, and he used his official powers to make sure they would be admitted.

However, Harris remembered few women of color being involved in the women's movement during those years, and she felt that some white women failed to appreciate the discrimination that nonwhite women experienced. She recalled Abzug, Friedan, Chisholm, Steinem, and many others confronting the issue of why few Black women and Native women joined them. LaDonna tried to communicate to these other early leaders why Native and other women of color were alienated from the feminist movement. She said:

> I haven't got an answer to it, but experiencing it was so hard to do, after
> being with those wonderful women. They always looked to me [to explain
> it], and Shirley Chisholm didn't quite have time to, being in Congress.
> Betty Friedan and Gloria Steinem particularly looked to me for how to
> reach those people, other women. We tried, but there's something about
> the attitude [of the white women] that I couldn't tell them; I could see [it]
> in them, but I couldn't tell them how to change it. Verbally they knew we
> should be doing this, but [they] didn't have any sense of how to interact
> with somebody different, didn't know how to interact with women different
> from them. I couldn't think of how to tell them to do it. There was certainly
> an arrogance about their feminism and that they knew everything. So we
> tried to have an experiment. This was horrible; we said, "Ok let's meet with
> them and talk it through and we'll meet with African American women."
> But I had an Indian point of view, so I knew how to interact with others, but
> I didn't know how to articulate it. They were too right, too smart.[12]

At one meeting between mainstream white feminists and African American feminists, the groups reached an impasse, and someone suggested that the women of color meet separately. When asked which group LaDonna would join, she said the women of color.

When reflecting on why some Native women feel estranged from the mainstream feminist movement, Harris recalled another meeting with African American women in the early days of the movement in the 1960s and 1970s.

The discussion was tense, and many of the Black women said they had to prop up their men and so needed to take a different approach. They also noted that when a Black man became successful, white women besieged him and wanted to date him.[13]

LaDonna's reflections can give us insight into how to forge a more unified movement by truly listening to one another and learning to interact with those different from ourselves without assuming any hierarchical positions. During this period of the early 1970s, Harris told a women's group to "become aware of their own divisions and not to change them, but to fashion them into weapons to meet their goals." She continued: "If we are to reach out to our sisters and brothers who do not yet stand with us, we must understand and speak to *their* experiences, *their* problems, *their* aspirations." She was keenly aware of both the differences and the commonalities among women.[14]

When LaDonna first married Fred Harris, she saw a wife's place as supporting her husband; but less than a decade later, she described women as "a secret servant class whose unpaid wages as homemakers allowed men to work in the marketplace." By the end of the seventies, she was both an activist in her own right and an unapologetic feminist. Like many who were fighting for the rights of African Americans, she also came to see the racism that she was simultaneously experiencing.[15]

On December 15, 1970, President Richard Nixon signed Public Law 91–550, returning 48,000 acres and Blue Lake to the Taos Indians. The U.S. government had seized them in 1906 as part of a move to establish a national park. In fact, at that time the Taos Pueblo had lost 300,000 acres of their land.[16] Fred and LaDonna Harris joined thousands of others in this struggle. Fred was very influential in this congressional fight, as was Americans for Indian Opportunity (AIO), the organization they founded together that same year.

One of LaDonna's many unsung interventions occurred in 1972, when AIM members occupied the BIA headquarters in Washington, D.C. She was in the building with the activists when they said they were willing to negotiate. Federal marshals were about to storm the Bureau. No one seemed empowered to negotiate with them, so LaDonna got on the phone with some Nixon officials with whom she had worked on the Taos Blue Lake case, and she told them they needed to have someone negotiate to avoid violence.

As in so many other instances, Harris led from behind. Often anonymously, she effected solutions to conflicts, took no credit, and moved on. Her leadership style resembled that of the remarkable Ella Baker, unsung heroine of the civil rights movement, who once told a filmmaker, "I found a greater sense of importance by being a part of those who were growing."[17] It is a fundamental aspect of her being to be compassionate, sensitive to others, and attentive to their needs and views.

Since its beginning, Americans for Indian Opportunity (AIO) has aimed to educate tribes, individuals, and organizations about their relationship to the federal government and the types of services available to them.[18] Due to LaDonna Harris's founding leadership and example, AIO's Ambassadors program embodies Indigenous feminism, as it is dedicated to leadership training of Native American professionals, enabling them to bring their tribal, Indigenous values to help their communities. Launched in 1970, the program is flourishing and has gone international, with ties all over the world with Indigenous people. They have established strong ties with communities in South America, Japan, Australia, and New Zealand, as well as many other countries.[19]

In "A Message from the Founding President of Americans for Indian Opportunity," Harris articulated her vision for the Ambassadors program:

> In traditional Comanche culture, each individual has their own special inner strength or "medicine." Different kinds of leaders are needed for different types of societal responsibilities. The Ambassadors will identify for themselves the types of leadership qualities and skills needed by our societies, and they will focus on how best to weave their cultural traditions into a contemporary context.
>
> Native peoples understand that relationships define our roles and shape our responsibilities to our communities. Tribal people know that these relationships and responsibilities are reciprocal and cyclical in nature. An understanding of our own identity and our pace among our own peoples creates pathways for us to strengthen ourselves, give back to our communities and broaden our horizons, giving us our role in the greater scheme of things and allowing us to be contributing citizens of our tribe and global Indigeneity.
>
> An eternal insult for Native people is that [non-Native] people don't see Indians as alive right now and still interested in cultural activities. Native people feel a generational connection and deep connection to the land. Native or Indigenous feminism differs from mainstream feminism because of the emphasis on the whole tribe and community rather than individual power. Survival also requires a sense of humor amid the overwhelming ignorance about Indians and denial of their humanity, where we are.[20]

Harris always had the hope that Americans for Indian Opportunity could be focused internationally to all Indigenous people. She remains the president of AIO, and Laura Harris, her daughter, is the executive director.

The Ambassadors program is a remarkable initiative, "an Indigenous values-based community capacity-building leadership development initiative launched in 1993. The Program helps early to mid-career Native American professionals strengthen, within an Indigenous cultural context, their ability to improve the well-being and growth of their communities."[21] The "Ambassadors" are selected from more than seven states and many different tribes. Members of each class of Ambassadors meet in four different gatherings, including a meeting in a natural place of beauty or historical-cultural consequence; an international setting in a different host country that is chosen for each class; either Washington, D.C., or New York; and in a tribal community (a reservation or urban community). Together, the group shares experiential-learning activities, mentorship, community-organizing training, communication-skills building, sessions with national decision-makers, and personal reflection.

The Ambassadors program is the only Native American leadership program that encourages participants to bring their traditional tribal values into a contemporary setting.

As a key element of the program, Harris has taught what she calls "Indian 101" for many years—material which she has blended into this program and which she illustrated in the film by that name. The program stresses the core cultural values of the Comanches that many other Native American Peoples share: relationships, responsibility, reciprocity, and redistribution. All these values are interconnected.

Each Ambassador participates for two years and remains in their community. Each class of AIO Ambassadors has visited at least one Indigenous community outside the United States, including in Guatemala, Mexico, New Zealand, Peru, Bolivia, and Venezuela. Many of the Ambassadors refer to LaDonna as Mama LaDonna, and she helps generate a powerful connection among the members of the group as they spend four gatherings together. Laura Harris, whom you will encounter more fully in chapter 6, is a superb facilitator and teacher who has been highly trained in group dynamics and experiential learning practices.[22] Her organization has now trained 250 alumni representing 150 tribes across seven states and countries. Her impact has been ongoing for decades in her dedication to Comanche values, Indian rights, environmentalism, sovereignty, and feminism.[23]

After Fred Harris ran unsuccessfully for president in 1972 and in 1976, he retired from politics and moved to New Mexico. His marriage to LaDonna faltered during these years, and they divorced in 1980. She had been a quintessential helpmate for Fred, and was as one reporter said, a "unique Senatorial asset."

When her marriage broke up, LaDonna was saddened. Their partnership, which had been so strong, began to weaken as she undertook more political battles herself. She ran for public office in 1980 as the vice-presidential candidate of the Citizen's Party. She and Fred remained friends, but she soldiered on alone.[24]

Unlike Wilma Mankiller, who always struggled with her role as a wife and with her husband Hugo's lack of support for her activism, LaDonna Harris had a loving partnership with Fred for over thirty years. Mankiller said that she did not want to be a wife who was a servant and completely submissive to her husband. La Donna did not experience this marital tension because her husband Fred was completely supportive of her ambitions. If he were in some ways threatened, he evidently disguised his feelings.

Both Harris and Mankiller were deeply committed to community develop-ment, and both were actively involved in the War on Poverty. Both saw women as especially effective in addressing issues involving families, children, health care, and poverty. Mankiller and Harris shared the views of early women's rights advocates that women were empowered as wives and mothers to protect their families through political action. For them this meant living feminism by en-abling communities to flourish by marshaling women's special intrinsic qualities and abilities.

In September 1993, Mankiller said that there was a Native prophecy "which foretold that this is the 'time of the women,' a time when women's leadership skills are needed . . . Women by and large, bring to leadership a greater sense of collaboration, an ability to view social, political, and personal concerns in a uniquely interconnected, female way."[25]

As Gloria Steinem remembers her, LaDonna has always genuinely respected others' views and believed relationships were "everything." She found her voice to be able to advocate for Native rights. Harris believes that "Native people are no longer victims and have passed the survival stage so need to be proactive: to have control over their own lives and resources as well as government, and that they have a lot to contribute by sharing their indigeneity."[26] Because of her tact, poise, and charm, LaDonna Harris could convince groups of people who disagreed vociferously. Her feminism is characterized by her commitment to hu-man connections, tribal values, social justice, and the environment.

To list all the leadership roles LaDonna Harris has played during her life to date is almost impossible. Harris agreed to be the U.S. vice-presidential candi-date for the Citizens' Party in 1980, running with Barry Commoner. She helped found the National Indian Housing Council, the Council of Energy Resource Tribes, the National Tribal Environmental Council, and the National Indian

LaDonna Harris with Madelyn May Goodhope, her great-great-granddaughter, taken by Carolyn Ross Johnston in 2017 in Albuquerque, New Mexico. Courtesy of LaDonna Harris.

Business Association, as well as serving on numerous national boards. She represented the United States to UNESCO and the Organization of American States Inter-American Indigenous Institute. She was a founding member of the National Women's Political Caucus, the National Urban Coalition, and Common Cause.[27] For over sixty years she has fought for civil rights and feminist causes as well as environmental and peace movements. On January 21, 2017, Indigenous Women Rise joined the national Women's March on Washington, D.C., to express their opposition to President-elect Donald Trump's proposals to block women's rights and Indigenous people's rights. Joining them were the Advance Native Political Leadership, Native Americans in Philanthropy, Native Voice Network, Native Voices Rising, National Indian Women's Resource Center, UltraViolet, and continental Network of Indigenous Women of the Americas. Sister marches took place in more than twenty cities across the country and across the world. LaDonna Harris was named honorary cochair of the event.[28]

LaDonna Harris was radiant when she was inducted into the National Native American Hall of Fame on October 13, 2018, at the Phoenix Indian School

Memorial Hall. Harris was surrounded by graduates of her Americans for Economic Opportunity Ambassador program, including McHalan McKosato (Sac and Fox). Cherokee/Choctaw singer Martha Redbone sang about the Indian boarding school era and played her hand drum. Emily Haozous, granddaughter of Allan Houser, said, "He built a real narrative of Native peoples as beautiful, graceful, and peaceful." At this same event, Gina Olaya, Wilma Mankiller's daughter, accepted an award for her gifted mother, and Jill Momaday accepted an award for her father, N. Scott Momaday.[29]

When LaDonna Harris turned ninety-three on February 21, 2024, she was as brilliant and vibrant as she was when she first arrived in Washington, D.C., in the 1960s. For more than half a century, she has served as a national leader of the feminist movement, as well as a leader for civil rights and tribal rights. Long before she started Oklahomans for Indian Advancement, and then Americans for Indian Opportunity, she already embodied the Comanche values of relationships, responsibility, reciprocity, and redistribution. All these values are interconnected within her lifelong tribal, Indigenous commitment to achieve social justice. LaDonna Harris always listens first, including to those who are different. This, too, is part of her legacy of effectively wielding Indigenous women's power.

CHAPTER FIVE

ADVANCING A POWERFUL LEGACY
KATHRYN HARRIS TIJERINA'S STORY

Indigenous feminist leadership is intergenerational in LaDonna Harris's family. She had three children: Kathryn, born on January 12, 1950; Byron, in 1958 and Laura, in 1961. Kathryn is ebullient, brilliant, funny, intense, and dynamic. She is a graduate of Harvard University, one of two American Indian women admitted her year. Then she earned a JD from Stanford Law School. At both of these institutions she experienced prejudice. When she complained to the dean at Harvard about so few American Indian students, the reply was that Black women were taking the minority places. In one of Kathryn's classes at law school, a Stanford professor once said, "Let's hear from the squaw now." When Kathryn was working at the University of Phoenix for thirteen years, her boss thought very highly of her, and one day he asked if she was a feminist. When she answered that she was, he was shocked. So she asked him in return, "Do you believe in equal pay for equal work?" He said, "Yes." "Well, I think *you* are a feminist," she replied. Kathryn has said in interviews, "How could I be LaDonna Harris's daughter and not be a feminist?"

What follows is a portrait of her life and family, much of it told in her words, some of it told in ours.[1] We include long narrative sequences from our interview with Kathryn Harris Tijerina because of her eloquence in recounting life with her parents in Washington, D.C., when her father was a senator, through her college and law school experiences, her years of activism in feminism, environmentalism, tribal sovereignty, indigenous arts, energy policy, and teaching, and her lifelong commitment to her family, the Comanche community, and the wider community.

TERRI BAKER: One of the things I want to ask you is about your family: who your family is, what tribe you are, and so on?

KATHRYN TIJERINA: I'm an enrolled citizen of the Comanche Nation, and the Comanches produce a lot of feminists, I believe, because traditionally we were a matrilineal tribe. The women owned the teepee and all the household goods, and men pretty much only owned their weapons and horses; everything else was owned by the women. A man would leave his family and go to his wife's family to live, and so women were very strong. I like to say Comanche women are kick-ass women; they tend to either be really sweet, like my mother is, or really mean. Those are sort of the two variations. Dolores [Sumner] of course was a sweet one, too. She used to call Mom her favorite cousin.

We weren't matriarchal, with women holding political power; the men were the peace leaders and the war leaders. We didn't actually have chiefs, which is a misunderstanding of Comanche political systems. You could be the lowest status woman in the tribe, and if a war leader was not behaving properly, and was bragging on himself or otherwise misbehaving, any woman could start teasing him and making fun of him and make him behave. Comanches were traditionally matrilineal with descent determined by women. So the women were really in charge of behavior. That's forgotten by some of the men in our tribe occasionally, but they never mess with any of the women, because the women still are pretty intense.

I was very fortunate to grow up with a very strongly feminist mother, and my dad who appreciated strong women. My dad's non-Indian; he's Scots Irish. As a result of how she was raised by her grandparents in a very traditional home, my grandmother had two non-Indian husbands, both marriages ending in divorce. To make a living, she went off and worked as a dietitian with the Indian Health Service. The Indian Health Service at that time required you to live on campus; you had to live there at the hospital, and so she went off to work full-time and worked for over thirty years with IHS. As a result, my mother was raised by her grandparents, with aunts and uncles and tons of cousins, and so it was very communal, the way Comanches ought to be raised.

My dad, even though he was non-Indian, learned to speak Comanche; so he's a fluent Comanche speaker and was fascinated with the history of Comanche people. He would go talk to all our elders and would record their conversations, and loved all the military and all those other kinds of historical things. Although he said he could never understand the Comanche religion. He said you had to be raised as a Comanche to understand the Comanche religion.

I was very fortunate when I was growing up that I always had cousins around me, and I would go stay with cousins and stay with my great-uncles and -aunts. Later on, when we moved to Cherry Street, we were just like a block away from the high school, and so our relatives, who were out on farms on Indian allotments out in the countryside, they would come and stay with us. This was in Lawton, Oklahoma, which is in the southwest part of Oklahoma. It was the third largest city when I was growing up. It was only about

60,000 people, so now I like to say I'm an urban Indian. I grew up in the big city of Lawton.

BAKER: Who was the oldest person you can remember? In American Indian communities, so much has been lost, and the oldest people are treasures because of memories.

TIJERINA: The oldest person would be my great-grandfather; he had cowboyed with Burke Burnett for a while. On his mother's side he's a descendant of Ten Bears, and his father was a Spanish captive whose original name was Sabino Romero. He was captured fairly late in his childhood; I think he was like eight or nine. He wasn't a particularly good captive at first. He fought against the Comanches and would act out, and so they called him Hoawah, which you'd translate as "The wild one," so that's his family. He's of the Yambarika Comanches, which was of course Ten Bears's band of Comanches. Yambarika means "Root eater"—there's a root that's like sweet potato that's called *yapi*, and apparently Yambarikas loved that. Comanche names tend to be about eating things. I think we were all foodies in the day. I had Papa with me as my great-grandfather until I was about, I think, ten when he passed away. But his wife, my great-grandmother, was with me until I was twenty-six. She lived for a long time. She was younger than he was to begin with, and he had had other wives as well.

You know, we were talking about non-Indian perceptions of Indian culture. Most anthropologists still say that there are a lot of polygamist societies throughout the world, but there are very few polyandry societies throughout the world. I always thought that was because these white men envisioned themselves with lots of wives, but they couldn't conceive of the idea of having a lot of husbands, so I think they missed a lot of societies. In Comanche culture, you had both multiple husbands and multiple wives. It was essentially a social security system, so that you would always have someone to hunt for you. My husband always loves the fact that anyone I take as sister is his wife; he enjoys that. The truth is that all his brothers and all my sisters' husbands are my husbands, as well. So when I tell people that Manuel is my favorite husband, they laugh and think, "Oh, isn't that cute," but I'm serious. Of course, I never really liked Jocelyn's or Laura's husbands that much, but luckily some of my sisters have good husbands.

How a family celebrates holidays depends on tribal traditions as well as host of other factors: whether a child attended boarding school, the location of the family, the unity or separation of family members, the reunion possibilities of holidays, and the memories that would surface. So Carolyn Johnston asked Kathryn how she celebrated holidays.

> TIJERINA: My mother loved holidays; she would always make a big deal of them. She would have decorations, so even for minor holidays like Valentine's Day or Halloween, she would go all out. We would have all sorts of decorations, and we would have family from both sides come over and share meals, so it was very important. She remembered when oranges were a scarce thing, so we would always have oranges and things like that in our stockings. One of the things I find funny about how Comanche translates into modern society is the word for "pear" in Comanche translates into "bears' fruit." And I was thinking, did bears particularly like pears? It turned out pears would come in these wooden crates with a picture of a bear on the front, so that's why they called it "bears' fruit."

The boarding schools and white education in general influenced marriage patterns, and so Carolyn Johnston asked Kathryn how she met Manuel, her husband.

> TIJERINA: We were law school sweethearts. My theory is anybody you can stand in law school, you can live with the rest of your life. For undergraduate I'd gone to the University of Oklahoma for two years, which is where I met Jocelyn. We then both transferred out—we'd decided it was time to have a new adventure. We were both going to go to Brandeis, but then while we were waiting to get the acceptance, I got admitted into Radcliffe, at Harvard. Back in that day your degree came from Harvard, but [women] were actually admitted to Radcliffe, which had a smaller admission rate than Harvard. So it was more difficult to get in.

> BAKER: Why did you want to go to college?

> TIJERINA: My dad had gone to college; my mother only had a high school degree. [At first] she only spoke Comanche; that was her primary language. When she went to first grade in public schools in Oklahoma—we were severely dyslexic in my family, [and] you may not know, dyslexia is a sex-linked gene, and is only passed on by the mother. Women and men can be dyslexic, but only women pass on the gene. When she was talking about the smallpox epidemic, my great-grandmother used to say "the small fox." So when I was little, I used to visualize seeing small foxes carrying the Comanches away. My mom with her dyslexia had a very difficult time and flunked the first grade. She survived mostly by figuring out her teachers and figuring out what her teachers wanted, and demonstrating to them she was smart and understood the material, even though she couldn't take tests well. She never went on to school after high

school; she graduated from high school, where she met my dad. She now, of
course, has honorary PhDs from New Zealand and from many of the main
schools here in the United States, and she is very well-regarded because of her
research and her advocacy for Indian rights, civil rights, women's rights, environmental rights, and the peace movement.

BAKER: You were involved in all those things as you grew up?

TIJERINA: I was. There are some fun pictures of us out demonstrating. My dad
first was elected to the state senate when he was twenty-seven years old. He
actually ran for state representative when he was twenty-one and lost that
election, and then was elected several times to the state senate, ran for governor
of Oklahoma and lost that election. Then he ran for U.S. senator and was twice
elected to the U.S. Senate from Oklahoma, as a new populist. He also ran for
president against Jimmy Carter, or as he liked to say, it was more of a short jog.
He was not elected president of the United States.

BAKER: Inclusivity in many tribes is important. Has inclusivity figured in your
life, given the many Comanche captives I learned about from your cousin, Delores, who was my friend from our Northeastern State University days?

TIJERINA: Oh, yes, absolutely, and it's also a Comanche value. We were very inclusive; we had all these captives who were Spanish, who were Americans, who
were Mexicans, who were Mexican Indians, all varieties. I think we had some
of the French who controlled Mexico for a while; we had some of those people,
because we have red-headed people with green eyes. Our culture is very much
about being flexible, being adaptable; we adapted [to] the horse right away,
and that spirit of inclusiveness—you know our core values are relationships,
responsibility, reciprocity, and redistribution. Those are all important concepts,
and that's the way my mother taught me to live.

Clearly, Kathryn's mother LaDonna instilled these values in her daughter,
which is a part of the intergenerational nature of women's power and tribal values. Kathryn also talked about her family and specifically mentioned the importance of who comes after you.

BAKER: You have a sister, is that right?

TIJERINA: I have a sister and brother; my brother is very severely dyslexic, even
more than I am. He only has a high school degree, but you would talk to him
and think he's a college graduate, because he's very articulate, and has a great
vocabulary and is very, incredibly smart. He went into TV production because

that was an area that he didn't need a lot of reading and writing. It's a visual area, and he excelled at that. He's now won four Emmys; they're group Emmys in the technical area, but that's still the pinnacle of his profession. We're very proud of him.

My sister is the baby of the family; she's eleven years younger than I am. She worked for Jeff Bingaman, who was the U.S. senator from New Mexico. She went over to the Smithsonian, where she was one of the very first staff people, even before Rick West was hired for the National Museum of the American Indian. We believe in the transition of leadership: you have to think of who comes after you. So, my mother hired her to groom her to be the executive director of Americans for Indian Opportunity, which she now is, and is doing a fabulous job of that.

BAKER: What was your first job, and some of the jobs you've had since then?

TIJERINA: When my dad was a U.S. senator, my very first job was working for Carl Albert, who was the Speaker of the House, and from Oklahoma. I had a summer job with him. So I can now do a bang-up tour of the U.S. Capitol, because that was part of my job. When tourists came in from Oklahoma, I would take them on a tour and talk about the art and the history of all the different parts of the capitol building.

The following summer I worked at the Senate (the vice president of the United States is also the leader of the Senate), so I worked in the Senate office of Hubert Humphrey, who was vice president, and I was the receptionist in his office. One of my most embarrassing moments was when someone called up for the administrative assistant, who was there in that office, and I asked, "Who shall I say is calling?" He said, "This is Hubert Humphrey." I didn't recognize his voice, so I was totally embarrassed. Those were great summer jobs, of course, as a kid.

I went on to law school after graduating magna cum laude from Harvard. I thought law school would be the next step. I did that in part because I wanted to be a sociologist, so I had gone to Oklahoma and had done a research project over the summer. As part of my senior thesis, I had to do an honors paper. I studied the police and Indians in Oklahoma. I chose Shawnee, because it was not one of the "bad" towns, I mean towns like Anadarko, towns like Ponca City, those were sort of known in Indian country to be really negative towns in terms of police–Indian relations. I think I was interested in that issue because I had a great-uncle who had been beaten to death by the Lawton police, my hometown police. And so because of that death, I always was very wary around police—because of that family history. Anything that worries me, I always want to study, so I thought, okay I should study up on Indian–police relations. What I found is that 50 percent of my sample in Shawnee, Oklahoma, over many years had died in police custody.

BAKER: And this was one of the good towns?

TIJERINA: Yes, this was one of the good towns. So that's one of the reasons I got my magna cum laude, because of that original research. But in the process, I also discovered that I needed to be more active. I couldn't just be a scholar and study things. I wanted to be more active.

In 2020, American Indians joined the Black Lives Matter protests in Minneapolis, after George Floyd was murdered by a police officer. In 1968, police brutality in the Twin Cities led to the creation of the American Indian Movement.[2] Kathryn Tijerina's personal story regarding the police and American Indians explains why she felt urgent concern in 2020, as she had for the previous fifty years.

TIJERINA: As a young child growing up in southwestern Oklahoma in the 1950s, I had a different attitude about police than most of the children I went to school with. Most of the white children thought of police as their friends. Police were someone who would buy them ice cream cones. Police would save their cats from getting stuck in trees.

That was not my experience. Growing up as Comanche, I was taught that it was not okay to be afraid of things. My Mother would make fun of me if I made a fuss about getting a vaccine shot. I was never taught to be afraid of snakes or spiders. But while I was never afraid of police exactly, I was always very wary of them. It was not something I was told. It was never discussed. It just was.

When I was older, I found out that my great-grandmother's youngest brother had died from being beaten by the police in my hometown. His name was Frank Red Elk. I never really knew Uncle Frank, but I loved his daughter, Zona, and everyone on that side of the family. His death and the unspoken grief of my family set me on a path of trying to understand more about police and law enforcement in general. In college, one of the things I liked in the late 60s and early 70s is cross disciplinary studies. So I majored in what was called Social Relations or "Soc Rel," which included all the social sciences from sociology to anthropology. I used that platform to study police and prison systems.

My first direct experience was going into a prison in Massachusetts. The prison was Bridgewater State Prison in Springfield, Massachusetts, and the year was 1969. The prison had male inmates, who included the criminally insane, inmates convicted of sexual crimes, and inmates convicted of political crimes, among others.

I had read about the various motives for locking people up. I was interested in learning if the prison guards believed in rehabilitating prisoners, or in keeping people in prison for the safety of society, or if they wanted prisoners to be punished for what they did. So I was able through the Phillips Brooks House to get the prison to agree to have me conduct a survey of the prison guard's attitudes. In exchange, I agreed to teach a class on Indian history to the prisoners.

My next step was in 1972, when I had the opportunity to do more original research. I was fortunate to get some funding from the U.S. Law Enforcement Assistance Agency and a grant from Equitable Life Assurance to look at "Native American and Police Relations." I knew that towns like Anadarko and Ponca City were known to be dangerous for Native Americans. But I wanted a more general sense of how things were. So I chose to study Shawnee, Oklahoma. I moved back to Oklahoma and started to interview Native American families in the area.

It was often hurtful and tough to dredge up this information. I found it a difficult process, and it must have been worse for those who were willing to talk to me. I found that of those I interviewed across time, over 51 percent had a family member or friend who had died in police custody. Some of these were people in jail who were, for example, denied medication. Or people who were found to have committed "suicide" while in jail. Others were like my uncle, Native Americans who were killed by the police.

For me this study was so traumatic that I made the decision that I could no longer just study a problem. I needed to find a way to be more of an activist. I decided to go to law school. In law school, I had the opportunity to participate in a police ride-along. While we were in the police station waiting for a call, one of the officers pulled me into his lap. He asked, "What do you say about that?" I answered, "I say sexual harassment," at which point he dumped me off his lap. Luckily, he was not the officer I rode with.

Because of Stanford Law School's proximity to Oakland, California, I got to know some of the Native American community there. I began to realize they had a serious problem with the police and the Native community. I was young and naive and hoped that education and training might have an impact on what was a systemic racist and militarized culture. There is a reason that they call some of the most aggressive officers "cowboys."

So, in 1974, I instituted a unit to train patrolmen in Indian Affairs in the Oakland Police Department. Although I was never trained as a trainer, I used my knowledge of the issues to conduct the training. Although the training was attended and the officers were attentive, I did not feel ultimately that I had an impact on their behavior. As far as I was able to ascertain, it did not notably help the Native community. It was heartbreaking.

Now I am sixty-six years old [in 2016] and retired after a long career in activism. I am thrilled at what is going on in 2020. Black Lives Matter is an organization that recognizes the systemic nature of the problem. It is also an organization mostly run by women. I am amazed and warmed to see so many different races in the street calling for fundamental reform.

I am hopeful that real reform will take place and that we can maintain the outrage for unwarranted police killings. I just wish that the people in the United States would also understand the number of police killings of Indigenous people. I am finally seeing a few Black women on the news who include LatinX and Indigenous people in their comments. Over all groups, Native Americans have the highest incident of death by police. In this Olympics that no one wants to win, the exception is young Black men.

Say the name. Frank Red Elk.

In an earlier interview, Terri Baker and Carolyn Ross Johnston asked Kathryn Harris Tijerina about many issues, including how young people decide what to do with their lives and why it is important for them to have models to follow.

TIJERINA: My dad, who had been the first person in his family to have graduated from college, then had gone on to OU (the University of Oklahoma) College of Law where he, at the time, had the best grade point average by anyone in the history of OU Law. That may have been broken by now, but at the time and for many years after, he had the highest grades. It was really the only thing I knew about, because that's what he did. So I thought, well I'll try that, so I went off to Stanford Law School, where I met Manuel, my favorite husband. He had gone to the University of Arizona in Tucson and had graduated college Phi Beta Kappa in three years with a double major, and he had almost gotten three majors. He was three credits short of having an additional major in math, just because he likes math. It was the fun thing for him to take. He was a very smart guy, which is how he survived growing up as a migrant farm worker. He would go as a migrant worker with his family and work in the fields from the time he was seven on, and that meant he would have to leave school before the end of the school year and start school in a different location than he would be the rest of the school year. So that was difficult academically, and yet he survived it and went on to law school.

The way that I first met Manuel was when we were in the same small section in law school, which meant that we went to all the first-year classes together, the same classes, and in some of the larger classes, like Civil Procedure, there would be other small groups that would join ours. We had a visiting professor, Willie Whitford, as our Contracts professor, and he called on Manuel. And he called him Mr. Titurveenee. Manuel got up, and before he answered the question correctly, which he eventually did, he gave the professor a lecture on the proper pronunciation of Spanish surnames, and I went, "Hmmm, this is an interesting person."

We've been married now for forty years, and I think one of the reasons we do well together is that his mother was a very strong woman. She had four children, and she got up and made breakfast for them before the crack of dawn, and then got out in the fields, and Manuel always said she could pick more cotton than his dad. She would work in the fields all day, then come home and cook again, and do laundry, and the housework, and whatever else that needed to happen. She was never given the opportunity to be something more than a farm laborer, but she was certainly one of the smartest and strongest people. I enjoy strong women, and I relate to strong women well.

BAKER: What do you think about women's history? What do you think it is? Is it American history, or is it a subset?

TIJERINA: I think women's history *is* history; history couldn't happen without women, and history has largely been taught without telling the story of women. Women have made incredible strides and changed the course of history often, and that has rarely been accurately reported, whether that's women in arts, or Native women, or any particular type of women. I think that they are key to history.

BAKER: Were you involved in the feminist movement?

TIJERINA: In the early 60s I was involved in the civil rights movement initially. We integrated Lawton, our hometown, before any of the national civil rights legislation and we did that primarily . . . my dad had been on the mayor's commission on integrating Lawton, but my mother helped create this organization, this sort of informal group of Black people, white people, and Indian people, which was a very unusual combination in Oklahoma.

BAKER: Why was that?

TIJERINA: Well, there was a lot of racism in Oklahoma growing up. It was different for Black people. For African Americans there were sundown towns in Oklahoma, which literally said you could come in and work, but by the time the sun touched the earth, you had to be out of town. They would not allow African Americans to be there overnight. That's the kind of harsh racism that came out of the Deep South. A lot of people who settled Oklahoma came from the Deep South. My dad's people came from Mississippi. So there was a very active racism against Blacks.

But there was also racism against Indian people. Sometimes it was direct, like with Black people, where it's "No dogs or Indians are allowed." I've seen signs like that in Anadarko, for example. We just talked about police–Indian relations, but there was also this kind of benign, subtle racism. For example, they would say things like, "Oh, you want to come to our church? You're Indian, how wonderful, what a wonderful heritage that is, but you know, you have your own church over here, and I think it would be really better if you went to your own church and not come to ours." That kind of racism was very prevalent in Oklahoma despite the very high rate of Indian people who lived there. In some ways it was a harder racism to combat because it wasn't as overt.

That covert racism just ended up making Indians feel bad about themselves. Somehow it was their fault rather than the fault of the system that kept them down. Particularly when Mother was organizing AIO, people would think Indians couldn't make As and that Indians weren't good enough to do well in school. My mother never believed that, and she wondered why people had those ideas. So she first started with this Honcho group, sometimes just called "the group," which didn't have a hierarchy, [as] it was a rotating social system. One time they would have the meeting in a Black home, one time they would have a meeting in a white home. They would serve food, they would get together, they'd talk about the issue. The issue was how to integrate Lawton. They would talk about, "Okay, this restaurant needs to be integrated. Okay, who knows the owner, who knows where she gets her supplies from, who knows where she banks?" And they would figure out through just sharing information with one another how to approach that person, how to pressure him through friends, through people with more power over them, to pressure them to agree to integrate.

BAKER: Do you think that's part of Native women's feminism?

TIJERINA: Yes, that collaborative spirit I think is absolutely a part of Native women's feminism. And food, you always share food. My mother excels at that kind of relationship building, getting involved, figuring out what people need and how to create change based on finding the right people to be the leverage to make that change. That collaboration. She's always worked with a group of other women who could support her in her work, so collaboration, I agree, is very much key.

You asked earlier about other things I've done in my career. After I left law school I worked for a nonprofit of eastern, mostly non-federally recognized tribes called CENA, and then I got offered a position with the Indian Policy Review Commission, which was a joint committee of the U.S. House of Representatives and the U.S. Senate. I came on as a staff person for Senator Abourezk of South Dakota, who is Lebanese American. I was also counsel to the commission. We did research on past legislation. Indians have more legislation about them that they have to deal with than any other group in the United States. We have a whole volume, literally a whole volume of U.S. statutes that just deals with Indian tribes. Our modern existence is very complex from a legal standpoint, and we were looking at old laws to get rid of the bad ones, and reinforce new laws, and find laws to deal with questions like divided strips of Indian land. So if an Indian person had 140 acres of land, which was a typical Indian allotment, they could pass that on to their eight children, then their eight children would pass that on to their eight children and so on. And after about the third generation you had a group of people who owned land in common, but you had to all agree on how to do something like lease it, and it was functionally impossible to control what happened on the land with any degree of efficiency.

These issues created a lot of problems throughout Indian country, and so that whole issue was addressed in one of the issues I dealt with when I was working on the Indian Policy Review Commission. Afterward, I went on to Senator Abourezk's personal staff, and then on to the Senate Indian Committee, where I was a counsel, and I was able to write laws and help pass the laws. Manuel at the time was working for Congressman Vincent Lieball, an important congressman on the Appropriations Committee and chairman of the committee that dealt with the federal government and postal service and the White House. It was kind of fun, because back in those days, you could actually get legislation passed. I'd run a bill from the Senate side, and he'd run it from the House side, and we'd get things passed by working together, so that was a lot of fun.

We gave ourselves a year after law school. We were essentially together three years in law school, so we took a year after law school to see if we still liked each other after that rarefied environment. Then we were married. We went back to the Deyo mission in Oklahoma to get married. My great-grandmother was there, and I invited girlfriends from OU and Radcliffe who came down and were part of the wedding party. And the women of the community did our food for the reception, and my mom took a *Vogue* pattern and made it into a Comanche dress with the little flaps on the sides and the little square cloth coming down on each side, and a whole bunch of her friends worked on the dress. Other than my wedding ring, I think the flowers and cake were most expensive. I think I paid $177 for my whole wedding; it was wonderful.

The marriage discussion led us to talk about American Indian religious freedom.

TIJERINA: When I was working in the Senate, a real issue was that Indian religious freedom was being denied because people didn't understand how different Indian religions were in terms of the place, and that place was very significant to Indian people. My mother, for example, and parents—both my dad and mom—had been instrumental in the return of the Taos Blue Lake, which was their sacred area. The people of Taos Pueblo had been trying for sixty years to get their land back, and they had won a land claim suit in the federal government saying, "Yes, that is their land, that the Forest Service illegally took that land from them." But they had only been offered money compensation, and they refused the money compensation, because that was their sacred site, and they wanted the land itself back. In the Nixon administration, my parents were able to pass a bipartisan bill to get that land returned, and it was the first time Indian land had ever been returned, and so it set a great precedent. As well as being very important for the Taos people, it set an international precedent, really, about Indian people being able to reclaim their land.

I was very aware of those issues, of the importance of religious freedom for Indian people, which should have been guaranteed by the U.S. Constitution, but which as a practical matter wasn't, because it didn't fit the Judeo-Christian sort of formula. I worked with some wonderful Indian people out of the Crow Reservation and other places, who were medicine people who came and advised us on how to do things. Then I wrote up the bill and worked with Senator Abourezk and others to get the bill passed in the Indian committee, and then in the full Senate. And then I wrote up the Senate report, and in a very unusual thing—usually the Senate doesn't have anything to do with the House, but I'd worked with the Indian members over in the House side, and they were very busy with something else they thought was more important at the time, and so they asked me to write up the report for the House side, as well—so I did that. And the bill got passed and signed into law.

At this point in her professional life, Kathryn began the move into management, which she enjoyed. She liked the more collaborative nature of management, and she enjoyed working with women. Her network was increasing, and currently is immense.

TIJERINA: About that time, I decided it was time to move on to the Department of Energy. I'd been thinking I was going to go into Indian law, and to practice law, but one of the things was that, while I found law intellectually very interesting, it was very confrontational. It was always win-lose.

I discovered that one could study management in college. I really didn't know that was an option. I discovered management after I got out of law school and had been working in Congress for a while, and found you could get to a win-win situation, and I found I liked that better. I went into the Department of Education, and they gave me a lot of management training while I was there. I worked in the Indian office, where I was basically the second person in charge of the office, and one of the things I liked about that was we were giving out grants throughout Indian country for renewable energy. We were working with the Council of Energy Resource Tribes, on oil and gas and uranium and some of the big-ticket things.

There had been a movement previously, which my mother pretty much had headed up, and she helped create. She has a history of creating organizations and spinning them off, so that the people for whom that's their passion, they should run it, and she'd just go and create a new organization. The Council of Energy Resource Tribes was one of those. We started off with getting ten cents for a ton of coal, and there was no place in the world where the owners of the land were so badly exploited, except for one place in Nigeria, I believe—they had even worse contracts than we did. It was a really prime example of [those situations where] we owned the land, it was our resources, and we were getting almost nothing, because the Bureau of Indian Affairs made the contracts for us, and they weren't being a good trustee. They were being piss-poor trustees in fact.

BAKER: Did you work with women on all these projects?

TIJERINA: The Department of Energy had almost no women. One of the things that happened to me [earlier was] there were some great women in the Senate, and I was collaborative with them.

I remember at one point I went to talk to Senator Abourezk, because there was an Indian man who was working with me who was doing exactly the same thing I was, and getting paid more than I was. So I went to Abourezk, and I had this very well thought-out argument for saying exactly why he should change that. My first sentence was, "He's doing exactly what I'm doing and he's getting paid more," at which point Senator Abourezk stopped me and said, "You're right; we should fix that," and he promptly gave me a raise. And I was so frustrated because I had this very, you know, well thought-out argument, and I didn't get a chance to make it, and his point was, "Hey, if you win, quit arguing." So that's one thing I had to learn.

Then at the end of my career with the Department of Energy, the head of the Indian Office, which was in the Intergovernmental Affairs department, had resigned, and so I was the acting director. Under the actual regulations of the federal government, if you're in the acting position more than six months, then you are legally required to get the position. So I went to the secretary of the Energy Department, and I said I would be very interested in getting this job. His response was "I know you are, Kathryn, but we need an older man for that position." So that would have been a fabulous lawsuit if I had been a litigious person. But I decided [against] suing, because at that point it was just his word against my word that he had actually said that. So I found someone whom I knew he respected highly and had that person call him and say, "You know, Kathryn could have had a very good lawsuit against you." And at the same time, I decided, "If they don't value my contribution, then it's time for me to leave." And that's when Manuel and I decided to move to New Mexico. We took a 50 percent cut in our incomes but had never been happier.

In the Department of Energy, I was almost always the only woman. There were mostly PhDs in the sciences, and it was a very difficult position in that regard, because it wasn't collaborative, and I enjoy those that are more collaborative. But at that point, I also became a member of the Women of Color, which was a national nonprofit organization, made up of African American women, Indian women, Hispanic women, and Asian American women primarily. My old boss at the Senate was a man named Alan Parker, and his wife was an African American woman. She started the group, and I was one of the founding members of the organization. So that even when I couldn't, in my day job, work with women, I ended up figuring out a way of working with them, because that was always sort of the way you got things done.

BAKER: Is there a difference between mainstream or white feminism and Indian feminism?

TIJERINA: Indian women have had a hard time joining white feminist organizations in general, because I think that white feminist organizations often have a harder edge to them. I don't know how to say it exactly, but they're more

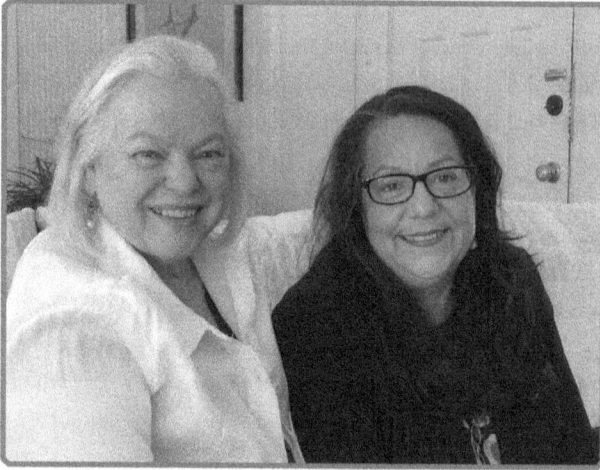

Kathryn Tijerina Harris and Laura Harris are enrolled citizens of the Comanche Nation. Photograph taken by Carolyn Ross Johnston in 2017 in Albuquerque, New Mexico. Courtesy of Kathryn Tijerina Harris and Laura Harris.

dealing with power, and sometimes even money, and less about social change and making change happen, or just sort of the motivation for it is somewhat different—and it's almost a culture, more than it is something that's articulated.

Despite that, my Mother was very involved. For example, she was a founding member of the Women's Political Caucus, which was an organization devoted to, at that point, electoral politics. The Women's Political Caucus was specifically to get women elected to positions of power, to electoral positions, to be elected for office. I had that in my background, so I was always open to women's groups. But I think American Indian women tend to be—I think all women are more collaborative—but I think [American] Indian women tend to take relationships and redistribution to a level that non-Indian women groups don't really see as clearly.

Although I think Gloria Steinem has been very collaborative, in part because of her relationship to Mom, whom she talks about in her most recent book. Gloria Steinem was open enough to learn a lot about Indian issues, and for a non-Indian she's got an excellent grasp of those issues. I grew up around Bella Abzug, and Shirley Chisholm, and Gloria Steinem. And interestingly, one of my favorites was Betty Freidan. She took me under her wing and turned me on to Doris Lessing, the author, and I read, I think it was *The Four-Gated City*. Betty Friedan was just very interested in spending time with me. The only thing I disapproved about her was that she was in that old mindset that we shouldn't support gay women, because men think that all feminists are gay anyway, and that would hurt the feminist movement. My theory was we should be inclusive, and if gay women need help, we should be helping them, because that helps all of us.[3]

CHAPTER SIX

LAURA HARRIS'S INDIGENOUS FEMINIST STORY

Laura Harris is a brilliant, compassionate, widely honored advocate for Indigenous rights and a committed lifelong feminist. Her Indigenous feminism applies traditional tribal values to meeting the needs of all Indian communities, and it extends across global contexts. She is a member of the National Congress of American Indians, the North American Indian Women's Association, and the Toyah Band of Comanche of New Mexico. These struggles are deeply personal for Laura Harris as the Indigenous feminist woman she was born and raised to be. As she said, "I am a troublemaker, did I mention that?"[1] Laura's kind of "troublemaking" is fighting against injustice and suffering. She is a rebel for social justice.

To prepare for her role as a leader in these intersecting struggles for social justice, Laura earned a BA in Political Science and Native American Studies in 1984. Because she felt she would need them, she also earned a Certificate of Study in the Spanish Language at Cuauhnahau Instituto (in 1983) and a Certificate of Study of Principles of Fundraising from the University of Indiana Center on Philanthropy (in 1991). She also traveled extensively in Latin America and continues to do so.

Laura's experiences in political campaigns, policy formation, and institutional development expanded her understanding of how change processes work and the values that ultimately matter. These experiences include her service as senior consultant for President Clinton's Initiative on Race (1997–1998), as senior adviser for Howard Dean's 2004 presidential campaign, as political director for the midwestern states in Bill Richardson's campaign for president (2007–2008), and as chair of the Native American Democratic Caucus of New Mexico (2006–2011). She put her skills as a trained fundraiser to work with the planning firm of Unger Thomas in West Hollywood, California, and the Democratic Foundation of Orange County, California. She also worked as development, public relations, and special events associate for the Smithsonian's Office of Institutional Initiatives, and she was part of the original staff of the National Museum of American Indian Campaign Office.[2] Laura worked for six years as the administrative correspondent and constituent liaison in Senator Jeff Bingaman's Washington, D.C., office. She also served on Barack Obama's Native American Domestic Policy Committee during his successful 2008 presidential campaign. Laura currently serves as the executive director of AIO and the Ambassadors program, the indigenous values-based leadership development initiative of Americans for Indigenous Opportunities.[3]

However, this extensive list of her leadership roles may be misleading because Laura Harris actually began her work as a rebel for social justice when she was just a child. She marched in front of the White House for women's rights, participated in antiwar marches, and testified before Congress. As Laura acknowledges, "Aside from having it in my DNA as a daughter of LaDonna Harris, I remember that it was shortly after I could read that I knew things were unfair. Every night at the dinner table we talked about things that were unfair. It was McLean, Virginia, where I grew up with a handful of Native Americans. Our neighborhood was very white." Laura was in elementary school when her father became a U.S. senator. She was teased by other children at her school, where they were taught a white-privileged version of American history and culture that made such injustices seem normal: "My fourth-grade teacher said, when we were studying the Civil War, that we couldn't blame those plantation owners for having slaves, because they needed help." However, Laura and her girlfriends pushed back, demanding equality for all, including girls.

> In third grade, [we] changed the dress code to [allow us to] wear a "pantsuit." We were very active, and we ran around and chased the boys and climbed on the monkey bars and spun around on the monkey bars. Somebody found out, and we got in trouble for wearing shorts under our dresses, which we weren't supposed to do. I asked, "In PE we're learning to spin around the bars—when we spin around on the bars would you rather the boys see our panties?" They couldn't answer that question. I asked a lot of questions. Around '67 or '68, we finally threw a fit, and they changed it. Those were the kinds of things I did, because I thought that's what you're supposed to do. I was opposed to prejudice of any kind. My third-grade teacher sent a girl who was a little special, a little slow, to the office on an errand. She told the rest of the class she was retarded, and I stood up and said, "Don't call her that."[4]

Laura attributes her strength to rebel against such injustices to being raised by two strong women, her mother and the strong African American woman who served her family as housekeeper, and who played a central role in raising her.

My teachers always really liked me but didn't always know what to do with me. I was a rebel. I had a sense of belonging to something larger. I knew I had a different worldview than others. I also grew up around strong women. When we moved to Washington, D.C., I was raised by an African American housekeeper who was a very strong, independent woman. She went with the family to protests. I felt that I was born a poor black child; I was one of them, born in the richest county in Virginia in a large, four-bedroom, three-story house in McLean, Virginia. Harriet Tubman was one of my heroes, and still is. We went to church, social events and a lot of protests, and our housekeeper joined us. There's a picture of the four of us at the White House, protesting for equal pay. I was involved from a young age in the feminist movement. In the movement of the sixties, white members were . . . many of the members were not very sensitive to people's color; they were racist. They didn't mean to be racist, but they were horrible.

Reflecting on her more recent experiences, Laura noted that feminist racism continues to be a problem that divides women.

We recently just had an issue: a friend of ours who works in a group, UltraViolet—which came out of the feminist network, which was predominantly white. She's part of that. She can talk about the women's political caucus and women's struggles, but she was talking about the black women peeling off, and she said she would peel with them, and the white women said it hurt their feelings. They really were like, "Oh my God, you feel that way too? We see you as one of us." But she didn't see herself as one of them, as she related to the black women.[5]

Laura Harris sees feminism and equality as part of Indigenous values, specifically her Comanche values. At one point, she said, she and her mother were "one person." To her, to be a Comanche means being a part of something larger, being part of nature, taking care of nature, being among strong women. However, she points out, sometimes Indigenous men have lost the thread of gender equality. Thus, for example, few Pueblo men will say they are in a matrilineal tribe. She calls tribes "the canary in the mine," as men have moved into low-paying blue-collar jobs, while women are solving all the problems and becoming more educated than the men. This trend has destabilized gender relations in some tribes, she says.

In an article she coauthored with her mother, LaDonna Harris, and sister,

Kathryn Tijerina, Laura Harris wrote about her pride in her own mixed Comanche Mexican heritage:

> I have always thought of myself as Numunuh (Comanche), though I basically grew up in Washington, D.C. and I have mixed blood. I'm particularly proud of my Spanish and Mexican Indian captive genealogy, which means our Comanche ancestors were strong warriors who valued the wealth of extended family. Comanche carry our inheritance with great pride, and no matter if we are able to tackle the challenges of citizenship in a progressive manner or not, I will proudly teach my granddaughter what it is to be a Numunuh, about her rich Comanche heritage—not just the songs and dances, but also our values, history of governance styles, and our past economic empire.[6]

Her pride in her complex family heritage leads Laura to stand up for other Indigenous leaders in their own fights for justice. When the AIO Ambassadors went to Bolivia, President Morelos hosted them. He is Indigenous himself, and his supporters had protested the privatization of water. For this reason, the U.S. State Department did not want the Ambassadors to give President Morales an award, and they tried to stop it.

What the State Department did not understand, however, is that tribal leaders act more as diplomatic generalists than as hierarchical leaders. As Laura Harris explains:

> In Americans for Indian Opportunity, we call our leaders "Ambassadors." We were thinking that tribal leaders acted more like diplomats. They have to be intergovernmental; they have to shoot basketball with the kids and eat lunch with elders, that they have to be generalists and holistic and that's what we found. They were successful because they were radical; they had a broad view. . . . We're the only national organization to talk about Indigenous values versus American values, and to define the differences. We have stopped saying, "We live in two worlds," since there's only one world, and you have to bring those values with you, and the only way to do that is to recognize them and articulate them, and then figure out how to bring those values with you in a modern context.

This is why the Ambassadors program aims to get away from narrow training of leaders so they can promote Indigenous values at a national and international level.[7] Based on her training in facilitation from CogniScope from CWA, Ltd., and faculty members in George Mason University's Department of Communications, Laura Harris designed the Indigenous Leaders Interactive System. This program is a consensus-building process that she and others use to help tribal governments and Indian organizations to build coalitions among various groups in order to address issues facing these tribal nations. The aim of this process is to strengthen the self-determination and sovereignty of Indigenous communities.[8]

In Laura Harris's view, feminist values are Indigenous values, and vice versa. However, some Indigenous peoples have lost this recognition, which must be restored within the leadership training process. As she explains:

> Feminism is certainly about equality and balance and Indigenous values. The Navahos articulated it so well, about being in harmony and morality and balance. We had to have balance to have a whole society. In leadership training we include women's issues as a primary concern, and [we] have a broader range of what women's issues are. A lot of men and women have lost that boundary. We need more leadership training and cultural emphasis so what they think of as feminist issues are very relevant to the needs of Native women. We also need to address cultural and sexual repression.[9]

Harris continues:

> We have lost that thread, that value, and here in New Mexico it's a prickly subject. Very early on, about five years ago or so, the buffalo people took on the Spanish [patriarchal] systems, so it's very rare to find a man who says it's matrilineal, but they'll be the first one to say, [when asked] "Do you own a house?" "Well, my mom owns a house" or "My wife owns a house." That's why . . . I talk about the racism in the movement, and also on the other hand . . . really colonialism and sexism are conjoined. And I really believe that. Women get things done. Christianity can also contribute to women's subjugation.

Based on her experience working through the Indigenous Leaders Interactive System and other AIO programs with various tribes, Harris is convinced that the reluctance of Indigenous men to share tribal leadership with women is causing other problems for their tribes. Nonetheless, she recognizes that these Indigenous socioeconomic problems reflect larger American injustices and cultural influences.

> When we went to the Makah tribe for a leadership program, we found that many men were running the tribe, and the balance was way off. They were driving on one wheel instead of four. They told us is that they were seeing a

trend—men moving more toward blue collar jobs, like full-time fishermen, and more women going to school, and almost always running all the companies. Not being the elected leaders, but running the programs, and it was beginning to cause a little bit of trouble because women were being more educated and men [becoming] more and more blue collar. It was causing a rift over who was the breadwinner.[10]

Even for a widely respected leader like Harris, how to address these issues is a problem for anyone outside a particular tribe. As she recalled:

> I was moderator for two women running to be governor. As a Comanche I have to be very careful to be culturally correct in talking about another culture. They were pretty straightforward in how men are appointed, and women have a lot of power, but you don't see it on the outside. Women run the inside, and it was suggested that we should have a chance to run the outside, too. Where are the women, she asked, and she got really upset about it and she said it in a really ugly, unsympathetic way, a little curt. I put her in her place and then later had to apologize. Those of us outside the culture don't have a place to judge. But you do see it more and more; women are running things, and tribal councils now have a summer institute in leadership.[11]

The Ambassadors program has become an extraordinarily successful program, with 250 graduates, all of whom are doing something for their communities. Laura described why this program works.

> In other leadership programs, participants build their resumes and then leave their home community, from where they were picked. They build their resumes and go off to a bigger and better job. In contrast, the Ambassadors create their own opportunity—one was working in the forest service, a great job, but after being in the program he decided to go back home. He landed in the tribal council. We find they either find a way to stay home or go back home. This is a revolution. We have fisherwomen, doctors, artists and a lot to go through the AIO programs, and they recreated the programs for young people. Someone in Oklahoma called LaDonna "Mama LaDonna," and it stuck, so now all of the Ambassadors use that term as endearing and part of the Native kinship relationship. As LaDonna says, "We are grooming our own revolutionaries."[12]

The AIO is dedicated to advance the political, cultural, and economic rights of Indigenous people in the United States and globally and bring Indigenous worldviews and tribal values to the needs of Indian communities in the twenty-first century. Sixteen participants composed each AIO leadership group that attended four or five gatherings. They were organized around "the Four Rs," which are relationships, responsibility, reciprocity, and redistribution, all widely shared tribal values that embody Comanche values.

LaDonna, Kathryn, and Laura Harris have worked in many avenues to further these goals. They often do a presentation called "Indian 101," the title of a film on LaDonna Harris. Its purpose is to educate everybody about Native people through a presentation on the history of American Indians, federal policies and their impact, contributions of Indigenous people, their current status and challenges, as well as stereotypes and misconceptions about them.[13] As Laura commented, "They don't know your tribe, don't know your government, think we live in a teepee. One of things I always include, it really gets the most surprise, is that Iroquois grandmothers made decisions, including about war. The biggest surprise to the audience is that Iroquois women were decision-makers with the Confederacy." Harris goes on to comment that "Euro-American academics have ruined everything" because they are convinced they have the truth. They distorted the history of Comanches and did not recognize women warriors or the fluidity of gender roles.

Deeply committed as she is to Comanche culture, Laura combines individualism and community in explaining that the more individualistic you are, the stronger you can be as a community member.[14] Everyone must remember that living according to the "four Rs" of Comanche values—Relationships, Reciprocity, Responsibility, and Redistribution—cannot stand with inequality. We must act to make these values real through our service to those who need help. This is why, on May 29, 2020, during the COVID-19 pandemic, Laura and her mother, LaDonna Harris, devoted themselves for the day to feeding the Native people of Albuquerque. Representing AIO, they joined with the NB, Notay Begah III Foundation, and local organizations and businesses in the drive-thru food distribution for Native families called "Helping Our Relations."[15]

In the ways they lead, teach, and serve, Laura, Kathryn, and LaDonna Harris exemplify the traditional, inherited power of American Indian women. And they work to pass on to the next generation that power and the confidence to use it for the good of the tribe, for the good of all Indian communities and Indigenous people around the world, for the good of all women, and for the good of the citizenry of the United States, with whom they hope to share the values of relationships, reciprocity, responsibility, and redistribution someday. One thing is clear—these Comanche women will continue to use their power in countless ways until their work is done.

CHAPTER SEVEN

THE PATH-LIGHTING POWER
OF CREATIVE VOICES
INDIGENOUS WOMEN'S POWER AS ARTISTS

Artistic works of all kinds exhibit and deploy Indigenous women's power, be-cause their creations celebrate and sustain tribal traditions while living within mainstream America. Artists use the power of their artistic talent to support their families and the life of their tribes. Visual artists—painters, potters, basket and fabric weavers—writers, and vocal artists exert significant power in Indian country. This is in part because artists bring the creative spark that lights the path to survival—for many tribal members, and sometimes just for the family who needs money for food.

Perhaps another reason for art's significance is because American Indians traditionally have created art as a function of excellence in the creation of the object, rather than only art for art's sake. For example, the artist created a cook-ing pot that balanced, held the heat, and was the right size for handling and for serving or eating from, and its external raised patterns made the pot easy to hold so that it did not slip from the hands. The pot was just right for its function, and its beauty was peculiar to the distinctive talent of the maker.

The same is true for literature. The poem as a creative work has function—it may be speaking about identity, history, healing, coming of age, how to survive on the plains or woodlands, and so on. This excellence in blending form and function is a part of the work's magic, its power.[1] The creative voice speaks to the poet, the poet writes or sings, and a poem is born. First, however, the voice has to speak to the artist, maybe in a dream or while looking at a leaf, perhaps after a time researching and thinking about a subject.

Smithsonian curator Rayna Green says, "The clay shapers, fiber twisters, pic-ture makers, and storytellers—the ones who said what was and what will be— they've always been important."[2] The point is that the women artists are the keepers of their culture. Green continues, "Thus the women have always kept the stories, in clay or reeds, in wool or cotton, in grass or paint or words to songs." And Green says they did this "because they wanted to preserve tribal culture, and because previous Anglo writers had gotten the stories so wrong that they wanted to set the record straight."[3]

Native women have always been wordsmiths because they have always been singers. They sang the songs of planting, cultivating, and harvesting, and they sang to bring a baby into life, to celebrate the coming into adulthood, to ease dying, to tame warriors, to soothe a baby, to entertain and distract people in times of hunger, to provide a rhythm and reminder of details as they worked, to heal, to curse, to remember. Just as in other cultures, the songs and stories are foundations for lifeways and markers of life cycles.[4]

Within Native holistic worldviews, women have always carried on traditional activities that expressed power. Following such traditional behaviors, within tribes today a woman may play many parts—scholar, wife, mother, artist, warrior, poet, lawmaker, and so on. One such creative Native woman who expressed many kinds of power is Paula Gunn Allen, who identified with her mother's nation, the Laguna Pueblo. She was a poet, novelist, critic, and activist who wrote of women's relationships to other women over time and space. Her poetry offers points of entry for all kinds of readers—remembrance, sisterhood, domestic memories, humor, frustration, and peace in being enfolded in the women's shared experience. Additionally, within the holistic and balanced worldviews of Native America, Allen's scholarship opposes the conclusions of the colonists. "[Sherry] Ortner's conclusion that menstruation was perceived as dirty and contaminating by tribal people and that they saw it in the same light in which it was viewed by patriarchal peoples is simply wrong."[5] Allen also points out that "the Arapaho felt that dying in war and dying in childbirth were of the same level of spiritual accomplishment." Furthermore, "the power of women can be controlled and directed only by other women who possess power that is equal in magnitude, but that is focused and under their control."[6]

Paula Gunn Allen, like many other American Indian women, never identified as a feminist. Clearly her understanding of power rendered this unnecessary. Allen's work not only provides information, but it also provides confidence in shared scholarship that may oppose the scholarly work of mainstream America. For scholars with that kind of confidence, the white male viewpoint is not the standard. The tribal viewpoint—including that of tribal women—is the standard. Her continuing influence on tribal scholars is vast and a lasting part of her power.

Native American Art and the Traditional Power of Women: "Medicine"

Joy Harjo who was named the U.S. Poet Laureate in 2019, and again in 2020 and 2021, also possesses what Indigenous people know as "medicine." Her body of work floats one along in lyrics that surprise, astonish, sadden, gladden—oh, all the things that splendid poetry does. However, an early poem, "I Am a Dangerous Woman," speaks particularly to the power that women possess, a power that is fierce. That power in modern times is understood as the power of the warrior-lawyers, warrior-scholars, and warrior-poets who care for Indian people in the ongoing Indian Wars. Consider the last stanza:

> i am a dangerous woman
> but the weapon is not visible
> security will never find it
> they can't hear the clicking
> of the gun
> > inside my head[7]

Of course, each reader will respond to this poem, as to any creative written work, in their own heart and mind. Although the reader may guess, the reader does not know the writer's full intention. The reader brings to any poem his or her own complex experience. Thus, readers may understand the poem differently, and the poet expects this. This is part of its medicine.

This medicine or power to retain identity and pass on cultural information provides the bedrock of Indigenous women's power. The exercise of power by tribal women in traditional arenas became increasingly important as European invaders decreased the power of Native men. In the nineteenth century, such struggles occurred in the women's movement, and in the mid-twentieth century the struggles continued with renewed energy. American Indian women, precontact and from the earliest days thereafter, were exercising power to assure tribal survival and lifeways within a colonizing tsunami that resulted in a European occupation that is still in place. American Indian women were simply born into power. However, American Indian men's roles and activities diminished, while the women's roles remained much the same, being modified as necessary over time. Today, American Indian women are still wielding power as they advocate both for other women and for their tribal people.

This is not to ignore the hard times that have fallen upon American Indian women. The Native cultures have been changed, modified by the colonizers. The egg is cracked. Domestic violence is present throughout Indian country, and so are the other ills of the mainstream society—alcoholism, drug abuse, disease, unemployment, and depression. The vicissitudes of life that increasingly developed in complex ways after Contact have affected all of American Indian life. Some Native people have fallen into despair. Others, however, have somehow called up the fortitude to work for the good in all aspects of life. Often such people have called on their traditions to create work so that they can participate in the competitive economy that surrounds them, and thereby feed and support families. Consider the dynamic of survival in the face of such dramatic opposition: wars, disease, slaughter, cultural genocide, and starvation.

Mainstream American society works and has worked historically to exclude American Indians, including from the arts. The exclusion is sometimes physical, as in removal and the restrictions to reservations in the nineteenth century. Sometimes the exclusion involves ownership of land. Sometimes exclusion is political, or cultural, or commercial, or spiritual, as can be seen in congressional delegations and museums. Because of casino gaming today, many American Indian tribes enjoy financial success. Indigenous artists benefit from this success, and their work lights a path of cultural inclusion for members of their communities.

An essential part of the appeal of art to a Native audience is inclusion. All human beings yearn for inclusion by some group. To read or see, to create or to appreciate American Indian art is to be enfolded in the American Indian community for a time. For the marginalized, this is especially significant. Belonging is a part of survival and often requires fortitude, because being a part of a marginalized group is not easy. Where does such fortitude to retain identity come from? I suspect that much of it comes in small, consistent doses to be found in inherited stories, songs, activities, instructions, foods—all the things that one inherits from one's ancestors. My mother, who learned fortitude at Goodland, passed on the fortitude to me. My mother Geraldine's mother, Maud, and Geraldine's grandmother, Lena, exemplified fortitude. You are who you are historically, as I used to tell my students. This is true for all people. And always you are navigating identity. Some of this inherited knowledge is so simple, but with the passage of time and continuing pressures on Indigenous cultures, details have been obscured.

National Treasures: Indigenous Women Culture Keepers

Consider perhaps the most famous of the many American Indian women artists, and what she did for the survival of her family, her pueblo, and eventually many American Indians. Maria Montoya Martinez of the San Ildefonso Pueblo in New Mexico was born in 1887, and lived until 1980. She created pottery that is internationally known, and she revived traditional techniques that were being lost. She and her husband, Julian, and other family members created distinctive blackware pottery. After extensive experimentation, Maria produced the first black-on-black pots for a museum in 1913. Her pottery resembled the burnished

black pottery that had been made since the seventeenth century, but she per-
fected her own distinctive style. Creating this blackware pottery is a very long
process that includes six distinct subprocesses.[8] Her husband, Julian, finished
the first decorated blackware with a matte background, an Avanyu design, in
1918. In 1954, Maria won the Craftsmanship Medal, which is the nation's highest
honor for crafts, from the American Institute of Architects. Many years later, in
1973, Maria won a grant from the National Endowment for the Arts to fund a
Martinez pottery workshop.[9]

Maria Martinez learned her traditional skills from her aunt Nicolasa, and later
with her husband, Julian. In the 1920s, the Smithsonian Institution archaeologists
asked Maria and Julian to reproduce 2,000-year-old black shards that had been
unearthed during an archaeological excavation in 1908. Over a decade of experimentation, they re-created the blackware using a technique that excluded oxygen
during the firing process. This made their pottery and skill famous.[10]

Maria Martinez influenced generations of potters in the Four Corners area,
both directly and indirectly. As the years passed, Maria influenced tribal potters
all over the United States, and they came to know that their pottery was valuable to mainstream collectors and museums, and that the ancient techniques in
pottery-making could be useful in supporting their families financially. At least
equally important, she influenced them to feel pride in their tribal traditions. For
example, Martinez especially influenced Pablita Tofoya Chavarria (1903–1979)
from Santa Clara Pueblo, who also became known for her black-on-black, carved
pottery. She signed her pottery "Pablita." One can see the Avanyu, or water serpent and wave design, on Pablita's pottery. Learning about the Avanyu is one of
the joys of knowing such pottery. Other tribes also have a water serpent, which is
dangerous. It is the flash flood that kills, or it may be a pond or creek that drowns.
The use of design is one of the ways that Native artists teach other artists and
encourage other American Indian artists to engage in research about their own
traditional symbols and stories. These artists create works that educate tribal
members and strengthen tribal identity. Educating tribal members about flash
floods by using the Avanyu probably saves lives. This educational element is an
important aspect of American Indian women's power.[11]

Thinking about the fortitude that such cultural recovery work requires, I often
spend time with the artwork of Cherokee artist Jane Osti, who also works to recover and pass on Native pottery techniques. For many years I have collected her
work, from the very earliest show in her garage, which featured pottery thrown
on a wheel, to the more recent pieces of hand-built, coiled, and decorated pottery. Her more recent pieces win big prizes and fetch significant prices at Santa

Fe Indian Market and other art sales and shows. Her pottery beautifies casinos and delights not only the eye but also the ears, the hands, the mind, and the heart. One rather mysterious blackware pot in my study echoes if I speak or sing when walking past it. Sometimes I stand and sing just to enjoy the echo. Another beautifully round and incised pot offers me pleasure when I cup it in my hands and run my fingers along its patterns of curves, angles, lines, and an incised hand that is not quite mine.

Because I have no artistic talent to create objects, I wonder how she learned to do this; how did she call up the commitment and the focus to seek such perfection? Because I knew Jane before she created such marvels. I know something of how difficult her life was. To speak to me of the influence of Osti's teacher, Anna Mitchell, I display a melon pot by Mitchell on a shelf along with Osti's singing pot, and across the room on another shelf, beside the black, round, incised Osti pot, sits the first pot I purchased from Anna Mitchell. They both speak to me. Mitchell's pot takes my heart back to the Cherokee Art Show, under the trees at the Cherokee Heritage Center. The day was hot, and Anna Mitchell and I sat in the shade as she talked about where she dug the clay on her property. We ate blackberry cobbler and enjoyed the slight breeze that moved the lightning bolts on our silver earrings.[12]

You see, art is memory and light, occasionally shade, grief, and laughter. Sometimes Osti's art sparks for me the brief recollection of meeting Sherilyn, who back in the 1990s carried the ingredients for martinis in her trunk to Jane Osti's invitational art show in her studio. Osti's art embraces me, and I hope her words from our conversation will invite you to think about her art and power, her medicine and that of other American Indian artists.

Why spend all this time and effort and toil? Why return again and again until it is *just right*—whatever that means at the time? What does it mean to be an artist, a Cherokee artist, an artist passing on the skills to ensure the commitment of another generation as well as honoring older generations? Jane talks about all of that. You just have to listen. Just like you have to listen to the songs of the pottery.

First, a little more about her: Jane Osti was born at Hastings Indian Hospital in Tahlequah, Oklahoma, and then lived at Rocky Ford, Oklahoma, north of Tahlequah. Jane Osti's mother died when she was five. Her father was a miner and rancher. She went to college in San Francisco at age thirty-three, and then she moved back to Tahlequah and attended Northeastern State University, where she earned a BA in 1989, and an MA shortly afterward. Cherokee pottery artist Anna Mitchell became her mentor and friend. Osti's work draws on prehis-

Jane Osti, a renowned Cherokee artist, is also an educator and has been honored with the title of Cherokee National Treasure. NB/ TRAN/Alamy Stock Photo.

toric Southeastern Woodland and Mississippian traditions. Osti has won many awards, including those from the Santa Fe Market, the Five Tribes Museum, the Eiteljorg Museum, and the Red Earth Indian Arts Festival. In 2005 she became one of the youngest Cherokee artists to be designated a Living Treasure by the Cherokee Nation of Oklahoma.

For the interview, we met in the Cherokee Arts Center in Tahlequah, where Jane has a studio. There were not many artists in the center that day, so we sat in the metal-working and print-making room, and we talked and laughed.

TERRI BAKER: Please talk about who you are and what you do for a living.

JANE OSTI: I am Jane Osti, and I've been doing art and pottery for about thirty years. I went to Northeastern State University, and you were one of my teachers. I graduated there with a bachelor's in Fine Arts and a master's in Education. Before that I went to Oaks Mission High School. I lived in the country and went to Indian Mission High School.

BAKER: What is your tribe?

OSTI: I'm a citizen of Cherokee Nation. I was born in W. W. Hastings Hospital way back in the 40s. Back then you had to be a quarter [Cherokee] to go there, since then they've taken away the blood quantum, and it's just ancestry now. That was the only health thing I knew as a child growing up, the only place we ever went, and that was seldom.

BAKER: Part of Indian Health Care?

OSTI: Right.

BAKER: Do you consider your profession to be an artist?

OSTI: Yes. I've been doing it for so many years, without any backup and, you know, just depending on my art for a living and to feed my creative soul and the financial needs of my family.

BAKER: Did you have an artistic mentor?

OSTI: Not until I was in my early forties. I had teachers I loved before that for painting. I was in my early forties when I met Anna Mitchell. She became my mentor and friend for life. She passed away a couple of years ago. She not only taught me about pottery and clay, but she also taught me about culture and just a way of being. She was a very special person in my life, and I miss her.

BAKER: We all miss her . . . So making this art, creating this art, I know from my relationship with other artists, it's a lot of trouble, takes a lot of time, a lot of focus. Why do you do what you do?

OSTI: Most days I can hardly wait to get up and do it; I do it because I love it, and mostly the added thing is it's part of my ancestors' ways, and being able to continue it and keep it going for next generations, that's a big incentive with teaching and with making the art. I've been teaching others for about thirty-seven years, even when I didn't know how but I thought I did. I was teaching anyway.

I was pretty much taught by Anna. I took clay classes and art classes in school. I started out using a wheel in the classes I took from Jerry Choate at NSU. I loved him as a teacher, too, and I loved throwing pottery on a wheel. But after I became aware of Anna's pottery and met her, I wanted to do coil pottery the way she did. I wanted to make things related to our Cherokee ancestry, so that was the path I started down.

BAKER: Do any of your family members create art?

OSTI: They have all tried, in the pottery. My daughter was pretty good at it, my grandson was pretty good at it, but Lilly my granddaughter is the only one that stuck with it for a while. She could be very good, if she had time, but she's busy pursuing education right now.

BAKER: Have you won prizes?

OSTI: Yes, I've won a lot of prizes, I've been really blessed. At Santa Fe Indian Market, Eiteljorg Museum Indian Market, mostly Indian museum shows or

Indian art shows, the Heard Museum to name a few. Basically, museums that have a real robust relationship with American Indian art.

BAKER: We are sitting in the Cherokee Art Center. What do you do here?

OSTI: This art center is the home for our Cherokee National Treasures mentor program. I'm most proud of that program. I'm on the board of Cherokee National Treasures. I am a Cherokee National Treasure. A few years ago, working with Counselor Victoria Vasquez, she and I put our heads together and came up with this program. We wanted to honor our elders, especially our Cherokee National Treasures, so that they could make quite a bit of money, or some money, teaching—and to preserve our culture at the same time. We wanted to make it as easy as possible. They're only required to have two students in this mentorship; they can have as many as they want, but they're only required to have two. And it pays them up to $1,000 per month for the months they teach, and they can teach up to six months a year. It has really helped. I know when I sold their work in my shop, every time they'd sell something they'd tell me, "Now I can buy propane or now I can get a roof," and I haven't heard that since this program started.

BAKER: Who are some of these treasures?

OSTI: Our eldest ones who have been teaching are Dorothy Ice, who is a loom weaver, a textile weaver; Thelma Forrest, a basket maker; and Bessie Russell. They're all National Treasures, and they're all close to eighty or more in years, young. They're all very vibrant and very good teachers. Knokovtee Scott was one of our teachers that passed away just recently, and he did shell carving. That is an art. He made us several future shell carvers—he ensured that we're going to have several shell carvers now. The same way with Dorothy Ice and Bessie Russell. Because of them, we have loom weavers and basket makers.

BAKER: You're really very intensely involved in the revival and maintenance of the Cherokee art tradition.

OSTI: Hopefully. I try to be, especially with the elders, I try to help. I always have time to listen to them, to what they want to tell me, and if they've got any concerns about the program or just on a personal basis. We've got pretty good relationships going on here.

BAKER: Do you consider yourself a feminist?

OSTI: I really haven't gotten out on the street and marched much, but very much so in my mind and my life—but I'm not out there on the front lines.

BAKER: You are on the front lines with your artwork and your work with the elders. That's really wonderful.

OSTI: I think we really accomplished something, being able to help them supplement their income, as well as preserving the arts and the culture.

BAKER: Do you think the casinos have helped? How does that work?

OSTI: Oh, yes! They buy our work. Simple as that. And they show our work in the clinics, the casinos, any of public places that they build and decorate with the 1 percent of the cost of the building. I was having to go out of state to do shows for years, in the 90s and early 2000s. I was doing maybe eight to ten, sometimes twelve shows a year out of state, until the Cherokee Nation got the casinos and started buying from us. Thank goodness, they did! I'd be too old to do that now. I couldn't do all those drives.

BAKER: You live here in Cherokee Nation, is that correct?

OSTI: Yes, I live here in Tahlequah.

BAKER: Do the Cherokee National Treasures still have events, a dinner?

OSTI: We have a banquet once a year, and everybody receives a gift card. Since Victoria is in the arts, and since she became a councilor, we've gotten a bigger budget. We were getting $5,000 a year, and now it's $115,000, and it allows for the classes being taught. It comes from Cherokee Nation businesses. It allows the teachers to be paid for teaching, and everybody gets a gift card, a $100 gift.[13]

BAKER: Thank you for doing this. Now will you show me your recent paintings?

Clearly Jane Osti's interview reveals the generational aspect of Cherokee art, which is also true of other American Indian art. Her words and history also show that she continues to live her identity, teach pottery-making skills to younger people, live her independence, and cooperate to support her elders as they teach younger artists. Those who recover techniques then pass them on to younger generations are ensuring tribal survival, and the younger generations who honor older generations are living their traditions. They are living their power as women. They also love their work, as do most of the women we honor in this book.

Younger Women Artists: Continuing Tribal Traditions in Modern Ways

Younger women artists also possess medicine, and such power manifests itself in many ways. I invite you to hear the song of Callie Chunestudy, who is a young artist and also a museum curator—feisty, funny, and informative. Callie is an artist herself, and so she appreciates the work involved in creating art—the focus, recovery of skills and techniques, the continuous learning that is involved. Callie agreed to be interviewed and answered our questions in emails.

Callie Chunestudy, an enrolled Cherokee Nation citizen, is a cultural specialist at the Cherokee Arts Center and Spider Gallery in Tahlequah, Oklahoma. Courtesy of Callie Chunestudy.

TERRI BAKER: Please talk about who you are, your tribe, and your current work.

CALLIE CHUNESTUDY: My name is Callie Chunestudy. I am a citizen of the Cherokee Nation and currently serve as curator for the Cherokee Heritage Center in Tahlequah, Oklahoma. I am also vice president of the Arts Council of Tahlequah (ACT), and a member of Southeastern Indian Artists Association (SEIAA).

BAKER: Are you married?

CHUNESTUDY: I am not legally married. I do however share a home with my male partner of fifteen years, whom I claim as my husband.

BAKER: Do you consider yourself a feminist?

CHUNESTUDY: I do!

BAKER: How do you define feminism?

CHUNESTUDY: To me, feminism is the celebration and respect of the female gender. An appreciation of our unique differences from men, working in unison with efforts to bring equal treatment of women to the workforce and society as a whole. Existence is comprised of balance: give and take, yin and yang. The imbalance of power and respect between the male and female genders is detrimental to all of creation. It has been far too long that women are underestimated, taken for granted, and unrecognized for their equal contributions and value in the world.

Cherokee society, before European contact, was matrilineal. Before patriarchal norms were set upon Cherokee people, women had just as much power and duties within their families, clan, and tribe. Some might say even more. Cherokee people certainly had traditional roles for men and women. Hunting, building, and the crafts that accompanied these tasks (bow-making, flint-knapping, etc.) were traditionally men's duties. Gardening, rearing children, keeping the home, and the respective crafts for these functions (basketry, pottery, etc.) were generally a woman's responsibility. However, when it came to switching roles, or taking on duties that may otherwise be outside the norm, it was not outrageously taboo in Cherokee society. It was accepted as the individual's calling or choice, and accepted by the community.

BAKER: Please talk about the exhibit about the Cherokee women that the Cherokee Heritage Center presented. Did you curate the exhibit?

CHUNESTUDY: "Earth Shakers" was co-curated by me and America Meredith, publishing editor of *First American Art Magazine*. America was on the advisory committee of the national Native women's art show "Hearts of Our People," presented by the Minneapolis Institute of Art. It is the first, large-scale, all female Indigenous art exhibition in the United States. We decided to answer that call at the Cherokee Heritage Center by creating an all–Cherokee women's exhibition.

Our exhibit features both female Cherokee artists and Cherokee women that have broken the gender ceilings in politics and the workplace. Mary Golda Ross is featured in the exhibit. She is the first Native American aerospace engineer. She is from right here in Park Hill, Oklahoma. The exhibit includes Cherokee National Treasures like Anna Sixkiller-Mitchell, [who] is featured for her revival of Cherokee pottery in Oklahoma. We did not want to limit the show to Cherokee Nation citizens, and have works and information on women from the United Keetoowah Band and Eastern Band of Cherokee Indians, as well. Wilma Mankiller is featured as the first female Cherokee principal chief (Western Cherokee Nation), and Joyce Dugan's biography and inauguration dress are displayed as well, as the first female Eastern Band chief. There are approximately seventy pieces in the exhibit, including works by Cherokee National Treasures, UKB [United Keetoowah Band of Cherokee Indians] Tradition Keepers, and EBCI [Eastern Band Cherokee Indians] Beloved Women.

It was very exciting creating an exhibit comprised completely of works by and about Cherokee Women. When I first proposed the exhibit, our director stated that he "had a problem having a show only for women." I think my head almost spun off, and he tried to rebound pretty quickly, saying that he thought people would then ask for an all-men's show. News flash: almost every show we've ever done is about a man or a group of men. They've had their turn. And as far as I know, this exhibit has not brought a clamoring group of men to our doors, upset that they don't have the limelight for two minutes. Maybe they know the Cherokee women would beat the tar out of them for something so disrespectful. He reluctantly relented, and we were allowed to do it, and we've had so many great responses from community members, leaders, and general visitors. Most of our advisory committee were women from all three Cherokee tribes.

I got a ton of inspiration from Theda Perdue's book *Cherokee Women*. Her leading her book off with the story of Selu, the first woman, is exactly why I began our exhibit with the same story. We also knew that we couldn't possibly include every amazing Cherokee woman in the space of the exhibit, so we installed a bulletin board for our visitors to post the name of their "Earth Shaker" on. All in all, I am proud to have been able to work on this project, and hope that other tribes across the nation have the opportunity to do the same.[14]

BAKER: Thank you for speaking to me. And I enjoyed the exhibit.

Callie Chunestudy, a member of a younger generation of artists and museum professionals, is unabashedly feminist, both within the ancient Cherokee tradition which she talks about and in the wider professional world. She works to recover and display the art, accomplishments, and history of Cherokee women, and through her exhibitions, she educates the museum audience, both American Indian and non-Indian. The educational aspect is important, because so much about American Indian tribal lifeways, customs, traditions, and details have been lost over the five hundred years of occupation by Europeans. The mainstream schoolbooks until just recently simply did not include much information about American Indians.

The consequence is that scholars have had to research and display the knowledge through art, which may be visual, structural, written. The art may be political, funny, sad, inspirational, enraging, ironical, educational—all the things that art is. Whatever it is, art makes us think and feel.

Chunestudy's curatorial efforts and her art encourage the audience to think and feel, sometimes in a humorous way. Another significant thing about Chunestudy is her membership on the board of the Arts Council of Tahlequah. This board is integrated, and its programs feature the artwork of Anglos, African Americans, American Indians, men and women. Callie's work is generational, respectful, and powerful. She clearly gives credit to those who have influenced her and fully embraces her power as a woman. Callie's artwork evolves from her tribal traditions and from the skills she learns from her Cherokee teachers, such as Bill Glass, who does wonderful work in pottery with glazes.

Cherokee artist Connie Jenkins (Te-go-nil) was born in Tahlequah, Oklahoma, in 1955. She is the daughter of Emma Sanders and Winfred Watkins. She went to the regional public school in Locust Grove for high school and attended Miami College in Miami, Oklahoma. She is self-taught as an artist and paints stunning works, especially of Cherokee women and children. She has won many awards, including at the Five Civilized Tribes Museum in Muskogee and from the Cherokee National Museum. Her works convey the power of Cherokee women who create and sustain life and are essential to the vitality and balance of the community.

Jenkins's painting, *Generations of Motherhood*, appears in *Earth Songs, Moon Dreams*.[15] Her figurine of a Cherokee woman on the Trail of Tears, titled *Keeping the Tradition*, is a powerful statement. The sculpture won first place, best in show, and the judges' choice at the Eastern Band of Cherokee Indians–sponsored Art Market.[16] The sculpture depicts a grandmother carrying a baby on her back. Jenkins has also painted *Sisters, Maggie, Bonded Emotions* and *Mother and Child*. Currently, Jenkins is raising her two grandchildren, Gracie and Bub. They travel with her and are with her while she paints.[17] Jenkins's celebration of women in her exquisite art is a part of her power as a woman and of her focus on survival of the tribe.

Born in 1922, Rowena Bradley was the third generation of basket weavers in her family. Mary Dobson, her grandmother, and Nancy Bradley, her mother, were gifted basket makers. Rowena is one of the few Cherokee basket weavers who employed the complex double weave technique in the 1930s and 1940s. She grew up in the Paint Town Community on Qualla Indian Boundary, owned by the Eastern Band of Cherokees. She made her first basket when she was around six. In her family, everyone participated in the making of baskets. Her father, Henry Bradley, principal chief of the Eastern Band, and her brother Jim gathered rivercane and dug for roots to make dyes. The weaving of baskets was the province of women. This practice is a tradition that extends back to prehistoric times.

Rowena Bradley remembered that "at the time my mother was teaching me how to weave the double-weave baskets, there were only two people I know of who could do this type of basketry: Mother and a very old lady by the name of Toineeta, who lived way up in the Soco community." These skills declined in the twentieth century, and they were rare in the 1930s. In *Weaving New Worlds: Southeastern Cherokee Women and their Basketry*, Sarah Hill included Nancy and Rowena Bradley, Arizona Swayney Blankenship, Aggie Wilnoty, and George and Rebecca Toineeta as those who made rivercane baskets at the time. Rowena made up designs of her own, like Chief's Daughter, Peace Pipe, Flowing Water, and Noon Day Sun.

Rowena Bradley remembered her mother's designs, and she wove the ones she remembered her doing. She used butternut, black walnut, and bloodroot, along with yellow roots to color the rivercane, as well as white oak, maple, and honeysuckle, which were soaked to absorb the dye. Bradley has won numerous awards, and some of her baskets are in the Smithsonian Institution.[18] Again, as with other tribal women, Bradley's work evidences the generational aspect of the passing on of traditions and designs. Her use of traditional materials and dyes also serves to sustain tribal lifeways.

In a scholarly study of Oklahoma Cherokee baskets, Karen Coody Cooper says of these artists that "their craft, due to basket maker persistence, represents one of the pinnacles of Cherokee cultural survival."[19] Cooper presents information about generations of women basket makers, examines commercial marketing ventures, considers issues surrounding the art, and provides many photographs and quotations from the artists. In noting the complexity of developing twilled patterns with dyed cane splits, Cooper says, "If you start out with the wrong count or the wrong order of splints, the design elements will not come together as desired."[20] In discussing the techniques of basket-making, Shawna Morton Cain, a Cherokee National Living Treasure (also known by the term National Treasure), talks about the importance of knowing math in basket-making when she says, "To do these designs you have to understand mathematics and you have to be able to divide and multiply."[21] In summary, Cooper's study shows that the art of basket-making requires mathematics, is generational, passes on tribal knowledge and traditions, and contributes significantly to tribal survival. This is American Indian feminism in creative action.

The Painters: Traditional Rituals, Possibilities, and the Power of Humor

Many Native women work as painters and exhibit their work in numerous shows and galleries. In her book *Earth Songs, Moon Dreams*, which collected American Indian women's paintings for the first time, Patricia Janis Broder reflected on the themes that their work reveals:

> An attitude of pride and respect for women pervades the Indian world and inspires paintings that are visual tributes to generations of American Indian women past, present, and future. In the American Indian world, women are respected and hold positions of honor. Many Native American peoples are matrilineal and matrilocal. Women who bear and raise children are honored for insuring continuance of life.[22]

Earth Songs, Moon Dreams offers beautiful illustrations of the work of women's painting and a convenient way to become familiar with artists, themes, techniques, and museum sites where the works may be seen. Some of the works are in private collections.

A number of tribal artists present motherhood, as does the Kiowa Lois Smoky, who was one of the original group of Kiowa artists working with Oscar Jacobson at the University of Oklahoma in the late 1920s. Smoky's paintings *Lullaby* and *Kiowa Family*[23] are examples of her work regarding mothers and children. Broder notes that male Kiowa artists originally treated Lois Smokey with disrespect, because traditionally men had been the creators of narrative paintings. Today, however, Broder says, Lois Smokey "has taken her rightful place as the pioneer mother of Plains Indian painting."[24] Lois Smokey exemplifies survival in the face of colonial attitudes, which her Kiowa male colleagues had accepted. Her power lives on in her influence on other artists.

The Cherokee/Osage artist Mary Horsechief also celebrates motherhood in her painting of a mother and child (author's collection). Her mother, Mary Adair (Horsechief), honors the Cherokee spiritual figure who gave corn to the Cherokee in her painting *Selu*.[25] Broder says that "women, both the spiritual figures of legends and the women of the traditional Cherokee world, are of primary importance in Adair's work."[26] Horsechief's work and that of her mother Mary Adair celebrate the feminine in tribal life and in the spirit life. Their work illustrates balance in life in this world and in the life of the spirit.

A number of women artists present details of ceremonies and spiritual connection, including Choctaw Valjean McCarty Hessing, in *Bear Dance* and *Mourning Rites*,[27] and Delaware Ruthe Blalock Jones, in *Delaware Woman with Ceremonial Doll* and *Shawl Dancers*.[28]

These and other American Indian women artists paint the details of ceremonies as part of their continuing effort to retain and celebrate tribal identity and lifeways. These artists image tribal lifeways that may be used for reference by other artists, and they cause audiences to pause and reflect on spiritual connections.

In all the paintings illustrated in Broder's book, you can see images of Indigenous women's tribal clothing at various moments in their lives, as in Comanche Marian Terasaz's *Comanche Girl*.[29] The Creek/Cherokee artist Joan Hill, in her painting *Morning of the Council*,[30] depicts the significant participation of women in tribal councils, thereby presenting the political power wielded by generations of Native women. The Creek/Seminole/Cherokee artist Dana Tiger, in her painting *Patrol of the Lighthorse*,[31] connects the past to the future in her depiction of a female and a male in the past tribal law enforcement agency. Although there is no documentation of the female Lighthorse in the nineteenth century, today, the Lighthorse (tribal law enforcement agency) has both male and female officers. As Broder notes, "By 1808, the Cherokee Nation had set down the first Indian code of laws and set up an agency to enforce these statutes. This agency created regulatory companies, known as the Lighthorse Patrol, to perform the function of police."[32] These artists present relationships of women and of the relationship between past and future, as well as presenting moments of exercising power in partnership with men. Clearly, these women exemplify women's power, in activities and underlying beliefs.

Muscogee (Creek) artist Phyllis Fife expresses and celebrates Indian humor in her work. One of her paintings, *Buffalo Two Chips*, depicts a "professional Indian."[33] Fife was born in Okfuskee County in Oklahoma and attended country schools, until as a teenager she attended the Institute of American Indian Art in Santa Fe. After graduation, she studied for a year at the University of California in Santa Barbara, after which she returned to Oklahoma and attended Northeastern State University and then University of Oklahoma, graduating with a BFA, and later earning an MA in education from Northeastern State University and a PhD in secondary education from the University of Arkansas. Fife retired as the director of tribal studies at Northeastern State University, where she taught in Native American studies and directed the National Symposium on the American Indian for several years. She is both an artist and an educator. Her work can be seen at the Philbrook Art Museum in Tulsa.

The Writers: Indigenous Women's Singing Voices

Much of the art of Native women is written—poems, stories, novels, plays, and nonfiction essays. These women sing powerfully as wordcrafters in American Indian country. Their work speaks to all readers—American Indian and non-Indian. The non-Indian reader may be looking for some kind of special spiritual knowledge (which I, Terri, have confessed before is a puzzle to me), or may be interested in other things—history, details of a ceremony, travel to another culture, adventure. These Indigenous women's written work offers knowledge, grief, hope, warnings, remembrance, and nostalgia. Women artists write about what it is to be human and American Indian in America.

The American Indian's world exists within a dynamic of conflict, as the dominant society has tried to erase American Indians and tribal people insist on surviving. This conflict moves the reader through the work, as does conflict in other literatures. Throughout the work of Indigenous women writers one sees, among other things, explanation, resilience, resistance, humor, and impatience with appropriation. Their work engages a reader because generally, though not always, they write in response to colonization. They write about survival of their tribes, the earth, their spiritual lives, their customs, their families—their way of life in the modern world. Their efforts are beginning to be rewarded by the dominant society.

Joy Harjo is the prime example. In her remarkable poetry and her way of playing the saxophone, she expresses both suffering and celebration of her people and of her own life. In 2019, Harjo became the 23rd Poet Laureate of the United States, the first Native American to hold this honor. In 2020 and 2021, she was again named poet laureate. Harjo has written eight books of poetry, as well as several plays and children's books, and she has recorded five albums. She has received numerous awards including two National Endowment for the Arts Fellowships and a Guggenheim Fellowship.

Joy Harjo is a member of the Mvskoke Nation. Born in Tulsa, Oklahoma, on May 9, 1951, she attended the University of New Mexico (for her BA), the University of Iowa (for her MFA), and the Institute of American Indian Arts. In her memoir, *Crazy Brave*, Harjo writes eloquently about her childhood and coming of age. She remembers her beautiful mother and her dynamic father, whose alcoholism led to her parents' divorce and much heartache. When her mother remarried, Harjo encountered another alcoholic who was cruel to her and her siblings. Harjo attended the Bureau of Indian Affairs boarding school in Santa Fe, New Mexico, for high school. Like Winnemucca and Zitkála-Šá, she writes of the trauma of their cutting her long hair, and of the harsh treatment the children received there.[34]

Harjo became pregnant as a teenager and married the child's father, moving to join him in Tahlequah. She eventually divorced him when he began to drink, as the other men in her life had done. She had an internal warning signal that kept her balanced, though she began to experience panic at times. She has two children: Phil Dyne (with Phil Wilmon), and Rainy Dawn (with Simon J. Ortiz).

Like Wilma Mankiller, Harjo was deeply affected by the radical movements of the 1960s, including the feminist movement and American Indian Movement, as well as the civil rights movement and the antiwar movement. She recalled: "There was also a revolution of female power emerging. It was subsumed for Native women under our tribal struggle, though we certainly had struggles particular to women. I felt the country's heart breaking. It was a breaking inside me."[35]

Harjo is strongly committed to women's rights and equality. Her poetry addresses colonization and imperialism as well as their effects on violence against women. She sometimes reminds us about the cost of the struggle of living in America, as she does in an early poem, "For Anna Mae Aquash Whose Spirit is

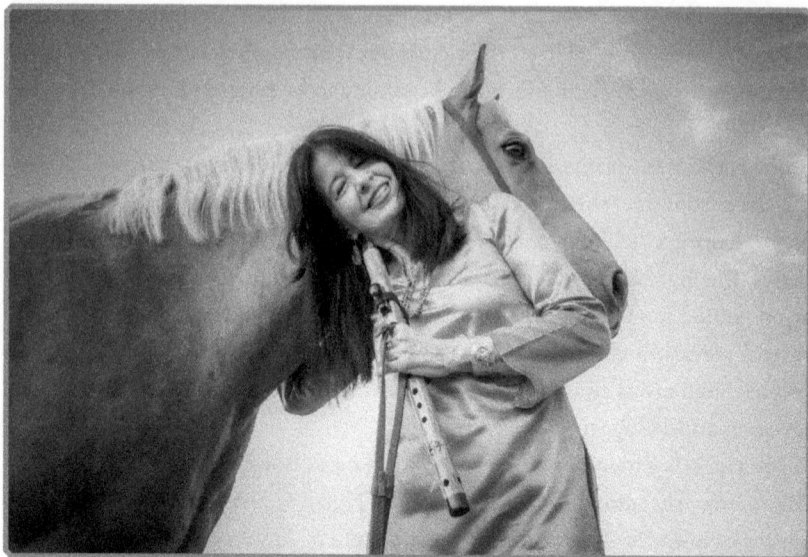

Joy Harjo is an internationally renowned performer and writer of the Muscogee (Creek) Nation. She served three terms as the 23rd Poet Laureate of the United States from 2019–2022. Courtesy of Karen Kuehn.

Present Here and in the Dappled Stars."[36] Anna Mae Aquash, a Micmac woman, was murdered in 1976 on the Pine Ridge Reservation in South Dakota.

Harjo is an activist for Native American rights and feminism and connects colonialism with women's oppression. In her poem "Bourbon and Blues" she writes:

> Some of us did not make it . . .
> I was a poet, mother and I was learning how to sing.
> We talked history, heartache, the blues, and what it means
> To be an artist with nothing to lose, because we lost everything,
> Here at the edge of America.[37]

Indeed, American Indians do live "at the edge of America." Our existence was nearly painted out early, and for the generation born in the late 1940s and early 1950s, only the white experience was to be found in schoolbooks. Harjo talks about this in a 1993 interview:

> Most of the poetry available to my generation was set in New England and was written by men, or women emulating the male experience. I always had to change myself to conform to the poem. But I loved the melodic tones, the

rhythm, and the music—those are the things that pulled me into a poem as much or more than the idea.[38]

Joy Harjo, taking from her early education what was useful to her and adding to it, like so many American Indians, went forward with her life and her gifts, and gave the world her poetry.

The reason why American Indian creative work is not generally included in U.S. classrooms (both in higher education and in K–12 public education) has to do with the anthologies used in most literature classes. These anthologies include a wide range of writing; some of the work included in anthologies may be composed by American Indians, but the average student reads and studies only those writings that the teacher assigns. The teacher assigns writing that is widely known and curriculum-approved, and with which the teacher is comfortable. Unless the teacher has learned about American Indian literature during her or his own educational experience—which is rare—discovering and understanding American Indian literature's significant details and techniques requires a lot of work.

Some American Indian literary information is included in *Merriam Webster's Encyclopedia of Literature* (1995), described on the cover as "A comprehensive and authoritative guide to the world of literature—authors, works, terms, and topics—from all eras and all parts of the world."[39] This resource was often to be found in university libraries. Magic realism is an entry, but it talks only about Latin American literature—with no mention of American Indian literature. It does not mention *Pretty-Shield, Medicine Woman of the Crows* (1932), an as-told-to autobiography by Frank Linderman, which had been republished in 1972. *Pretty-Shield* recounts an event that certainly could be interpreted as magic realist in the story of Lost-boy, and it is significant in its accounts of pre-reservation life, which embraced such events.[40] In contrast, the entry for "trickster"[41] does include a good deal of American Indian information. All in all, as a research tool for American Indian Literature, *Merriam Webster's Encyclopedia* is somewhat useful.

However, the teacher would have to know the terms to research, whether from her family experience or education. Familiarity with literary terms in American curricula design largely means familiarity with Anglo or British literary terms. From the late 1940s through the early 2000s, using the criterion of "civilized," if one does not write like white Europeans and usually white male Europeans, the writing is characterized as "uncivilized" and thus, not worthwhile.

In 1994, Andrew Wiget published a *Dictionary of Native American Literature*.[42]

This book is very helpful, but again, the teacher has to be determined to research Native American literature and to include it in the class assignments. Of course, some teachers are determined and do so; however, curriculum requirements are usually test-driven, and there is little time for study of additional material in the classroom.

This lack of inclusion in literary-research resources and time for teachers is an aspect of marginalization. Teachers in public education and higher education use such resources, as do editors of anthologies, and so the beat goes on from one generation to the next. This goes to the issue of worthiness. That is, what is worthy to be included in a literature course with restricted time and tests? Is it the work that repeats and supports the mainstream traditions of Europe and European American writers and the "winners," or the work that supports the traditions of the conquered?

This question is important to understanding and appreciating American Indian women's artistic power, because these writers and other artists often have engaged in processes of cultural recovery through listening, recording, and remembering stories from family and tribal elders, through research in libraries and archives, through visits to important historical sites, such as Spiro Mounds in Oklahoma, or Cahokia near St. Louis. Being in the landscape nurtures understanding of the literature and the cultures that produced it. Then, through publication or exhibiting, artists educate. Any passionate reader knows that the written word may take one into a world created by the writer: ancient Rome, ancient Cahokia, seventeenth-century England, Jamestown, the Elizabethan world, the world of Miss Marple, and nineteenth-century Indian Territory.

The writer creates verisimilitude through detail. The American Indian writer who is creating a past world has to engage in some form of recovery to find that detail. The Choctaw writer LeAnne Howe describes her process of recovery in her "Author's Note" at the end of her novel *Shell Shaker*.[43] The information included in such notes is invaluable to other writers, as they engage in their own research and create their own works of art. For example, while many cultures, including American Indian cultures, have charms and spells to attract a lover, in *Shell Shaker*, LeAnne Howe writes that Choctaw women did not use such spells: "Either it is there at first glance, or will never be."[44] Possibly, she recovered this detail before she included it, or she may have known the detail from her own life experience.

Some poets sometimes write about the absurdities of Euro-American encounters with Indians and their spiritual beliefs. Judith Ivaloo Volhorth, an

Apache/Comanche, presents a poetic conversation of this kind in "Black-Coat Meets Coyote *Conversations of the Absurd.*"

Linda Hogan, a Chickasaw citizen, reminds readers about survival as generations continue in her "The Direction of Light":

> Children grow inch by inch
> like trees in a graveyard,
> victors over the same gravity
> that pulls us down.[45]

Marilou Awiakta, an Eastern Cherokee sends a warning about the importance of "taking care of the earth."[46]

Wendy Rose, Hopi/Miwok, in "For the White Poets Who Would Be Indians,"[47] addresses the subject of appropriation, which is pervasive, sometimes dangerous, even lethal, and almost always irritating. This appropriation exists in many ways as a manifestation of continued thievery.

Louise Erdrich writes about the American Indian experience of negotiating and navigating life in the United States. She belongs to the Turtle Mountain Band of Chippewa Indians (Anishinaabe, also known as Chippewa and Ojibwe). She was born in Little Falls, Minnesota, in 1954. She was in the first class of women admitted to Dartmouth College, receiving a BA there in English. She also received an MA in the writing seminars at Johns Hopkins University. She has written novels, poetry and children's books, including *Love Medicine, Tracks, The Beet Queen, The Bingo Palace, The Round House, The Night Watchman*, and *The Sentence*, among many others. Erdrich has won many awards including the National Book Critics Circle Award for Fiction (with Michael Dorris), National Book Award for *The Round House*, and Library of Congress Prize for American Fiction. She married Michael Dorris in 1981, and they separated in 1995. He died by suicide two years later. They raised six children, three of whom Dorris had adopted as a single parent, and three of their biological children. Erdrich is the oldest of seven children herself. She is a gifted writer and one of the most significant Native American writers of the contemporary period. She creates the world in her novels through the use of verisimilitude.

Louise Erdrich's Indigenous feminine power is reflected in her fiction, as she examines complex familial and sexual relationships within Native families, drawing on her Chippewa heritage. Her novel *Future Home of the Living God* (2017) is a dystopian feminist work about the enslavement of women by fundamentalist Christians who force them to procreate. In her earlier novels *Tracks* (1988), *The*

Blue Jay's Dance (1996), and *Tales of Burning Love* (1997), Erdrich explores explicitly feminist themes of identity and exploration.[48]

Breaking a Path Forward: Singing in the Mainstream

Many American Indians wish to present their artistic talents within mainstream venues. Barbara McAlister has done just that as both a visual artist and a vocal artist. She is a member of the Cherokee Nation, and her family traces its Cherokee lineage back to Sequoyah and Old Tassel. She traces her Scottish heritage back to Ludovic Grant, a trader who intermarried with a Cherokee woman in the eighteenth century. McAlister's grandmother graduated from the Cherokee Female Seminary in Tahlequah in 1902, and then taught school for two years.

Throughout her life McAlister has produced paintings in the Bacone style focused on American Indian images. Her paintings have been exhibited in a number of museums, including the Jacobson House Native Arts Center at the University of Oklahoma in Norman. In 2020, the Five Civilized Tribes Museum in Muskogee, Oklahoma, exhibited a retrospective of her work which drew a large audience to Agency Hill.

In addition to being a painter, McAlister is a world-renowned mezzo-soprano who has performed over thirty-five opera roles. She said during her interview with me on May 30, 2020, "I was on contracts in Germany for ten years, singing every day except Sundays unless we had a concert." During the interview McAlister talked about her professional journey, as I asked her how she moved into the world of opera from Muskogee, Oklahoma, after having graduated from Oklahoma City University. She told me that she had learned to love opera from her parents, and she followed her passion.

BARBARA McALISTER: I began during college singing summer musicals one summer, opera apprentice another summer, back and forth. After college I went to L.A. as some of Clu [Gulager]'s acting friends suggested it. So I studied and performed there, studying with Lee Sweetland and his dear wife, Sally. They were my master teachers. I auditioned and was accepted into the Los Angeles Music Theater and Workshop with a full scholarship and thirteen weeks of daily training. It was a prestigious school. I then did a national tour of *Sound of Music*, understudying Sister Berthe. I then sang with the Sacramento Music Theater in chorus and solo as Sister Berthe. Great time!

TERRI BAKER: When did you begin in opera?

McALISTER: My career took its turn into opera when I auditioned for the National Zachary auditions and won first prize, a trip to audition in Germany for opera companies. During 1979, in March, it was the *Tiger den Koblenz*, I was with that for three years and sang several roles. Then I auditioned for *Passau*, and got it, then I was in Flensburg for three years, then Bremerhaven for three years—my favorite theater. I sang great roles. I guested with Opera de Monte Carlo. I moved to New York. Then I began at Boston Opera New England.

Barbara McAlister is a Cherokee artist, teacher, and world-renowned mezzo-soprano. Courtesy of Barbara McAlister.

BAKER: So, you traveled around a good bit? Talk about that please.

McALISTER: All of opera in the USA for solo is by auditions. Unless you are at the top and get a phone call. So I was hired in Europe to guest with Teatro lirico di Toscanini, a wonderful touring opera group from Bulgaria. A couple of years with them, and back and forth to the USA. I sang guestings in France and Italy in a German opera. All those years, I was based out of New York City. I was hired at Tulsa Opera, and Washington Opera in D.C., and worked with the great composer Menotti. One of my dreams. Also, Monte Carlo—a dream.

BAKER: You were very active. What happened then?

McALISTER: Then I was probably sixty, and age discrimination starts barking at the door, so I auditioned for the Met extra chorus. Four hundred auditioned for very few openings. I got in. As extra chorus you know the exact days you are needed, so in between, I could audition. I was hired to sing with Hong Kong Opera, then back to New York. I was hired to perform as a soloist at Carnegie Hall in a Mozart work, with songs arranged by the composer-arranger Mark Hayes, in 2009. From 2001 on, I did many performances at the Met in chorus. One of the neat things throughout my career is the people I've met along the way. They include my dear colleagues, really famous people like Zeffirelli, and top singers. During my early career I met Carol Burnett, Ginger Rogers, Ann Blyth, John Saxon, Werner Klemperer.

BAKER: What you are doing now.

McALISTER: In 2009 I moved back to Muskogee, my birthplace. Not long after returning, I was hired by my tribe where I have been teaching and mentoring solo singers.

BAKER: So tell me about your students.

McALISTER: Oh, my students are doing so well! They give two recitals a year. Katelyn, Austin, and Bretly received college scholarships at Oklahoma City University and the University of Arkansas. One just received a choir extra scholarship at Northeastern State University. One student was accepted by NYU, but opted out, and will attend the University of Tulsa program. Sean had a lead in Tulsa Opera, *The Snow Queen*. Three years ago, I had five students with Tulsa Youth Opera. My students are all in choirs and musicals at high schools around this part of Oklahoma. Last year, two were awarded the First Timothy Long Award. Each received $1,000. This year two students, Aislyn and Bretly, will receive the second Timothy Long Award and will each receive $1,000. Katelyn was hired by River City Players at Northeastern State University last summer. I am proud of them all. I also have private students. Tulsa Opera has hired me to give master classes.

BAKER: Thank you so much for your work and for your interview.[49]

McAlister's life and career exemplify the possibilities for American Indians, and certainly the possibilities for Native women artists. McAlister's life also shows the focus by tribal members on their American Indian history and connections. She is celebrated by the American Indian community, and she has performed several times at the National Museum of the American Indian. As discussed earlier in this book, the Cherokees have experienced unspeakable suffering and have continued to survive. McAlister inherited the power of Cherokee women and went forward with her personal journey. Her accomplishments have been rewarded both by her tribe and the governor of Oklahoma, who in 2019 awarded her the Governor's Arts Award. In May 2020 the mayor of Muskogee presented her with the key to the city. She has proudly shown me a picture of her grandmother who attended the Cherokee Female Seminary, and I have attended some of her performances and recitals by her students.

Barbara McAlister is intent on passing on to the next generation her techniques and strategies, so that they may pursue their goals. She had help from mentors and teachers along the way, as she indicates in her interview. However, she was courageous in going forward, taking chances as she auditioned for parts, traveling the world. Throughout it all, she has remained devoted to the heritage and well-being of the Cherokee tribe. Like the other Indigenous women artists whose voices, work, and lives this chapter explores, as well as all the Indigenous women this book celebrates, McAlister is a modern woman with roots in the power of American Indian women that traces back to precontact times. She has found and followed her path fearlessly, and she has shown that path to a younger generation.

These Indigenous women artists are certainly the "keepers" to which Rayna Green refers. Through their efforts in a variety of fields of artistic work, they have engaged in the preservation of American Indian culture, working intergenerationally through recovery of techniques, details, ceremonies, behaviors, and stories from older generations and from research, while passing on their knowledge to a younger generation helping them learn to participate successfully in the larger American society as artists. The efforts of these diverse women artists speak powerfully, drawing on their shared Indigenous women's traditional "medicine" powers to remember, to heal, and to support new growth. If you read, listen, and observe carefully, they say, you may discover how to follow the path marked by those who have gone before, and to break a new path forward for yourself, your family, your people, and all of those who will be touched by the love power to which your work gives voice.

CHAPTER EIGHT

STORIES OF SOVEREIGNTY, SURVIVAL, AND CULTURAL PERSISTENCE
INDIGENOUS WOMEN'S POWER-BASED LEADERSHIP

In contemporary struggles for tribal sovereignty, cultural persistence, and survival of the earth and of the people, Native women who maintained their inherited tribal traditions of power and gender equality often serve as leaders. Some of their stories tell of fights for land and water rights, and for the recovery of their history. Others tell of attempts to eliminate violence against Indigenous women and to assure their reproductive health and welfare. These Indigenous women leaders come from many nations and many generations. The youngest leaders of this impressive group of women led a fight for water, and older women leaders came to their support.

Standing Rock Rises against the Dakota Keystone XL Pipeline: The Story of Jasilyn Charger, AnnaLee Rain Yellowhammer, and LaDonna Brave Bull Allard

Jasilyn Charger and AnnaLee Rain Yellowhammer were teenagers when they led a battle for water rights and tribal sovereignty against combined corporate and government forces who aimed to build the Dakota Keystone XL Pipeline across their tribal lands on the Standing Rock Reservation in South Dakota. They were tired of their lives being filled with abuse, and tired of attending the funerals of their friends who committed suicide. Jasilyn Charger was nineteen when she learned her best friend had killed herself. Charger is Cheyenne River/Lakota Sioux. She said, "I don't blame my Mom." Her mother was murdered. "The abuse lives in our blood." She also said, "Who better to speak for the past than the voice of the future?" She had left the Cheyenne River Reservation in South Dakota for Portland a few months earlier. In the summer of 2015, she returned to attend the funeral of a friend who had committed suicide. Two days after she arrived, another friend killed herself. More suicides followed. By the end of the summer, thirty Cheyenne youths had attempted suicide and eight completed suicide. Charger formed a youth group with White Eyes, a teenager, and their friend Trenton Casilla-Bakeberg. They raised money for youth trips and basketball tournaments.[1]

As the suicides diminished, the youth groups called One Mind Youth Move-

146

ment turned to political concerns. Young Native women led the movement against the Dakota Access Pipeline. A battle for tribal sovereignty revolved around water rights. The Keystone XL Pipeline was being built under the Cheyenne River upstream of the Standing Rock Reservation. Commissioned in 2010, the Keystone XL, the pipeline's fourth phase, attracted massive protests. These young Indigenous women spent that fall as part of the local campaign against the Keystone XL Pipeline, whose route would cut under the Cheyenne River just upstream from the Standing Rock Reservation, where Energy Transfer Partners was trying to build the Dakota Access Pipeline. They set up a tiny "prayer camp" just off the access route, on the north end of the Standing Rock Sioux Reservation. Supported by these camps, the protests grew, uniting conservative farmers, old radicals of the American Indian Movement, urban environmentalists, and traditional chiefs of hundreds of tribes. The youth group moved their camp into the ravine beside Cannonball River on the extreme western end of Standing Rock Sioux Reservation.

An older Indigenous woman leader, LaDonna Brave Bull Allard, founded Sacred Stone Camp on April 1, 2016, which immediately attracted the young activists. She was Standing Rock's historic preservation officer. The youth group joined her and other older activists, and they lit the sacred fire together. In Sioux tradition, there is a Lakota prophecy of the black snake that brings darkness and sickness. The prophecy said the seventh generation, those born between 1980 and 2000, would rise up and defeat the snake, bringing balance back to the earth. The message was clear: the struggle against the pipeline was part of the same, all-too-familiar struggle against alcoholism, suicide, and drug abuse. The youth group saw the pipeline as the snake, and they organized a distance run to Omaha to deliver a letter of objection to the Army Corps of Engineers, doing the run in relays. They stayed in churches, community centers, private homes, and women's lodges. The young people "carried a staff that represented their ancestors." Eryn Wise, a twenty-six-year-old activist who was raised by her grandmother on Jicarilla Apache Reservation, was a primary leader of the youth group.[2]

On July 26, 2016, the Army Corps of Engineers approved the Dakota Access easement. The elders began to claim more interest and control, and they visited the protest camps. They paid for emergency services and portable toilets. They acknowledged the young people as the prophesized "seventh generation." Chief Arvol Looking Horse gave the youths a *chunupa*, the ceremonial pipe, a symbol of knitting together the human community and nature, as well as the ancestors with the now-living. The group became known as the International Indigenous Youth Council. Activist groups like Black Lives Matter joined in, and African

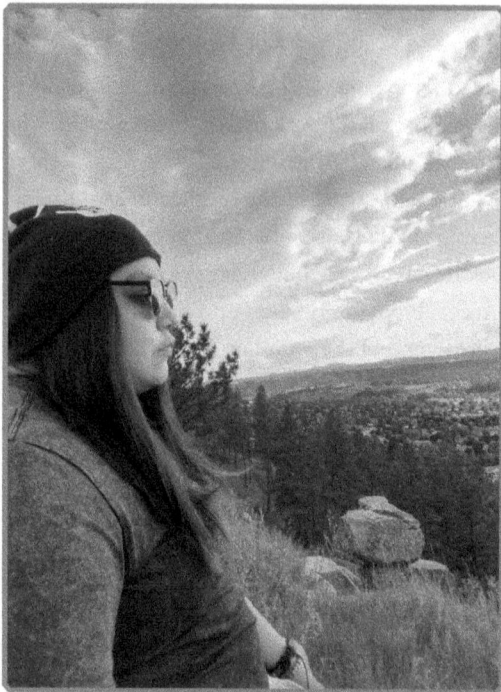

Jasilyn Charger, a member of the Cheyenne River Sioux tribe, was a youth founder who ignited the Standing Rock Pipeline Resistance Movement. She is a land and water defender, the cofounder of the International Indigenous Youth Council, the One Mind Movement, and 7th Defenders. She is a youth leader of Earth Guardians, Indigenous rights activist, and advocate for LGBTQ rights. Courtesy of Earth Guardians.

American medics went to Standing Rock to serve as volunteers. Veterans and "water protectors" joined the protest in December 2016.

However, on December 4, 2016, the police brutally attacked the campers. The Army Corps of Engineers announced a decision to deny an easement for the Dakota Access Pipeline route. The youth group organized a run to Washington, D.C., to be held from April 2016 to February 2017. A youth group named ReZpect Our Water demonstrated at the camps. In April 2016, Joye Brain of Indigenous Environmental Network and tribal historian LaDonna Brave Bull Allard established a water protectors' camp as a center for direct actions, resistance, and defense of sovereignty. Brenda White Bell, a descendant of Sitting Bull, spoke on their behalf at the UN Permanent Forum on Indigenous Issues on April 25, 2017.

In May 2016, thirteen-year-old AnnaLee Rain Yellowhammer (Hunkpapa, Standing Rock Sioux) and 30 young people launched a petition that opposed the pipeline. In April 2016, they ran 2,000 miles cross-country from North Dakota to Washington, D.C., carrying a petition with 140,000 names, and they delivered it to the Army Corps of Engineers. Estimates are that over 550,000 people eventually signed the petitions to stop the pipeline.

Cheyenne River/Lakota Sioux 2016

Jasilyn Charger said in Dakota/Lakota, *mni Wiconi* means "Water is life." Anna-Lee described "the way young people acted as defenders of Mother Earth and saying no to Big Oil."[3]

In the following extended account, Jasilyn recalled the relay run to Washington, D.C.:

We had young people really putting their lives on the line and expressing through their bodies. A lot of them couldn't really speak or they were really shy, but we express our points of view by using our bodies, and we get that message across the country. Being a part of that development and being a part of that monumental, life-changing event, that's a milestone. That's a great big achievement for our people. You don't really see us very often, in social media or out in the world, but we make it known that we as a people don't agree with this. We will run to you; we will use our bodies and our voices. At that time, nobody was really paying attention to us, nobody wanted to listen, and the tribal governments were fighting with each other about whose fault it was and who was going to take the lead, who was going to do what, who was going to go to court hearings. We were kind of tired of it.

We were going to stand together, but in the beginning, we didn't know each other. We decided to do a long run across the country to bring attention to the Standing Rock situation. At the beginning, none of the runners knew each other, they didn't grow up around each other. It was their first time meeting, and you know, we got through it together. If something came up, we got through it ourselves.

We got a lot of criticism from older people—lots of men, lots of non-natives, like "why are you running?" When we got to Washington, D.C., we actually met with the two star general of the Army Corps of Engineers. We got to meet with representatives from Congress, and the Bureau of Indian Affairs. We got to meet with all of the representatives that were in the White House, and a few senators who were representing Native communities, who fought for Native causes. No adults got to go into the meetings; it was all young people.

The second youngest runner said, "I'm running for my children." She was only like four years old at the time. It was really powerful for me to see that she recognizes that there is an extension of her spiritually, there's gonna be descendants. For us to think about that was really a powerful thing because seven generations ago, people died for us because they knew that they wanted us to have a life in western society. They wanted us to have a voice, they wanted us to have everything that we needed, and they wanted us to all know that we mattered. It really touches hearts, when someone says that. It comes from our elders shouting, "this is for our seventh generations," but to have that seventh generation speak for itself is a really powerful thing to do, and we constantly encourage it.

When we left Standing Rock in August, there were only 30–40 people in the camp, but when we came back there were thousands of people at our camp. I never thought it would get as much attention as it did. I think that as Standing Rock got bigger over the months and as it got colder, it was really hard for younger people to be heard. The adults were really taking over, which really challenged me as an organizer. They wouldn't let us in the meetings, they wouldn't let us listen in on the council meetings or be a part of them because they said we were too young or we were women. So that was a big barrier for us. To get around it, we created our own council where we could facilitate ourselves and govern ourselves in the way we wanted to be represented. The older ones didn't really take too well to that; they thought we were challenging their authority, which as Indigenous people, we don't do. You listen to your elders and you're taught to obey, so a lot of people were really angry. But then people were like, "if you're going to do this, we are going to help you build it," and that's the effect that we wanted. We want people to help us rather than govern us and try to lead us . . .

At Standing Rock, we planted a seed in someone and it's their choice what they do with it. If you give that seed a chance to grow, something really beautiful comes out, something really amazing. You really give them that fire, the fire to really have that courage. It's like giving birth to a baby—you have a seed and its inside your heart and your body. But how do you get that outside and into other people, into the world, and into the community? It's a birthing process. It's a movement about water. Women, we carry water when we carry our children, they're swimming in water, they're grieving in water. For us, water is our first medicine, it's what our children need, it's what's in our bodies. We are people of water. It's so easy to get caught up into the greed and the really masculine part of the world . . . We forget to have compassion and look at the world with femininity and compassion.

If we come at it as a united front, our organizing can be so much more. I'm really looking forward to building with this movement and building with these young people and giving them a chance to shape their own future, to take our future back, and make what we want out of it for our kids, for our next generation. I'm looking forward to really holding people accountable, teaching them to be confident and strong, but also to have compassion and understanding for other people.[4]

Young Native women continued to play a major role in the protest. Kate Iron Eyes, a twelve-year-old Lakota young leader and organizer spoke about the legacy of Indigenous women's activism in an interview with *Truthout* in 2016. Naomi Klein interviewed her on a video on Facebook that attracted a million viewers. International Indigenous Youth Council was founded by Jasilyn Charger. Tara Houska (Ojibwe Couchiching First Nation of International Falls, Minnesota) was the national campaign director of Honor the Earth. Eryn Wise (Jacarilla Apache and Laguna tribes) was the council communications director. By September 2016, over three hundred recognized tribes were represented in three of the camps, which included three to four thousand pipeline resistance supporters. Nonetheless, in October 2016, protesters were removed.[5]

Earlier in 2016, they had had a victory when they sued the Army Corps to stop construction. James E. Boasberg, a federal judge, had ordered the U.S. Army Corps of Engineers to conduct a more extensive environmental impact statement. Jan Hasselman, attorney for Earthjustice, represented the tribe. The Corps announced that they would seek alternative routes.

About that victory, Madonna Thunder Hawk, an organizer with the Lakota People's Law Project, said that the court's decision and a recent federal ruling that ordered the shutdown of the Dakota Access Pipeline in North Dakota had been cause for celebration. Just not too much. "It's a war for us," she said. "There are some victories, but the war continues." Tribal activists gained international attention after they blocked roads outside Mount Rushmore to condemn President Trump's visit to what they called stolen lands. They won a fight to shut down an oil pipeline that crossed sacred ground in North Dakota. The pipeline was shut down for at least thirteen months while the environmental impact report was prepared. In addition, Dominion Energy and Duke Energy canceled the Atlantic coast pipeline project in the wake of the recent decision. However, President Trump signed an executive memo to review and approve the pipeline. By 2017, oil was flowing through the pipeline.[6]

Shortly after Joe Biden became president in 2021, he signed an executive order revoking the permit of the Keystone XL Pipeline to carry Canadian crude oil to the United States, but by then, great damage already had been done.[7] This continuing struggle is over tribal sovereignty, and preservation of Native history and artifacts, as well as water. Indigenous people's sovereignty includes tribal lands, fishing and hunting rights, water and mineral rights, criminal jurisdiction, religious ceremonies and rituals, ancestral remains and sacred objects, tribal identity and membership requirements, family issues, economic enterprises, and the hope of rising young leaders that the future of their people can be better than the lives they are allowed to live now.

Elouise Pepion Cobell's Story of Lamentation and Celebration: Recovery of Indian Trust Fund Money

When Elouise Pepion Cobell (Yellow Bird Woman), the great-great-granddaughter of Mountain Chief, the hereditary chief of the Blackfeet (or Blackfoot people), awoke to learn that she had just been awarded a MacArthur Genius Prize of $300,000, she knew how she would spend it. She would seek justice for her Blackfoot Nation. In the winter of 1883–1884, five hundred members of the Blackfeet Nation starved to death as they waited for supplies at the old agency at Ghost Ridge, where the Indian agent lived. They were not permitted to hunt and thus were totally dependent on federal supplies. The reservation land has rich reserves of oil and gas, but the Blackfeet Indians did not receive their royalty payments, and the Department of Interior had never given the Indians an accounting for their payments for over a century. The plight of the Blackfeet people resembled that of the Indians in Oklahoma who lived in poverty in the nineteenth and twentieth centuries, even though their lands held massive amounts of oil and other minerals.

Like Zitkála-Šá ("Red Bird"), a Yankton Dakota Sioux woman who lived from 1876–1938, Elouise Pepion Cobell was dedicated to fighting for the rights of American Indians and for the education of their children as authors and teachers. Zitkála-Šá wrote a moving account of how Oklahoma Indians lost their land and failed to receive royalties from the oil on it, forcing them into abject poverty. Her findings led to important reforms when she served as adviser to the U.S. government's Meriam Commission in 1928.[8] She researched the corruption against Indians in Oklahoma in the 1920s. When oil was discovered on the lands of Indian allotments, the Indians were victimized and even killed for their land. Zitkála-Šá's book *Oklahoma's Poor Rich Indians: An Orgy of Graft and Exploitation* documented these outrages.[9]

In the earlier period of Indian removal of the southeastern nations to Indian Territory, the U.S. government had pledged to give them money and land for new homelands. Their relocation to Indian Territory concentrated many different nations on land then presumed to be worthless. However, when oil and

Zitkála-Šá, also known by her anglicized and married name, Gertrude Simmons Bonnin, was a Yankton Dakota writer, editor, translator, musician, educator, and political activist. Courtesy of the Smithsonian Institution.

other natural resources were discovered, the U.S. government gained control of these resources through fraud and chicanery. They also did not make good on their promises to pay millions of dollars to the nations. With the Dawes Act, the remaining territory of the tribes was allotted, and the Department of Interior presumably held the revenue "in trust."

Therefore, the land which was to be theirs "as long as the rivers flow" was stolen repeatedly.

Finally, on June 22, 2016, Congress passed the Indian Trust Reform Act, and the Department of Interior appointed a trustee to address the problem.[10] This enabled an opening for Cobell to sue the federal government.

After exhausting other measures Elouise Cobell sued the U.S. government in the largest class action lawsuit in American history. She filed the suit in 1996. Cobell spent the majority of the $300,000 she received in 1997 with the John D. and Catherine MacArthur prize on the litigation. Ultimately, the court battle lasted over thirteen years. Finally, Cobell won the case in 2009 after seven trials and ten times going to appeals courts.

In 2010, Congress passed legislation awarding $3.4 billion for mishandling American Indian trust funds going back to 1887, and President Barack Obama signed the bill. The award followed a 13-year litigation and 6 months of negotiations before the congressional ratification in 2010. One and a half billion dollars was awarded to the members of the class (300,000) beneficiaries, $1.9 billion for a land consolidation program, and $60 million for a college scholarship fund for Indian youth.

A federal judge gave final approval to authorize payment on June 20, 2011. This $3.4 billion government settlement was the largest ever in American history. After her thirty-year battle, Elouise Cobell died victorious later that year, on October 16, 2011, having devoted her life to achieving justice for her people.[11]

The Story of Ada Deer: Leader of the Fight for Restoration of Menominee Federal Recognition

Ada Deer was born in Keshena, Wisconsin, in 1935, to a non-Indian mother who told her, "Ada Deer, you are an Indian and you were put on the planet for a purpose." This is how she has always lived. She became the first Menominee to receive a BA from the University of Wisconsin–Madison, and in 1961, the first Native American to receive an MSW from New York School of Social Work (later Columbia University School of Social Work). She settled in Minneapolis, and in 1991 she became the head of the Native American Rights Fund. Shortly thereafter, she became the first female Native head of the Bureau of Indian Affairs.[12]

Among Ada Deer's many achievements, one of the most important was her leading role in bringing the Termination Era to a close. Ironically, her Menominee tribe's success made them a target for termination, and elites within the tribe wrote the final termination plans. However, the Menominee suffered greatly from their termination, which led to widespread

Ada Deer, member of the Menominee tribe, was the first woman to head the U.S. Bureau of Indian Affairs and the first Native American woman from Wisconsin to run for U.S. Congress. Courtesy of Wisconsin Historical Society.

poverty. Deer worked along with Sylvia Wilber and Shirley Daly to lobby politically and to energize the grassroots movement within the tribe for restoration
of federal recognition to the Menominee tribe. She cofounded DRUMS (Determination of Right and Unity for Menominee Shareholders) to combat Menominee Termination and subsequent control of tribal resources by a nontribally run
corporation. It will come as no surprise to readers of this book to learn that the
DRUMS organization included a substantial enrollment of women. Due to their
activist advocacy as well as that of their allies, President Richard Nixon signed the
Menominee Restoration Act in 1973.

Because of effective leadership, Ada Deer was elected to many tribal bodies,
including the Menominee Common Stock Voting Trust and the Menominee
Restoration Committee. She also lobbied Congress and testified to multiple
congressional committees, like the Senate Committee on Interior and Insular
Affairs[13] on the disastrous effects of termination for the Menominee and other
Native peoples. Like LaDonna Harris, Deer worked steadfastly both within her
tribal unit and across organizations. She was on LaDonna Harris's board of directors for Americans for Indian Opportunity (AIO). Complementarily, when
Fred Harris was in the U.S. Senate, he and LaDonna had aided Deer greatly in
the Menominee Restoration effort.

Ada Deer was a brilliant political strategist and a skilled diplomat. She served
on many organizations' boards, including the Girl Scouts of America and the
U.S. Department of Health Education and Welfare's Urban Indian Task Force.
As a Fellow at the Harvard Institute of Politics at the Kennedy School of Government, she showed others how to lead with a similar kind of effectiveness.
When advocating for tribal sovereignty and Native people's rights, she always
addressed her appeals to congressional members, church leaders, and to members of the various organizations with which she worked.[14] This has widened her
base of support immensely and given legitimacy in the media for what otherwise
might have been interpreted as a militant campaign.

Ada Deer began teaching at the University of Wisconsin–Madison in 1977,
with the title of distinguished lecturer. She became director of the American Indian Studies Department in 1991. She started the first program at the university
to provide Native American reservations with social work training. Because of
her many accomplishments as well as her Indigenous women's leadership style,
President Bill Clinton appointed her to be Assistant Secretary of the Interior,
and then as the first Indigenous woman to head the Bureau of Indian Affairs. Ada
Deer lived with purpose and fought unceasingly for Indigenous rights, including
prisoners' rights.[15]

The Story of Debra Haaland: The First Indigenous Woman to
Serve as Secretary of the Interior of the United States

Nominated by President Joe Biden, Deb Haaland was confirmed on March 15, 2021, as the first Native American Interior Secretary. In 2018 she and Sharice Davids of Kansas, a member of the Ho-Chuck Nation of Minnesota, had become the first two Native women ever elected to Congress. Haaland is a member of the New Mexico Laguna Pueblo, and her district included the city of Albuquerque and many of its suburbs.

Following in the path of Ada Deer, Haaland is having enormous influence in the U.S. government's relationship with Indian nations. Historically, the Interior Department has been a major tool of oppressing American Indian people—this changed on her first day in office. The Department of the Interior controls one-fifth of all U.S. land and offshore holdings. Haaland's role will be significant in the allocation of natural resources, climate change issues, and endangered species policies.[16] Of crucial importance is the fact that the Department of the Interior includes the Bureau of Indian Affairs.

Deb Haaland grew up in a military family. Her father was a Marine, and her mother is a Navy veteran. A single mother of her daughter Somah, Deb struggled to support her and to put herself through college. She received a BA from the University of New Mexico and then earned her JD from the law school at the University of New Mexico. She was elected to the Laguna Development Corporation Board of Directors, and she was involved in overseeing business operations of their gaming enterprise. True to her Indigenous tradition, she was influential in implementing environmentally friendly practices. On August 28, 2021, Deb Haaland married Skip Sayre, her long-time partner, in Santa Ana Pueblo, New Mexico. Sayre is the chief of Sales and Marketing for Laguna Development Corporation, which operates three casinos and two travel centers.[17]

When she served in Congress, Haaland worked for environmental justice and to address the situation of large numbers of murdered and missing Indigenous women.[18] A month after she became the Secretary of the Interior, she formed a new unit within the Bureau of Indian Affairs to address the crisis of missing and murdered Native Americans. Long a champion of civil rights, she approved the new constitution of the Cherokee Nation, which includes provisions protecting Cherokee Freedmen.[19] Secretary Haaland also created the Federal Indian Boarding School Initiative, whose task is to investigate the abuse in the now defunct residential boarding schools that Native American children were forced to attend under the 1819 Civilization Act Fund. One of their goals is to search those residences for the remains of Indian children.[20]

A member of the Pueblo of Laguna and a thirty-fifth generation New Mexican, Debra Haaland served as the 54th U.S. Secretary of the Interior. She is the first Native American to serve as a cabinet secretary. Courtesy of Debra Halaand's Office of the Interior.

Women from Zitkála-Šá to Angie Debo, Elouise Cobell, and now Debra Haaland have sought to regain the trust money of American Indian people and to ensure their tribal sovereignty, right to their lands and natural resources, access to health care, and respect for their human rights. Debra Haaland has the power as Secretary of the Interior to make dramatic changes in ways that were impossible before. She is putting Indigenous women's traditional powers to care for their people and for the land into action on a once-unthinkable national and international scale.

The Stories of Sarah Deer and Luana Ross: Ending Violence against Native Women

In their activism and in their writing, Sarah Deer and Luana Ross focus on eliminating violence against Native women. Ross (Confederated Salish and Kootenai tribes) is especially concerned with the consequences of colonialism and the resulting confinement of Native people in boarding schools, jails, prisons, orphanages, and reservations. According to Amnesty International in 2007, Native American women are two-and-a-half times more likely than other U.S. women to be sexually assaulted; more than one in three will be raped in her lifetime. Colonization nearly destroyed traditional Native family and community structures and destabilized gender relations that had been equal. Europeans and European Americans considered Native women "violable," and their domination became a symbol of American dominance over Native communities. This is why colonialism attacked women's social status within their communities. Currently, 57 percent of men who sexually assault or rape Native women are white. Sexual violence has been a tool of genocide and colonialism, and it continues to work in this way to this day. Thus, Ross argues, Native nations must address gender violence to combat the continuing consequences of colonization.[21]

Dr. Luana Ross has conducted extensive research on the experiences of Native American women in prison, leading to many publications, including a book, *Inventing the Savage*.[22] As Ross writes there:

> The history of colonization of America's Indigenous people is a tragic one. From the time of European contact to the present day these people have been imprisoned in various ways. They were confined in forts, boarding schools, orphanages, jails, and prisons and on reservations. Historically Native people formed free, sovereign nations with distinct cultures, and social and political institutions reflecting their philosophies. Today, Native people are not free. They are a colonized people seeking to decolonize themselves.[23]

Ross has received numerous awards, and she has published many articles.[24] She contends that engagement with the term "feminism" is not a "white thing," and that colonialism takes place in gendered and sexualized forms that reconstitute both individual and communal Indigenous identities in disempowering ways.[25]

Sarah Deer (Muscogee), who received her BA and JD from University of Kansas, has been working for over twenty-five years to eliminate the rape of Native women. She compares the ways in which American and Native American judicial systems have dealt with sexual violence toward Native women and finds that the mechanisms for dealing with rape have not worked. She offers a Native woman–centered approach to rape and sexual violence by calling for community accountability and a reexamination of the nature of contemporary criminal jurisprudence.

With Bonnie Clermont, Sarah Deer authored the Amnesty International 2007 report, "Maze of Injustice," which documented sexual assault against Native American women. She won a MacArthur Fellowship for "empowering tribal authority and reshaping landscape of support and protection of American women at risk for domestic and sexual violence." Deer is now chief justice for Prairie Indian Community's Court of Appeals. Native women on reservations suffer one of the highest per capita rates of violent crime in the world because of limited jurisdictional powers, lack of resources, and limitations on sentencing authority. Tribal courts are unable to prosecute these crimes, and federal prosecutors decline to take up more than half the cases under their authorization.[26]

This is why Sarah Deer has reframed the problem of sexual violence in Indian country as an international human rights issue. She was instrumental in the passage of two landmark pieces of federal legislation: the Tribal Law and Order Act of 2010, and the 2013 reauthorization of the Violence against Women Act, which restored some of the authority that had been taken from tribal governments by

Oliphant v. Suquamish (1978). These two Acts give tribal courts the power to prosecute non–Native Americans who assault Native spouses or dating partners, or who violate a protection order on tribal lands.[27]

Here is a story within Sarah Deer's story: Until Oklahoma's statehood in 1907, about one half of eastern Oklahoma belonged to the Five Civilized Tribes. However, Congress passed the Oklahoma Enabling Act in 1906, which was interpreted as disestablishing the reservations and enabling statehood. A recent Supreme Court decision has been interpreted as acknowledging that the nations in Oklahoma are still on reservation land in matters of criminal jurisdiction. The case involved Jimcy McGirt, who was convicted of sex crimes against an underage child on lands that are part of a former reservation, and he was given a life sentence when convicted in state court. In a 5–4 decision the U.S. Supreme Court decided *McGirt v. Oklahoma* (Case No. 18-9526) in favor of the Creek Nation, concluding that a large section of Oklahoma, including much of Tulsa, is still a reservation for the purposes of criminal prosecutions. Native people on the land subsequently cannot be tried by state courts; they must be tried in tribal or federal courts. (This ruling does not apply to non-Natives.) *Sharp v. Murphy,* a previous recent Supreme Court ruling, concluded that the Oklahoma Enabling Act did not disestablish the reservations. In both cases, Justice Neil M. Gorsuch, a westerner, sided with the tribes, as he has in previous cases. For example, he sided with tribes in a case in which a Native American was cited for illegal hunting in Wyoming, and another case in which taxes were imposed on a business owned by a member of the Yakama Nation.[28]

The most recent Oklahoma case references the U.S. government's long history of brutal removals and broken treaties with Indigenous tribes, and grappled with whether the lands of the Muscogee (Creek) Nation had remained a reservation after Oklahoma became a state. Sarah Deer wrote: "Reading it, the understanding of what happened to our people was nice to see acknowledged at this level of the government. It's not something we've seen from the Court very often. It has a lot of meaning."[29]

Stories of Groundbreaking Scholars and Teachers: From Sarah Winnemucca and Zitkála-Šá to Clara Sue Kidwell, Beatrice Medicine, Henrietta V. Whiteman Mann, Brenda Child, Renya Ramirez, Mishuana Goeman, and Jennifer Nez Denetdale

In the second half of the twentieth century, Native women began to recover their history, writing from American Indian perspectives. They earned PhDs, medical degrees, law degrees, social work degrees, and nursing degrees, and they became teachers and scholars. The topics on which these young Native scholars focus range from family histories, boarding school experiences, and consequences of U.S. federal policies and warfare, to biographies, autobiographies, and tribal histories. Scholarship on American Indians today is a large, impressive field of study. Native women have made a tremendous impact by recovering the history of Native people.

Scholars and storytellers in the post–World War II period who are preservers of American Indian history and culture have published widely, founded American Indian Centers, Native American Studies programs, preserved tribal and family histories, and contributed to Indigenous theory. They tell the stories of their nations, family histories, suffering and resilience, boarding schools, sexualities, native feminisms, and cultural persistence.

Since Native languages were not written (except Cherokee, after Sequoyah invented the Cherokee syllabary), tribal histories previously were conveyed in the oral tradition. After the American Revolution, Indian history was written from the perspective of the Indians' relationship with the federal government. Occasionally figures like Pocahontas and Sacajawea appeared, but the lives of the majority of Native women were unrecorded in accounts written from an Indian point of view—with a few exceptions, like those by Sarah Winnemucca and Zitkála-Šá. In 2005, at the U.S. Capitol Statuary Hall in Washington, D.C., a statue of Sarah Winnemucca representing Nevada greeted visitors for the first time. Her autobiography, *Life among the Paiutes*, is the first work written by an American Indian woman, and the first by a Native American west of the mountains. As authors and teachers, both Winnemucca and Zitkála-Šá were dedicated to fighting for the rights of the American Indians and for the education of their children.[30]

As Paula Gunn Allen explains, "Women's traditions are largely about continuity, about "all that goes into the maintenance of life over the long term," and specifically in Plains cultures, "power was and is gained, accrued, mediated, and dispenses only through the grace and beneficence of female influence."[31] Five hundred nations lived within the North American continent when the Europeans arrived. They shared a belief that men and women were equal and must remain in balance. Therefore, women shared political, economic, and spiritual power. The Europeans sought to subordinate women and disempower them as a strategy for dispossession of Indian land. War, disease, Christianity, and federal "civilizing" policy diminished the power of women in the tribes and left them vulnerable to a heightened risk of violence. At the time of contact, estimates are that there were 5–15 million Native people in the area now called the United States. By 1900, approximately 250,000 remained.[32]

Throughout her remarkable years of teaching, writing, founding programs, and as a museum curator, Clara Sue Kidwell (Anishinaabe-Choctaw) has been a national treasure. She was born in Tahlequah, Oklahoma. She is a major scholar, feminist, and professor of Native American Studies. She received both a BA and PhD from the University of Oklahoma. She began teaching American Indian Studies in the 1970s. She taught at Haskell Indian Junior College, the University of California at Berkeley, Dartmouth College, and University of Oklahoma. She founded the American Indian Center at the University of North Carolina. Kidwell has published extensively.[33]

Kidwell served as assistant director for cultural resources at the National Museum of the American Indian, and was involved in moving a million pieces from the George Gustav Heye Center, a branch of the Museum of the American Indian in New York to Washington, D.C. She believes that recovery of traditional forms of gender equality is an essential first step to developing and then articulating a coherent Indigenous female cultural sexual identity. Despite some Native women's resistance to join with feminist agendas, a number of Native American feminist scholars like Kidwell perceive an important linkage between "matriarchal" Native women's traditions and the goals of feminism.[34]

Beatrice Medicine (Standing Rock Sioux) was an eminent Native American female anthropologist and founder of Native American Studies. She was born at Wakpala on the Standing Rock Reservation in South Dakota. In her numerous books and articles, she studied the human behavior of racism and stereotyping, as well as Native women's lives before and after the nineteenth century. Her book *The Hidden Half: Studies of Plains Indians Women* (coedited with Patricia Albers) was one of the first studies to address the lives of Native American women.[35] Medicine emphasized the survival of Native languages and culture, and she spent fifty years teaching at numerous institutions.

In 1974, along with her cousin Vine Deloria Jr. in 1974, Medicine served as an expert witness in trials related to the battle at Wounded Knee that occurred in 1973 (*United States v. Banks and Means*). She was committed to serving Native communities on issues related to bilingual education, tribal identity, and addiction and recovery. For many years, she was actively involved in civil rights issues in Seattle, Vancouver, and Calgary. She worked for the rights of women, children, and gay, lesbian, and transgendered people. Her extensive scholarship on gender, and on American Indian women's sexuality and spirituality, illuminated how she lived and embraced feminism. Her Lakota name, Hinshaw Wasti Agli Win, translates as "Returns Victorious with a Red Horse Woman."[36]

Beatrice Medicine taught at Indian schools and colleges and universities across Canada and the United States. She worked to support opportunities for multicultural and bilingual education for minority students, especially those of Native American background. Although she retired on August 1, 1989, her final book was published a year after her death in 2006. She received many awards and honorary degrees, but the honor Beatrice Medicine treasured most was being chosen as the Sacred Pipe Woman at the 1977 Sun Dance.[37]

Henrietta V. Whiteman Mann (Cheyenne) saw herself as a modern Indian woman following one of the traditional Cheyenne woman's roles as a perpetuator and keeper of traditions. Dedicated to education, she contended that it is essential to use the "white man's educational system without internalizing his culture. We have had to formulate some sophisticated concepts of survival, and those are what I try to provide to Indian students." As a result of Mann's activism and her colleagues' urging, today Montana requires teachers that teach on or near Indian reservations to take six credits of Native American Studies as a requirement for their teaching certificate. Montana is the only state in the country to make that a requirement. Mann was only one of two Native Americans ever to be elected to the National Academy of Education.[38]

As Professor Whiteman Mann describes her life:

> I did what was expected of me and I really had to work hard, I had to work hard to be 100 percent for being a woman and I had to work another 100 percent for being an American Indian. But I've always been proud of who we are and so I worked hard, my life has been one of service because that's who we are as American Indians, we lived a life as service, we give, but my life has also been very fulfilling because I have not only told our story but I have told the story to our children, my life has been about serving your children, your grandchildren, our children as the first children of this land, that is what has made my life so exciting but that has given me purpose, that has been my entire purpose in life.[39]

In a statement from the information service of the University of Montana, Whiteman Mann writes: "I feel that Indian women are in some ways better suited to the educational world than Indian men, as in many Native cultures we've been the perpetuators, the keepers of the stories, the traditions, the religions, which certainly are educational roles. . . . The University—the white culture—may list me as the Director of Native American studies or an assistant professor, but those are only words. What I am—what I have always been—is a perpetuator, a keeper."[40]

Brenda Child (Red Lake Ojibwe) has been engaged in writing a new constitution for the 12,000-member nation.[41] Child has published widely, exploring ways Ojibwe women have strengthened their communities for centuries, from mediating between tribes and fur traders, to organizing to ameliorate urban Indian poverty after World War II. In the recovery and preservation of the history of Native women, the experiences of the federal and missionary boarding schools have inspired many books. Early scholarship on the boarding schools (which also included missionary boarding schools) focused on these assimilationist goals and exposed the physical and psychological brutality of the practices at the schools.[42] Beginning in the 1980s and 1990s, studies like those of Brenda Child began to analyze the children's agency, personal experiences, resistance, and ways in which they made the experience at the boarding schools their own.[43]

These studies of the boarding school experiences acknowledge the brutality and damage to Native children, but they do not portray them simply as victims who were brainwashed to abandon their languages, ceremonies, and tribal values. The personal testimonies, stories, poetry, and histories of those who went to the boarding school reveal tremendous pain, loneliness, and longing for home. They also reveal great resilience and resistance. Sometimes the Indian children openly rebelled by having stomp dances and green corn ceremonies. Many ran away from the schools. As Geraldine McKinney's moving accounts of her experiences reveal, some children were able to make the time at boarding school serve their future needs, regardless of the pain and loneliness they felt because of being away from home. As Daniel Heath Justice writes, "[They] remind us that our histories are more than tragedy, more than suffering, more than the stories of degradation and deficiency that settler colonialism would have us believe. They remind us that we're the inheritors of heavy, painful legacies, but also of hope and possibility, of a responsibility to make the world better for those yet to come."[44]

Young scholars and teachers are retrieving and preserving Native women's history and exploring new areas of study.[45] Renya Ramirez (Ho-Chunk) imagines her grandfather's life in the context of Ho-Chunk kinship systems, and this has led to her own Native feminist methodology. A granddaughter of Henry Roe Cloud, who has been conceptualized as assimilationist, she rejects the categories of traditional and progressive in reclaiming her family history, repositioning Cloud within the context of his relationships with the adopted Roe family, including his adopted white mother, Mary Roe Cloud.

Professor Reyna Ramirez traveled to Yale University's Sterling Library, as her mother had also done, to use the same archive to write about her parents. Her mother did not finish this project, so her daughter followed and wrote the book her mother had hoped to write, publishing *Standing Up to Colonial Power: The Lives of Henry Roe and Elizabeth Bender Cloud* in December 2018. Reyna's grandparents, Henry and Elizabeth Bender Cloud, had struggled within the sys-

Mishuana Goeman, Tonawanda
Band of Seneca, Hawk Clan, is a
professor of Gender Studies and
American Indian Studies, and
Special Advisor to the Chancellor
on Native American and Indigenous
Affairs at UCLA. Courtesy of
Mishuana Goeman.

tem against colonialism. Renya's
mother, Woesha Cloud North,
chose a more radical approach.
Like Wilma Mankiller, she joined
Native activists during the Alcatraz occupation (1969–1971) and
supported their fight for self-determination, tribal sovereignty, and justice for
American Indians. Now her daughter continues this intergenerational commitment to Indigenous rights and identifies herself as an Indigenous feminist.[46]
Renya Ramirez's areas of research include Ho-Chunk biography, urban Native
Americans, diaspora, transnationalism, Native feminisms, gender and cultural
citizens, and the relationship between Native Americans and anthropology, citizenship, and antiracist education. She has published widely.[47]

Mishuana Goeman, a member of the Seneca Tonawanda Band, focuses on
feminist intervention into an analysis of colonial spatial restructuring of Native
lands and bodies in the twentieth century. She is a professor of Gender Studies
and American Indian Studies at UCLA, and Special Advisor to the Chancellor
on American and Indigenous Affairs. Her book *Mark My Words: Native Women
(Re)Mapping Our Nations* features literature written by Native women to argue
that women's writing centering on Indigenous knowledge is necessary to help
support decolonization by remapping settler geographies. The essays address
violence against Native women—violence perpetuated through erasures, the
education system, the formation of nation-states, and through historical narrative—to create a Native feminist standpoint that is useful in decolonization. Professor Goeman contends that a move toward Native feminist spatial practices is
an important step in restructuring lands, bodies, and communities.[48]

Goeman is developing a community-based digital community project,
Mapping Indigenous, that is working toward creating a self-represented sto-
rytelling, archival and community-oriented maps that unveil multilegend
Indigenous landscapes, as well as developing curricula for K–12. She gives
us a powerful reimagining of what the Native landscape looks like by exam-

ining the literary narratives of the urban Navajo powerhouse Esther Belin. She imagines new conceptions of space to create and re-create our daily relationships with land, people, and ancestors. Her recent book *Settler Aesthetics: Visualizing the Spectacle of Originary Moments in "The New World"* (2023) analyzes the continuity of imperialist exceptionalism and settler-colonial aesthetics in Terrence Malick's 2005 film, *The New World*.[49]

Professor Jennifer Nez Denetdale's book *Reclaiming Diné History: The Legacies of Navajo Chief Manuelito and Juanita* is a superb study that combines family history, oral history, and extensive research in all previous histories of the Diné people. Her recovery of the lost history of Chief Manuelito and Juanita is groundbreaking. She explains the importance of gender balance and complementarity: "Concepts of sexuality are important for understanding the Navajo worldview in which duality and complementarity organize the world. In the Navajo perspective the world is largely divided into male and female—and it is through the capacity to procreate, through the sexuality, that new life is brought forth." In their creation story, Changing Woman is the mother of all Diné. Denetdale recalls how Manuelito explained to William Traux at Fort Defiance in 1874 that Changing Woman's birth, her rite of passage to womanhood, and then her pregnancy brought about harmony in the world. The Sun was the father of her twins, who found their father and with the help of Spider Grandmother, then began to rid the world of monsters.[50]

In her portrait of Juanita, Denetdale recovers her importance in the tribe's history, including her participation in the delegation to Washington, D.C., as well as her importance as wife, mother, weaver, and culture bearer.[51] Denetdale reminds us that Indigenous women's roles are modeled on those of female deities

Jennifer Nez Denetdale is a professor of American Studies at the University of New Mexico. A strong advocate for Indigenous peoples, she is the first Diné/Navajo to earn a PhD in history. Photography by Ramona Emerson, Reel Indian Pictures. Courtesy of Jennifer Nez Denetdale.

like those who are prominent in Navajo creation stories. While Navajo women experienced many changes under colonialism, they look to women's roles in the traditional stories as guidance for their lives.[52] These traditional narratives provide spiritual and physical renewal, and they reaffirm community and kin relationships. Denetdale recalls the statement of Keith Basso, who claimed the Apache "speak the past into being to summon it and give it dramatic form so we can participate in our ancestors' quest for survival and the need to create a sense of community and kin." N. Scott Momaday, the great Kiowa essayist and story-teller, similarly proclaims, "We are what we imagine ourselves to be."[53]

Like those who went before them, all these contemporary groundbreaking scholars and teachers focus on retrieving tribal and family histories, and they realize the ways in which gender, violence, and colonization are inextricably connected. Recovery of tribal history is essential in the struggle to achieve sovereignty.[54] Recovery of women's history and traditional power is as essential to this struggle as this struggle is to their people's survival and flourishing.

Emily Haozous's Story: Leading Native Health Care

Emily Haozous's grandfather was Allan Houser, who was a Chiricahua Apache and one of the most famous painters and sculptors of the twentieth century. His father was the grandnephew of Geronimo. When Emily's grandfather was near the end of his life, battling cancer, she spent long periods with him and helped care for him. This had a profound impact on her and inspired her to pursue a life in medicine, especially nursing. She saw how the hospice people were so caring and nurturing, and she wanted to go into nursing and oncology, and especially to focus on cultural sensitivity in that field. A member of the Chiricahua Fort Sill Apache, Emily is a registered nurse, research scientist, and associate professor at the University of New Mexico College of Nursing. She has a passion for bring-ing equitable health care to all corners of Indian country. She trains health-care workers to be culturally sensitive to Native patients. This can make the differ-ence between a patient's living or dying. Her research analyzes cancer disparities in American Indians and Alaska Natives. She continues the Apache traditions of powerful women healers.

Historically, Apaches lived within the ethos of supernatural power as they still do. That is, everything in life involved supernatural power. As Kimberly Moore Buchanan points out, "Power was to be used for the benefit of the entire tribe, not for selfish purposes." Buchanan's study treats Apache women as providers, producers of clothing and shelter, fire builders, leaders, supporters, fighters,

A member of Chiricahua
Fort Sill Apache, Emily
Haozous is a descendent
of Geronimo and the
granddaughter of famous
artist Allan Houser. She is
an associate professor at the
University of New Mexico
College of Nursing, and
eminent scholar focusing
on oncology and health disparities. Photograph taken
by Carolyn Ross Johnston
in Santa Fe, New Mexico,
in 2017. Courtesy of Emily
Haozous.

medicine women, and as wives and mothers.[55] Apache wives brought wealth to their families, as the tribe was matrilocal, which means that the man lived with his wife's family, brought wedding gifts to the family, and economically supported the family with his hunting, raiding, and warring skills. Therefore, Apache women were powerful and valued. While male and female children were valued equally, "daughters were considered to be greater economic assets due to matrilocal practices. Within the Apache belief system, White Painted Woman personified the Apachean respect for females."[56]

Using one's power for the benefit of the tribe and for the benefit of American Indian people in general is a constant thread in Indigenous women's power. This is why Dr. Emily Haozous returned to New Mexico, where her Apache ancestors originally lived. Originally, the Apache Nation lived in what is now southwest New Mexico, southeast Arizona, and northern Mexico. The tribe as a whole was referred to as Chiricahua Apache. It was composed of four bands named Chiricahua, Warm Springs, Bedonhke, and Nednais. Emily lives in Santa Fe with her husband and two sons. When asked about her sons, she literally glowed and spoke lovingly about them, their extraordinary gifts, and their differences in temperament. Literally, she sees them as the lights of her life.[57]

In her interview in 2017 with Terri Baker and Carolyn Johnston, Emily Haozous said she is a feminist, and that this means being connected to the community and sharing her knowledge and empathy with the members of her community. Clearly, hers is not an individualistic kind of feminism. Feminism to her means equality of men and women, and balance is a key to the flourishing of the community.

For Emily, the two major forces in her life were her father, Robert Haozous, and her grandfather, Allan Houser. She said her father gave her unconditional love and inspired confidence that she could accomplish anything she attempted. Her grandfather was a wonderful artist who also supported her in her aspirations, and he instilled in her a deep sense of history and connection to the Apache people.[58]

Among medical caregivers, Haozous believes that nurses are the ones closest to the patients and families. Indian families assume they have the role of caring for the ill person, and sometimes they might be reluctant to involve the hospice people, so she wanted to be able to harmonize the two groups so they could best care for both the patient and the families.[59] Emily chose to go to college and graduate school and to devote herself to teaching and research. She recently completed a large research project on over 167 urban Indians in the Santa Fe area, half of whom were found to suffer from hunger. She has a holistic view of health that includes the economic aspects, cultural values, and family support networks or absence of such networks. She is deeply committed to enabling communities to flourish by marshaling women's special intrinsic qualities and abilities. She promotes cultural humility in her teaching and practice, and she advises nurses to go into the community and say, "Teach me." She realizes the distrust that Indian people may have of health-care providers and attempts to eliminate discrimination in that care, as well as discriminatory or stereotyped presumptions. She says, "Culture is the lens through which we experience the world, and so culture is also the lens through which Native people experience diagnoses, palliative care, and treatments."[60]

Haozous believes that the goals of feminism are relevant to Native women's lives: issues of equity in employment, freedom from violence and rape, and gender equality. When asked if she is unapologetically feminist because of her education and being affected by movements of the sixties, she said that her cousin has no education, yet holds the same values as she does.

For Emily Haozous, integrating American Indian values with contemporary research methods to address health issues in Native populations is central to her life's work. She is dedicated to giving back to her community, especially in times of crisis, as in severe illnesses. She is interested in both the prevention and the treatment of patients and families of patients. At the same time, she is uninterested in her own "power." She would rather focus on empowering members of her tribe and larger community. Professor Haozous has written extensively in journals, and given scores of community presentations, in addition to teaching in the university. She has focused on cancer pain and symptom management, cancer prevention, early detection, and eliminating health disparities in American Indians and Alaska Natives.[61]

The Fort Sill Apaches descend from Geronimo, who was driven out of New Mexico and imprisoned, before eventually being released in Oklahoma. Their ancestors were taken from one U.S. Army installation to another, from Florida to Alabama for twenty-eight years, before ending up in Oklahoma. Each year, Emily Haozous joins other Fort Sill Apache tribal members in a Mountain Spirit Dance in Oklahoma. In 2011, the federal government designated a thirty-acre area of land in New Mexico for the tribe to form a reservation.[62]

Native Women Leaders Keep the Sacred Fire Burning

As the stories in this chapter show, Native women's lives have been profoundly affected by colonization, violence, dispossession of land, and the disturbance of gender balance and equality. Many of these experiences led to lamentation. However, these stories show that there also are reasons for celebration. Native women and men have resisted and fought for tribal sovereignty, for water and land rights, against violence, and to nurture children and the earth. They have preserved memory, language, and culture. Native feminisms enable an understanding of how gender, race, and colonialism are interconnected, and thus how sovereignty and balance can be achieved once again. When the Cherokees left on the Trail of Tears in 1838 from Red Clay, Tennessee, they carried some of the sacred ashes to Indian Territory. They breathed life into the embers of the sacred fire, as Native women have for centuries, thereby sustaining the life of the people. The Native women featured in this and the previous chapters have kept these embers burning, never giving up their people's traditional pattern of gender power and balance in living.

CHAPTER NINE

CONCLUSION

Not long ago, Terri's friend Marnie Cope gave us a story about her chickens. She closely observes and cares for her flock of about thirty chickens, even nursing the old ones as they are about to die. It seems that for a while the flock was without a rooster who would normally lead, so one of the hens took over. Terri began calling her Feminist Hen. When Marnie scattered food for them in the chicken yards, Feminist Hen would go about, rounding them up and encouraging them to eat. When Marnie provided fresh water to the flock, she would move them to the water. In the evening, Feminist Hen drove her flock to the hen house and oversaw proper roosting protocol. Then one day a chicken hawk attacked the flock swooping down into the chicken yard and scattering the frightened hens. But Feminist Hen rushed the marauding hawk, flying at the predator with claws outstretched. In the face of the attack, Chicken Hawk was driven off. Feminist Hen had saved the flock, and peace descended.

This story is about caring for and protecting family and community. It is also about stepping up in the face of necessity. Stories can transform, and they can heal. In this book, Native women tell their stories in their own voices through memoir, interviews, poetry, art, song, and framing a new history. They tell stories of lamentation, celebration, and hope. They also tell how they live feminism.

LaDonna Harris said, "Everybody has medicine." Medicine is that essence of a person which is a unique spiritual gift or talent. Good medicine is sacred, healing power. Wilma Mankiller speaks of it as "being of good mind." Both Harris and Mankiller, along with many other Native American women, have shared their remarkable medicine with us. This book honors all these Indigenous women who have continued to tend and to share their life-giving, life-sustaining medicine. Our central idea, confirmed by their stories, is that these Native women's power has been based on their medicine within their people's traditional lived pattern of gender balance.

From the period of first contact, Native women shocked the Europeans because of their high status in the tribes, and the equality of men and women. The women of the Six Nations in upstate New York dramatically influenced early

Euro-American women's rights advocates, including Lucretia Mott and Lydia Child, when they saw through them a vision of gender balance and equality being lived. Native women also played key roles in the feminist movement of the 1960s, and they were present from its beginnings. For example, Wilma Mankiller sat at the table in San Francisco where young women who became leaders of feminism's revival shared experiences and planned actions, and she maintained a close, cross-difference friendship with Gloria Steinem for the rest of her life. La-Donna Harris also was a founder and guide of the contemporary feminist movement, and she served as co-chair of the 2016 Women's March in Washington, D.C. Across the years, Native women have played leading roles in advocacy for change on issues that affect all women, including reproductive control of their bodies and lives, the elimination of violence against women (rape, murder, and domestic violence), equal pay, freedom from sexual harassment, and equal access to education and political power.

Some American Indian women have been uneasy at times about being designated as "feminist," but their support on these issues has been unwavering, because respect for women's value and gender equality has always been their people's tradition. Many American Indian women view the emergence of sexism among Indian men as a result of colonization and oppression, because before European contact, their Indigenous traditions embodied women's empowerment and equality. The boarding schools to which they were often forced, and always encouraged to send their children were meant to continue and to expand the process of colonization and oppression, but many of the children clearly themselves subverted these policies, and as adults, they worked to strengthen tribal identity, as exemplified by Geraldine Hall McKinney's story. Moreover, Geraldine used her boarding school education, in combination with the traditional women's power she learned from her mother, to assure that her daughter, Dr. Terri McKinney Baker, would persevere to become a highly educated woman, a teacher of Native American students, an activist, and an intertribal leader for Indigenous peoples' empowerment who worked effectively with other Indigenous women to change lives.

This book presents the stories of generations of powerful American Indian women. Often these Native women "lead from behind the scenes." That is, while working in their professional capacities and in their relations with their communities, they are visible to some degree, and few people realize the extent of their efforts and their effectiveness. The women in this book feel a calling to work for the good of tribal people and other vulnerable people, and they do so. Their work is informed by the knowledge of who they are as well as their continuing efforts to discover more about their identities. The powerful women who came before, those who died, and those who persevered despite the obstacles to tribal survival continue to inform the lives, the relationships, and the decisions of these powerful modern women. Native women live their identities in ways that have become available to them from their family situation, their personal medicine, their education, and their relationships with their tribes. Although they may be invisible to mainstream America, as are most Native American Indians, they serve on advisory boards, they consult nationally on important issues that fall within their professional expertise, they serve their tribes in administrative offices and in academic settings, and they tell true stories and make art that reflects, expands, and communicates Indigenous experience.

American Indian women learned what it meant to be male and female from their mothers, as well as from their people's creation stories, ceremonies, and tribal life. Before contact, their spirituality centered on nature, female and male divinities, and a belief that everything was connected and that they were related to all life, animals, plants, and stars. Medicine men and women played a large role in their lives, and their thought was not based on Cartesian dualism, but rather was cyclical and holistic. Femaleness was greatly valued, feared, and respected in the Indigenous nations. Women were empowered by stories about female creators, warrior women, fire-bringers, and mothers who sacrificed so that their people could live, who gave the gifts of corn and the sacred pipe, including divine beings like Spider Grandmother, Selu and Kanati, Corn Mother, Buffalo Calf Woman, Changing Woman, and White Painted Woman. In part because of shared female and male reverence for female divinities, Native women held policymaking power in the governing of the tribes.

Living Indigenous Feminism: Stories of Contemporary Native American Women honors the voices and actions of modern Native women who have continued to live in ways that reflect all these forms of traditional female power. Our hope is that these stories, which show the remarkable diversity of these Native women's beliefs, ways of living feminism, service to their nations, and pride in their Indigenous identities, will inspire others' empowerment and action. A renaissance of tribal sovereignty, identity, and memory increasingly sweeps across the United States through the leadership of new generations of Native American women.

ACKNOWLEDGMENTS

First, I wish to thank my coauthor Terri Baker, with whom I worked on this book for eight years. Sadly, she died on October 15, 2022. This book is dedicated to her. We had a wonderful adventure researching and writing this work. She is greatly missed. I am indebted to Tom Baker, her husband, who has enabled this book to come to fruition. On April 18, 2024, he suddenly died.

I wish to thank Nathaniel Holly at the University of Georgia Press, who is responsible for making this book possible. He is imaginative, brilliant, and a marvelous editor. I am also grateful to my friends who read and commented on the manuscript: Wayne Flynt, Judith Green, Patricia Perez-Arce, David LaVere, and my sister Nancy Smith. I thank Nancy Schuler for her endless patience and help with technical issues. I am also grateful to Laura Price Yoder, Lea Johnson, Melissa Buchanan, Zubin Meer, and Ben Shaw for their many contributions to this book.

I am eternally grateful to Wayne Flynt and Leon Litwack, who have been re-markable mentors to me for decades. I wish to thank Marion and Elie Wiesel for their constant encouragement and support. For their insights and enduring friendship, I thank Xavier Landon, Jeffrey Kennedy, Ed DeAvila, David Woods, Theda Perdue, Jewel Spears Brooker, Santiago Nunez, Ralph Brooker, Ann Hunter Simpson, Mark Tluszcz, William Adams, Kerry Buckley, Jean Rasor, Jim Huskey, Michael Solari, Philip Mattar, Catherine Griggs, James Goetsch, Maggi Morehouse, Jared Stark, Linda Lucas, Claire Bell, Chris Payne, John Galloway, Greg Padgett, Davina Lopez, Mara Soudakoff, Rodney and Margo Fitzgerald, Peggy Newton, Vais Salikhov, Randy Browne, Beth Paulk, Shelby Hall, Mike and Susan Abram, Bill Murrah, Betty Henault, Travis Absher, Shannon Green, Jesus Subero, Marnie Cope, Connie Henshaw, Scotti McKinney, and Charlie Baker, son of Terri and Tom Baker. I also thank the readers of the University of Georgia Press who were enormously perceptive and generous in their commen-tary on the manuscript.

I wish to thank LaDonna Harris, Kathryn Harris Tijerina, Laura Harris, Jane Osti, Callie Chunestudy, Barbara McAlister, Emily Haozous, Joy Harjo, Wilma

Mankiller, Mishuana Goeman, Jennifer Nez Denetdale, Jasilyn Charger, Ada Deer, Deb Haaland, Jocelyn Payne, and Virginia Sixkiller.

I am grateful to my parents, Alta Ross Johnston and father Eugene Johnston, nieces Patricia Higgens and Jennifer Smith, and Matt Higgens for their support and insights. I am grateful for the wisdom of *all* the Indigenous women featured in our book including the members of the Eastern Band of Cherokee Indians and the Cherokee Nation of Oklahoma.

AUTHORS AND FRIENDS

Terri McKinney Baker and Carolyn Ross Johnston

Terri Baker retired as chair and professor from the Department of Languages and Literature at Northeastern State University in Tahlequah, Oklahoma. She taught classes for the Languages and Literature Department and classes cross-listed for the American Indian Studies Program. Along with Connie Henshaw, she published *Women Who Pioneered Oklahoma: Stories from the WPA Narratives*. Working with Professors Joseph Faulds, Bridget Roussell Cowlishaw, and Christopher Malone, she edited and published *Vision and Voice: A College Reader/Rhetoric* (in three editions, in 2004, 2006, 2009). Earlier, along with Professors Joseph Faulds and Steve Poulter, she edited and published a freshman reader, *Seminary Leaves: A Northeastern State University Anthology*. She has published essays, poetry, and has written and produced two plays, one at Northeastern State University and one by request of the Choctaw Nation of Oklahoma, which presented it at their annual September holiday festival. Additionally, she wrote, directed, and produced a film for classroom use, *Soul Treaties: Oklahoma's Native American Literature*. As a museum professional, she acted as the research consultant for Ed Wade and Associates, a private consultant team that produced a national touring interpretive art exhibition, "Beyond the Prison Gate: The Fort Marion Experience and Its Artistic Legacy." As a part of an NGO, Rural Development Leadership Network, along with other Native women, she presented a workshop at the United Nations Commission on the Status of Women. Terri Baker's higher education degrees came from Southeastern Oklahoma State University (BA, in English and speech), University of Utah (MA in English), and Louisiana State University (PhD in English). Terri Baker was a citizen of the Choctaw Nation of Oklahoma and lived in rural northeastern Oklahoma. After this full life of leadership, service, and creative engagement, she died on October 15, 2022. She is greatly missed.

Carolyn Ross Johnston is professor of History and American Studies, and Elie Wiesel Professor of Humane Letters, at Eckerd College in St. Petersburg, Florida. She has written five previous books—including *Jack London: An Amer-*

ican Radical?; *Sexual Power: Feminism and the Family in America* (nominated for a Pulitzer Prize); *Cherokee Women in Crisis: Trail of Tears, Civil War, and Allotment*; *My Father's War: Fighting with the Buffalo Soldiers in World War II*; and *Voices of Cherokee Women*—as well as numerous articles. For twenty-four years, she taught winter term courses with Nobel laureate Elie Wiesel at Eckerd College. After receiving her PhD in history from the University of California at Berkeley, she taught at Colorado College for two years, followed by forty-six years thus far at Eckerd College. She has taught Native American History and Native American Thought for thirty years. She also teaches American social and intellectual history, women's history, the sixties, "Rebels with a Cause," environmental history, and American Studies courses. She is a recipient of a Danforth Fellowship and a Woodrow Wilson Fellowship. She received the Robert A. Staub Award for Excellence, the Lloyd W. Chapin Award for Excellence in Scholarship and the Arts, the John M. Satterfield Award for Outstanding Mentor, and the John M. Bevan Award for Teaching Excellence and Campus Leadership. Both Terri and Carolyn have been state presidents of the American Association of University Professors. They have fought for civil rights, women's rights, and Indigenous rights. After completing *Voices of Cherokee Women*, Carolyn's research in the Mankiller papers at the Western History Collection inspired her to write this book.

NOTES

Notes on Terminology

1. Johnston, *Sexual Power*, viii.
2. "Matriarchy," *Merriam-Webster*.
3. Sanday, *Women at the Center*.
4. Sanday, *Women at the Center*; Mann and Goettner-Abendroth, *Matriarchal Studies*.
5. Gottner-Abendroth, *Matriarchal Societies Studies*; Mann and Goettner-Abendroth, *Matriarchal Studies*.

Introduction. Cultural Survival and Indigenous Women's Traditional Power

1. Andres Resendez comments that "if we were to add up all the Indian slaves taken in the New World from the time of Columbus to the end of the nineteenth century, the figure would run somewhere between 2.5 and 5 million slaves"; Resendez, *Other Slavery*, 5.
2. Perdue and Green, *Columbia Guide*, 76–77.
3. Mankiller et al., *Reader's Companion*, 190. Rayna Green, historian, and curator wrote, "A feminist revolution here would simply honor American tradition, not overthrow it."
4. Wagner, *Untold Story of the Iroquois Influence on Early Feminists*.
5. Landsman, "'Other' as Political Symbol," 247–284, 258–259; see also Hallowell, *James and Lucretia Mott*.
6. Wagner, "Is Equality Indigenous?"; "7. 19th Amendment."
7. Karcher, *First Woman in the Republic*, xii, 10–12, 32, 86–87, xxviii.
8. Child, *History of the Condition of Women*.
9. Landsman, "'Other' as Political Symbol," 259, 267.
10. Landsman, "'Other' as Political Symbol," 247–284, 267.
11. Landsman, "'Other' as Political Symbol," 267–268.
12. Haraway, "Primatology Is Politics by Other Means," 77–118, esp. 114.
13. Landsman, "'Other' as Political Symbol," 273–274.
14. Landsman, "'Other' as Political Symbol," 273–274.
15. Johnston, *Voices of Cherokee Women*, 75.
16. Johnston, *Voices of Cherokee Women*, 199–200.
17. Debo, *And Still the Waters Run*, 91.
18. Crow Dog and Erdoes, *Lakota Woman*, 206.
19. Mankiller, *Reader's Companion*, 198.

Chapter 1. My Mother's Story: Geraldine Hull McKinney

1. Baker, "Song for Two Voices," 78–79.

2. Josephy, *500 Nations*, 147–148.

3. Lomawaima, "Preface," xiii.

4. Lena's bride price story appears in shortened versions in Baker and Henshaw, *Women Who Pioneered Oklahoma*; Baker, "Cherries in Wildcat"; Bauer-Maglin and Radosh, *Women Confronting Retirement*.

5. Thornton, *American Indian Holocaust and Survival*, 114. See also DeRosier, *Removal of the Choctaw Indians*, 116.

6. Kappler, *Laws and Treaties*, 311.

7. Debo, *And Still the Waters Run*, 11.

8. Debo, *And Still the Waters Run*, 13.

9. *Congressional Record*, 39th Congress, 1st session, 1866, CH 40, 241, 236–239.

10. Foreman, *Down the Texas Road*.

11. For the Menominee in Wisconsin, the property was timber, as Ada Deer recounts. Deer says, "In the 1870s, the federal government restricted reservation logging to Menominee men, but whites could get access to tribal timber by marrying Menominee women. By the 1930s, many Menominee had white fathers or grandfathers"; Deer and Perdue, *Making a Difference*, 4.

12. See Grann, *Killers of the Flower Moon*; for a detailed account, see Aldrich, "A History of the Coal Industry."

13. Shirley, *Law West of Fort Smith*, 22.

14. McReynolds, *Oklahoma*, 297.

15. Morgan and Morgan, *Oklahoma: A History*, 154. See also Kidwell, "How America's Destiny Became Manifest," 274.

16. Debo, *And Still the Waters Run*, 290–317.

17. Shirley, *Law West of Fort Smith*, 21.

18. Foreman, *Down the Texas Road*, 10–11.

19. Debo, *And Still the Waters Run*, 19–21.

20. *Annual Report of the Board of Indian Commissioners 1885*.

21. Debo, *And Still the Waters Run*, 21–22.

22. See McCoy, "Choctaw Gift from 1890s," 12.

23. Conley, *Cherokee Nation*, 188.

24. Debo, *And Still the Waters Run*, 278.

25. *Oklahoma Forts, Military History and Civil War Map*.

26. *Civilization Fund Act*, chapter 85.

27. This story has appeared in a slightly different version in Baker, "Cherries in Wildcat."

28. Milligan and Shepherd, *Choctaw of Oklahoma*, 243.

29. Hiemstra, "Presbyterian Missionaries and Mission Churches," 459–467.

30. As an adult, I talked with my mother about Goodland at her kitchen table, and in Tahlequah recorded one interview on VHS tape. Both brief and longer excerpts from the interviews have appeared in the following publications: Baker and Henshaw, *Women Who Pioneered Oklahoma; Journal of Gilcrease Museum;* "Green Country."

31. Self, "What Really Made," 1–2.

32. Debo, *And Still the Waters Run*, 279.

33. Glancy, "Death Cry for the Language," 11–12.

34. Snell, *Grandmother's Grandchild*, 107.

35. Mihesuah, *Cultivating the Rosebuds*, 19.

36. Mihesuah, *Cultivating the Rosebuds*, 21.

37. Mihesuah, *Cultivating the Rosebuds*, 23.

38. Lomawaima, "Preface," xiii.

39. Lomawaima, "Preface," xiv.

40. Lomawaima, "Preface," 88.

41. Lomawaima, "Preface," 90.

42. Snell, *Grandmother's Grandchild*, 109.

43. Email reply to Terri Baker email requesting information, June 29, 2018.

44. Milligan and Shepherd, *Choctaws of Oklahoma*, 240–241.

45. Milligan and Shepherd, *Choctaws of Oklahoma*, 242–243.

46. Personal papers of Geraldine Hull McKinney, Collection of Terri McKinney Baker.

47. Personal papers of Geraldine Hull McKinney, Collection of Terri McKinney Baker.

48. Kidwell, *Choctaws in Oklahoma*, 224.

Chapter 2. My Own Story: Terri McKinney Baker

1. Baker, "Medicine Man Blues" (unpublished poem by Terri Baker).

2. Baker and Henshaw, *Women Who Pioneered Oklahoma*. A selected list of publications and presentations follow. Poems appeared in such publications as Wingsard and Isom, *Literature: Reading and Responding;* Blackburn, *Writer's Forum;* Ringold, *Nimrod: Oklahoma Indian Markings;* Ringold and Isom, *Nimrod: Oklahoma Indian Markings;* Bauer-Maglin and Radosh, *Women Confronting Retirement.* Three plays were produced, two during the Choctaw Labor Day Celebration in Tuskahoma, Oklahoma, by request of the Choctaw Nation of Oklahoma 1999, and one at Northeastern State University in 1998. A documentary about American Indian literature for classroom use was produced in 2000. Various presentations were made during the Annual Symposium on the American Indian by request of the American Indian Heritage Committee on which she served. During the 1990s, Dr. Baker was active in the Women's Caucus of the South Central Modern Language Association, once serving as chair of three sessions and presenting papers in the American Literature sessions. Dr. Baker presented papers at the Southwest Popular Culture Association; Dr. Baker presented at the University of Arkansas Annual

American Indian Symposium. After retirement, Dr. Baker continued publishing and presenting the results of her research.

3. "Symposium on the American Dream," which was the theme of the National Symposium on the American Indian one year that Terri Baker, along with the American Indian Heritage Committee, helped produce annually at Northeastern State University.

4. Baird, "Are the Five Tribes," 6.

5. Baird, "Are the Five Tribes," 9.

6. Katanski, *Learning to Write "Indian,"* 3.

7. LaVere, *Contrary Neighbors*, 7.

8. King, "Coalition Wants 'Misleading' Statue Removed," 1.

9. King, *Strength to Love*, 2.

10. The University of Oklahoma Press, the University of Nebraska Press, the University of Georgia Press, the University of New Mexico Press, the University of North Carolina Press, the University of Mississippi Press, and the University of Alabama Press.

11. *Choctaw Nation of Oklahoma.*

12. *Choctaw Nation of Oklahoma.*

13. Bradford, "Of Plimoth Plantation."

14. Bradford, "Of Plimoth Plantation," chapter 10.

15. A version of this analysis appears in the afterword by Terri Baker in Soderlind and Carson, *American Exceptionalism*, 245–246.

16. Dunbar-Ortiz, *Indigenous People's History*, 199. For more on double consciousness, see Du Bois, *Souls of Black Folk*, 10–11.

17. Kidwell, "How America's Destiny Became Manifest," 270.

18. Resendez, *Other Slavery*, 17.

19. This story appeared in part in Baker, "Hungry Ones."

Chapter 3. Wilma Mankiller's Story: Leading with Indigenous Women's Power

1. Snodgrass, *Beating the Odds*, 206–210.

2. For a discussion of consequences of relocation, see Dunbar-Ortiz, *Indigenous Peoples' History*, 174.

3. Mankiller and Wallis, *Mankiller*, 145–147, 150, 154, 157, 159. Chapter 11 is titled "Dancing on the Edge of the Roof."

4. Mankiller and Wallis, *Mankiller*, 157.

5. "Notes for Mankiller Autobiography"; and Mankiller and Wallis, *Mankiller*, 210–212.

6. Mankiller and Wallis, *Mankiller*, 154–155.

7. Mankiller and Wallis, *Mankiller*, 157.

8. "Notes for Mankiller Autobiography."

9. Mankiller and Wallis, *Mankiller*, 98–116, 143, 99–100. Indian tribes in California had experienced violence and brutality. Two hundred and seventy-five thousand Indians lived in California when the Spanish established their first settlement there in the mid-eighteenth century. From the time of the missions through Mexican rule and

into the Gold Rush, Indigenous people in what is now called California experienced brutality, land theft, starvation, enslavement, and genocide. A University of California study found that in the 1850s at least 1,000 Indian women were so brutally raped that most of them died. Four thousand Indian children were kidnapped and sold into slavery. In many communities in California in the 1870s, bounties were offered for Indian scalps and severed heads.

10. Mankiller and Wallis, *Mankiller*, 162.

11. Mankiller and Wallis, *Mankiller*, 163, 190, 186–187, 186–196.

12. Mankiller and Wallis, *Mankiller*, 190, 193, 195–196, 192, 200–202. See also Blansett, *Journey to Freedom*, for an excellent biographical study of Oakes and the occupation of Alcatraz. Blansett also discusses Oakes's activism after his daughter Yvonne's death including the Pitt River campaign in which Mankiller was involved.

13. Mankiller and Wallis, *Mankiller*, 195, 203–204; Mankiller's brother Richard was at Wounded Knee in 1973. See also Blansett, *Journey to Freedom*, 200–208, for more background on the Pitt River campaign.

14. McReynolds, *Oklahoma*, 224.

15. Johnston, *Cherokee Women in Crisis*, 104.

16. Holt, "New Thing in Our Country," 261.

17. Mankiller and Wallis, *Mankiller*, 226.

18. Mankiller, *Autobiography*, 222–226.

19. Steinem, "Leaders as Guides of Return."

20. Steinem, "Leaders as Guides of Return."

21. One Fire Development Corp., "About."

22. Hoskin, "Chief Chat."

23. Mankiller and Wallis, *Mankiller*, 235–238.

24. Mankiller and Wallis, *Mankiller*, 243–252.

25. Ramirez, "Race, Tribal, Nation, and Gender," 22–40; Mihesuah, *Indigenous American Women*.

26. Jeffries, "Re-membering Our Own Power," 160–195; especially 182–183.

27. Wilma Mankiller Collection, WHC, box 41-19; Mankiller and Wallis, *Mankiller*, 168, 214.

28. Box 8-1 Mankiller Collection, WHC.

29. Mankiller and Wallis, *Autobiography*, 246.

30. Letter of Wilma Mankiller to Bruce Weinhert in Westlake Village, Calif., June 1, 1992.

31. Mankiller Collection, WHC, box 41-45.

32. Mankiller and Wallis, *Autobiography*, 235, xxi–xxiii, 233.

33. Mankiller and Wallis, *Mankiller*, 238–239.

34. In 1985, Wilma had succeeded Chief Ross Swimmer, when he resigned to accept the appointment as assistant secretary of the U.S. Bureau of Indian Affairs. Wilma then succeeded him as the principal chief of the Cherokee Nation. She was the first

woman to hold that office in modern times. She was elected in 1987 and re-elected in 1991. By 1995, Wilma's health had begun to be a problem and she retired from public office.

35. *Spin and Marty* were shorts, set in Triple R Ranch, a western-style summer camp, that aired during the Mickey Mouse Club in the 1950s. Cotter, *Wonderful World of Disney Television*, 187, 189, 191.

36. Crawford, "Campus Protest."

37. Mankiller and Wallis, *Autobiography*, 29.

38. Chavez, *Cherokee Phoenix*.

Chapter 4. Comanche Feminist Power: LaDonna Harris's Story

1. Harris, *Comanche Life*, xiii, xix. See also Harris and Wasilewski, *This Is What We Want to Share*, 7.

2. The following text is a transcript of the following interview: Baker and Johnston, July 19, 2017.

3. Interview with Baker and Johnston, July 19, 2017.

4. Janda, *Beloved Women*, 27.

5. Interview with Baker and Johnston, July 19, 2017.

6. Interview with Baker and Johnston, July 19, 2017; see also Janda, *Beloved Women*, 27.

7. Janda, *Beloved Women*, 29–31.

8. Janda, *Beloved Women*, 29–31, 55; "LaDonna Harris (Indian Powerhouse)."

9. Janda, *Beloved Women*, 53.

10. Blansett, *Journey to Freedom*, 101–103; see also Stockel, *LaDonna Harris*, 96–98.

11. Interview with Terri Baker and Carolyn Johnston, July 19, 2017. Betty Friedan took Kathryn Harris, LaDonna's daughter, under her wing, and LaDonna recalled "minding" Friedan's rips and hems on occasion before an event.

12. Interview with Terry Baker and Carolyn Johnston, July 19, 2017.

13. Interview with Terry Baker and Carolyn Johnston, July 19, 2017; Janda, *Beloved Women*, 56.

14. Interview with Baker and Johnston, July 19, 2017; Janda, *Beloved Women*, 56–57.

15. Janda, *Beloved Women*, 57–58.

16. Janda, *Beloved Women*, 61–63.

17. DeLong, "Ella Baker."

18. Janda, *Beloved Women*, 63, 68, 73.

19. Interview with LaDonna Harris, July 27, 2018.

20. "About the AIO Ambassadors Program."

21. "Mission of the Ambassadors Program."

22. "Mission of the Ambassador Program."

23. Chavez, "LaDonna Harris."

24. Janda, *Beloved Women*, 74, 47, 76. Fred Harris died on November 23, 2024. https://www.frenchfunerals.com/obituaries/fred-roy-harris.

25. Mankiller and Wallis, *Mankiller*, 242, 246–247.

26. Interview, July 19, 2017; see also Steinem, *My Life on the Road,* 251–253, for insight on LaDonna Harris's gift of living in the modern world with her Native consciousness.

27. "LaDonna Harris (Comanche) Biographical Profile."

28. Staff, "Indigenous Women Rise"; "Early History," National Women's Political Caucus. She was a founding member of the Women's Political Caucus in 1971, along with Gloria Steinem, Bella Abzug, Shirley Chisholm, Dorothy Height, Eleanor Holmes Norton, and Jill Ruckelshaus.

29. "Twelve Ways to Be Inducted."

Chapter 5. Advancing a Powerful Legacy: Kathryn Harris Tijerina's Story

1. The following interview took place on June 14, 2016, between Dr. Terri Baker and Kathryn Harris Tijerina in Santa Fe, New Mexico. The occasion came about through relationships. Jocelyn Payne, Terri's friend and colleague at Northeastern State University in Tahlequah, Oklahoma, was Kathryn Harris Tijerina's roommate in college at University of Oklahoma before they both transferred. She introduced Terri to Kathryn. The interview took place at La Fonda Hotel. Kathryn received questions in advance.

2. Phillips, "Longtime Police Brutality."

3. Kathryn Tijerina to Terri Baker and Carolyn Johnston, June 14, 2020. See also Lakota People's Law Project, "Native Lives Matter." Interview: Baker and Tijerina, June 14, 2016; Interview with Baker and Johnston, July 19, 2017.

Chapter 6. Laura Harris's Indigenous Feminist Story

1. Interview with Baker and Johnston, July 19, 2017. Laura Harris has been widely honored for her leadership, including as recipient of the New Mexico YWCA 2001 Women on the Move Award.

2. Interview with Baker and Johnston, July 19, 2017.

3. "Laura Harris," Land Peace Foundation; Interview with Baker and Johnston, July 19, 2017.

4. Harris et al. "Applying Indigenous Values to Contemporary Tribal Citizenship," 316–330.

5. "Laura Harris," Land Peace Foundation; Interview with Baker and Johnston, July 19, 2017.

6. "Laura Harris," Land Peace Foundation.

7. "Laura Harris," Land Peace Foundation.

8. "Laura Harris," Land Peace Foundation.

9. Interview with Baker and Johnston, July 19, 2017.

10. Interview with Baker and Johnston, July 19, 2017.

11. Interview with Baker and Johnston, July 19, 2017.

12. Cobb-Greetham, "LaDonna Harris," 219–225.

13. Interview with Baker and Johnston, July 19, 2017.

14. Interview with Baker and Johnston, July 19, 2017.

15. *ABQ Journal* Staff, "Drive-Thru Food Event for Native Families."

Chapter 7. The Path-Lighting Power of Creative Voices: Indigenous Women's Power as Artists

1. See Wade, Haralson, and Strickland, *As in a Vision*, 26, for a discussion of American Indian consciousness and aesthetic perception. See also Kidwell, "Systems of Knowledge."

2. Green, *That's What She Said*, 2.

3. Green, *That's What She Said*, 3.

4. See Wade, Haralson, and Strickland, *As in a Vision*. This book contains a significant selection of traditional tribal literature, artwork, analytical essays, and a glossary. The book shows connections among art, literature, history, and anthropology.

5. Allen, *Sacred Hoop*, 253.

6. Allen, *Sacred Hoop*, 254.

7. Green, *That's What She Said*, 129.

8. Peterson, *The Living Tradition of Maria Martinez*.

9. Hyde, *Maria Making Pottery*; see also Schaaf, *Pueblo Indian Pottery*.

10. Harvard Radcliffe Institute, "Martinez."

11. Shaaf, *Pueblo Indian Pottery*.

12. A version of this appeared in Terri Baker, "Hungry Ones."

13. Interview with Osti, January 22, 2020.

14. Interview with Chunestudy, July 18, 2019.

15. Broder, *Earth Songs, Moon Dreams*, 147.

16. Snell, "Keeping the Traditions."

17. See *Phoenix* Archives, "Cherokee Artist Wins Awards."

18. Fariello, *From the Hands of Our Elders*. See also Hill, *Weaving New Worlds*.

19. Cooper, *Oklahoma Cherokee Baskets*, 9.

20. Cooper, *Oklahoma Cherokee Baskets*, 15.

21. Cooper, *Oklahoma Cherokee Baskets*, 15.

22. Broder, *Earth Songs, Moon Dreams*, xv.

23. Broder, *Earth Songs, Moon Dreams*, 9, 11.

24. Broder, *Earth Songs, Moon Dreams*, 10.

25. Broder, *Earth Songs, Moon Dreams*, 151.

26. Broder, *Earth Songs, Moon Dreams*, 150.

27. Broder, *Earth Songs, Moon Dreams*, 182, 186.

28. Broder, *Earth Songs, Moon Dreams*, 141, 142.

29. Broder, *Earth Songs, Moon Dreams*, 127.

30. Broder, *Earth Songs, Moon Dreams*, 157.

31. Broder, *Earth Songs, Moon Dreams*, 163.

32. Broder, *Earth Songs, Moon Dreams*, 162.

33. Broder, *Earth Songs, Moon Dreams*, 267.

34. Harjo, *Crazy Brave*, 158.

35. Harjo, *Crazy Brave*, 139.

36. Harjo, "For Anna Mae Aquash."

37. Harjo, *American Sunrise*, 61–62.

38. Smith, "Joy Harjo."

39. *Merriam Webster's Encyclopedia of Literature.*

40. Linderman, *Pretty-shield, Medicine Woman of the Crows*, 195.

41. *Merriam Webster's Encyclopedia of Literature*, 1130.

42. Wiget, *Dictionary of Native American Literature.*

43. Howe, *Shell Shaker*, 225.

44. Howe, *Shell Shaker*, 20.

45. Hogan, "Direction of Light," 32.

46. Awiakta, *Seeking the Corn-Mother's Wisdom*, 6.

47. Rose, "For the White Poets," 86.

48. Snodgrass, "Tales of Burning Love," 176.

49. Terri Baker conducted the interview with Barbara McAlister via email and telephone during May 2020.

Chapter 8. Stories of Sovereignty, Survival, and Cultural Persistence: Indigenous Women's Power-Based Leadership

1. Elbein, "Youth Group That Launched a Movement." See also Wamsey, "Court Rules Dakota Access Pipeline."

2. Elbein, "Youth Group That Launched a Movement." See also Wamsey, "Court Rules Dakota Access Pipeline."

3. Charleyboy and Leatherdale, *#NotYourPrincess*, 84–85.

4. Charleyboy and Leatherdale, *#NotYourprincess*, 84; Change.org (The World's Platform for Change); Our Climate Voices, "Jasilyn Charger | Cheyenne River Sioux Tribe."

5. Elbein, "Youth Group That Launched a Movement." See also Wamsey, "Court Rules Dakota Access Pipeline."

6. Elbein, "Youth Group That Launched a Movement." See also Wamsey, "Court Rules Dakota Access Pipeline." See also Todrys, *Black Snake Standing Rock*, for an excellent detailed account of Jasilyn Charger, LaDonna Allard, Lisa DeVille, and Kandi White and other Native young people who were activists as water protectors at Standing Rock.

7. Monga and Eaton, " What Is the Keystone XL Pipeline."

8. Zitkála-Šá, *Oklahoma's Poor Rich Indians.*

9. Nabokov, *Native American Testimony*, 281, 300–303.

10. "Indian Affairs," U.S. Department of the Interior; home page, National Congress of American Indians.

11. Janko, "Elouise Cobell." The documentary about her is also a good resource. Janko, "100 Years."

12. Deer and Perdue, *Making a Difference*, 7–8.

13. Bowers, " Women of DRUMS," 56, 149–151, 159–160.

14. Bowers, "The Women of DRUMS," 54, 163–164, 188.

15. Deer and Perdue, *Making a Difference.*

16. Roth, NPR.

17. *The Paper, Albuquerque Independent Community News*, Albuquerque, N.Mex., August 29, 2021.

18. "Secretary Deb Haaland," U.S. Department of the Interior.

19. "Secretary Haaland Approves New Constitution," U.S. Department of the Interior.

20. Hauser and Paz, "U.S. to Search Former Native American Schools."

21. Gurr, *Reproductive Justice*, 105–109.

22. Ross, *Inventing the Savage*, 3. She has a PhD in sociology from the University of Oregon, and has been a professor at the University of California at Davis and UC–Berkeley. She was born in 1940. Dr. Ross is currently associate professor of Women Studies at University of Washington, has been in American Indian Studies as an adjunct professor since 1999, and is the codirector of Native Voices Graduate Program. Since her tenure with Native Voices, Dr. Ross has produced several award-winning films including *A Century of Genocide in the Americas, White Shamans and Plastic Medicine Men,* and *The Place of the Falling Waters.*

23. Ross, *Inventing the Savage*, 3.

24. "Luana Ross," University of Washington. Ross was also awarded a Newberry Library Fellowship and a Ford Foundation Fellowship. She has published numerous articles including "Race, Gender, and Social Control: Voices of Imprisoned Native American and White Women" in *Wicazo Sa Review* (1994); and "Native Women, Mean-Spirited Drugs, and Punishing Policies" in *Social Justice* (2005). She has also contributed chapters to important Native Studies and sociology texts, including *Reading Native American Women* (2005); *Native American Voices: A Reader;* and *States of Confinement: Policing, Detention, and Prisons* (2000).

25. Lewallen, "Strategic 'Indigeneity,'" 11.

26. *Maze of Injustice.*

27. "Sarah Deer," University of Kansas; Deer, *Beginning and End of Rape.* See also Smith, *Sexual Violence and American Indian Genocide.* Smith is not an Indigenous feminist because she is not a member of any tribe, but she has contributed scholarship to issues of concern to Native women. Andrea Smith received her BA from Harvard University; a master of divinity from Union Theological Seminary; a PhD in the History of Consciousness from the University of California, Santa Cruz; and juris doctorate from University of California, Irvine School of Law. She attracted attention for having claimed Cherokee identity without proof or acceptance by the Cherokee Nation. She taught at University of Michigan and currently teaches at University of California, Riverside. She has been active in fighting to end violence against women of color and their communities.

Recently the murder and disappearance of Native women has gained national attention with several articles in the *New York Times.* See Healy, "Rural Montana." The sixteen-year-old Selena Not Afraid disappeared near Billings after a New Year's Eve party when the van she was riding in pulled into a rest stop. Twenty-eight have gone missing, and the family fears sex trafficking, murder, and classifying missing as runaways by the law enforcement agencies.

Last year 5,590 Indigenous women were reported missing to the FBI National Crime Information Center.

> April 12, 2019
> Maya Slam, "Native American Women Are Facing a Crisis,"
> "since 84% of Indigenous women have experienced physical, sexual or psychological violence in their lifetimes. This is according to National Institute of Justice. Moreover, one in three Native American women have been raped or experienced attempted rape according to Justice Department, a statistic which is more than twice the national average. 13% how many sexual assaults reported by Native America women result in arrest according to the Justice Department. 35% for Black women, and 32% for white women. 506 Indigenous women and girls have disappeared or been killed in 71 urban American cities in 2016 according to the November report of Urban Indian Health Institute.
>
> In 2016, 5,712 Indigenous women and girls were reported missing; only 116 were logged by the U.S. Department of Justice federal missing persons databases according to National Crime Information Center."

28. Richardson, July 10, 2020.

29. Healy and Liptak, "Landmark Supreme Court Ruling."

30. Hopkins, *Life among the Paiutes*; James, *Notable American Women*; Zitkála-Šá, *Oklahoma's Poor Rich Indians*. Sarah Winnemucca lectured widely throughout the United States. She met Elizabeth and Mary Peabody Mann, advocates for women's rights, who helped her prepare her autobiography. She built a school with her brother at Lovelock, Nevada, for Native children. In the 1920s, Winnemucca was active in the women's rights movement and created the Women's Welfare Commission through the General Federation of Women's Clubs, which encouraged the Indian Reorganization Act of 1934 under Franklin D. Roosevelt's New Deal.

Both Zitkála-Šá and Sarah Winnemucca espoused tribal values of balance and gender equality, and fought for sovereignty and decolonization. Their Indigenous feminism was anti-colonialist and anti-imperialist. They shared a struggle against racism and violence against women, and they celebrated women as nurturers, mothers, healers, conservers of culture and agents of service to the community. Zitkála-Šá attended a Quaker missionary school, White's Manual Labor Institute, in Wabash, Indiana, when she was eight. Shortly after she arrived at the school, they cut her hair. She described the trauma of having her long hair cut: "And now my long hair was shingled like a coward's. In my anguish I moaned for my mother, but no one came to comfort me. Not a soul reasoned quietly with me, as my own mother used to do; for now I was only one of many little animals driven by a herder" (*My Life: Impressions of an Indian Childhood*, 27).

Zitkála-Šá later graduated from Earlham College in 1897. Then she taught at Carlisle and challenged attempts to erase Indian language and culture. She thought these practices promoted cultural genocide. She resigned and moved to Boston to write and study the violin. She worked on an opera, the Sun Dance, which was performed on the Ute Reservation in Utah and performed on Broadway in 1938. She also founded the National Council of American Indians in 1926 and advocated for citizenship rights and cultural preservation. Sarah Winnemucca and Zitkála-Šá struggled with integrating many various identities as an Indian. They were highly educated, published books, taught Indian children, and were active in the movement for women's rights in the United States. Both brought traditional tribal values into the struggle to change U.S. policy toward American Indians.

31. Allen, *Sacred Hoop*, 82, 205.

32. Thornton, *American Indian Holocaust and Survival*, 26–32, 104–113.

33. Bataille and Lisa, *Native American Women*, 171–173. Kidwell's books include *The Choctaws in Oklahoma: From Tribe to Nation, 1855–1970*; *Native American Studies*, with Alan Velie and Robert Con Davis-Undiano; *Native American Theology*, with Homer Noley and George E. Tinker; *The Choctaws: A Critical Bibliography*; and *Choctaws and Missionaries in Mississippi*. She wrote many articles dealing with American Indian women.

34. Bataille and Lisa, *Native American Women*.

35. "Beatrice Medicine," Women's Intellectual Contributions to the Study of Mind and Society. Medicine received her BA in anthropology from South Dakota State University, her MA in sociology and anthropology from Michigan State University, and her PhD from the University of Wisconsin. Her book *Learning to Be an Anthropologist*, a selection of her writings, was published by the University of Illinois Press in 2001.

36. "Beatrice Medicine," Women's Intellectual Contributions to the Study of Mind and Society; "NEW: Human Rights Advocate."

37. "Guide to the Beatrice Medicine Papers."

38. Mann, *Cheyenne-Arapaho Education*. Mann was selected as the Cheyenne Indian of the Year in 1983, and honored in 1987 as the National American Indian Woman of the Year. She served as the deputy to the assistant secretary of Indian Affairs, director of the Office of Indian Education Programs, Bureau of Indian Affairs in 1986. Mann received her BA in English from Southwest Oklahoma State in 1953, an MA in English from Oklahoma State in 1970, and a PhD in American Studies from University of New Mexico. She taught at the University of California at Berkeley, Harvard University, and the University of Montana. In 1991–1992, she served as the national coordinator of the American Indian Religious Freedom Coalition in the Association on American Indian Affairs. She was only one of two Native Americans ever to be elected to the National Academy of Education.

39. Transcription of Mann's speech from Lonelodge, "American Circle of Honor."

40. Barsness, *Henrietta Whiteman*.

41. "Brenda Child," University of Minnesota. With Brian Klopotok, she published

Indian Subjects: Hemispheric Perspectives on the History of Indigenous Education in 2014. Child published *My Grandfather's Knockings Sticks: Ojibwe Family Life and Labor on the Reservation,* which won the American Indian Book Award and the Best Book in Midwestern History Award. She served as the president of the Native American and Indigenous Studies Association in 2017–2018. Brenda Child has written extensively on the impact of boarding schools on Native families, and how Ojibwe women strengthened their families as mediators. For example, her book *Boarding School Seasons* used letters between parents and their children in boarding school to explore impact of institutions. The book won the North American Indian Prose Award. She is Northrup Professor and chair of the Department of American Studies at the University of Minnesota. She served on the board of trustees of the National Museum of the American Indian, Smithsonian, and as the past president of the Native American and Indigenous Studies Association. She was born on the Red Lake Ojibwe Reservation in northern Minnesota.

42. See Lomawaima, *They Called It Prairie Light: The Story of Chilocco Indian School*; works by Child et al., "In the White Woman's Image."

43. Taylor and Wride, "'Indian Kids Can't Write Sonnets,'" 25–53. Students at the boarding schools were expected to become either laborers if male or servants if women. Their training was essentially aimed at cultural extermination, but the consequences were often unintended. Those who made the experience their own acquired skills in English, academic preparation, leadership, and resilience. Many of them forged friendships across tribal boundaries and often for life. Some of them became the tribal leaders in the twentieth century like Geraldine McKinney, and lived feminism as they devoted their lives and talents to the good of their tribes and community. What was intended to exterminate their culture strengthened their beliefs and loyalty to family and tribe; they brought their knowledge and skills home.

44. Justice, *Why Indigenous Literatures Matter*, 2, quoted in Taylor and Wride, "'Indian Kids Can't Write Sonnets,'" 40.

45. Lewallen, "Strategic 'Indigeneity,'" 11.

46. Ramirez, "Writing as Granddaughter and Academic."

47. "Renya Ramirez," University of California, Santa Cruz. Ramirez is a professor of anthropology and humanities at UC–Santa Cruz. She received a BA from UC–Berkeley, and MA and PhD from Stanford University. Ramirez received numerous honors including a Rockefeller Grant, 2001–2003; a UC Mexus Grant in 2005; and grants from UC–Santa Cruz in 2006, 2007, and 2009. She is the author of *Standing Up to Colonial Power.*

48. Goeman, *Mark My Words.* Goeman received her PhD from Stanford University's Modern Thought and Literature program and was a UC presidential post-doctoral fellow at Berkeley. She is a professor of Gender Studies and American Indian Studies (https://theasa.net) UC–Los Angeles. She has published numerous peer-reviewed articles in journals such as *American Quarterly, Critical Ethnic Studies,* and *Wicazo-Sa.* Dr. Goeman is the 2024–2025 president of the American Studies Association (ASA).

49. "Mishauna Goeman, Ph.D," University of California, Los Angeles.

50. Denetdale, *Reclaiming Diné History*, 52–59. Jennifer Nez Denetdale is the first Diné-Navajo to earn a PhD in history. She is an associate professor of American Studies at Northern Arizona University. Her book *Reclaiming Diné History: The Legacies of Navajo Chief Manuelito and Juanita* was published in 2007. She is the director of the University of New Mexico's Institute for American Indian Research and the chair of the Navajo Nation Human Rights Commission. She has advocated for Navajo women and the LGBTQI, and received the UNM Faculty of Color Award for her teaching, research, and service in the academy. Her book *The Long Walk: The Forced Exile of the Navajo* for young adults was published in 2007. She is the director of UNM's Institute for American Indian Research, and the chair of the Navajo Nation Human Rights Commission. She received an award for Excellence in Diné Studies by the Navajo Studies Conference. She was selected to deliver the inaugural address to the 23rd Navajo Nation Council in January 2015. She received the UNM Presidential Award of Distinction in 2017.

51. Denetdale, *Reclaiming Diné History*, 88, 92, 128–129.

52. Denetdale, *Reclaiming Diné History*, 128–129.

53. Denetdale, *Reclaiming Diné History*, 128–129, 134.

54. Goeman and Denetdale, *Native Feminisms*, 9–13, 10. Mishuana R. Goeman and Jennifer Denetdale summarize the usefulness of Native feminism in recovery of traditional values and the process of decolonizing:

> While acknowledging these strains of feminism that work at odds with Indigenous sovereignties and understanding the debates among Native women about the usefulness of the term and its application to our intellectual labors and applications to our Native nations and communities, we affirm the usefulness of a Native feminism's analysis and, indeed, declare that Native feminist analysis is crucial if we are determined to decolonize as Native peoples. . . . For Native women there is not one definition of Native feminism; rather there are multiple definitions and layers of what it means to do Native feminist analysis. However, as Native feminists, our dreams and goals overlap; we desire to open up spaces where generations of colonialism have silenced Native peoples about the status of their women and about the intersections of power and domination that have also shaped Native nations and gender relations.

55. Buchanan, *Apache Women Warriors*, 14, 34.

56. Buchanan, *Apache Women Warriors*, 13–15. Women had free choice to join the men on raids and warring; however, women also had to care for children and were valued as childbearers. When husbands were killed, women could join revenge raids, and in battles, women often fought alongside their husbands. The mothers of fighting women cared for the children during such times. Two women enjoy particular attention in the book: Dahteste and Lozen. Both were with Geronimo when the band came in and were sent first to Florida and then to Alabama. After release from Alabama, Dahteste lived on the Mescalero Reservation until she died. Lozen died in captivity in Alabama.

Both women traveled with Geronimo, accompanying him on raiding and warring parties, fighting with the men, acting as messengers, and negotiating for the band.

57. Haozous interview, May 16, 2017.

58. Haozous interview, May 16, 2017.

59. Haozous interview, May 16, 2017.

60. Haozous interview, May 16, 2017. She received her BA from UC–Santa Cruz and her PhD from Yale University in 2009. Her dissertation examined cancer and barriers to cancer care for American Indians in the Southwest. She holds a Regent's Lectureship at the University of New Mexico.

61. Haozous interview, May 16, 2017.

62. Carcamo, "Fort Sill Apache." Jeff Haozous, Emily's cousin and previous chair of the Fort Sill Apaches, led an initiative in 2015 to establish a casino. The tribe sought recognition as a nation in New Mexico and received it. The Apache Casino Hotel is in Lawton, Oklahoma.

BIBLIOGRAPHY

"7. 19th Amendment: Suffrage and the Power of Women's Votes (with Sally Roesch Wagner and Melanie Campbell)" (podcast). Ms. Magazine. 58:59. August 24, 2020. https://msmagazine.com/podcast/episode-5-100-years-of-the-19th-amendment/.

"About the AIO Ambassadors Program." Americans for Indian Opportunity. Accessed August 21, 2024. www.aio.org/about-the-aio-ambassadors-program.

ABQ Journal Staff. "Drive-Thru Food Event for Native Families in ABQ." *Albuquerque Journal.* May 28, 2020. www.abqjournal.com/news/local/drive-thru-food-event-for -native-families-in-abq/article_1683dc9d-4902-5b03-bde1-18694512a511.html.

Adams, David Wallace. *Education for Extinction: American Indians and the Boarding School Experience 1875–1928.* Lawrence: University Press of Kansas, 1995.

Ahmed, Sara. *Living a Feminist Life.* Durham, N.C.: Duke University Press, 2017.

Albers, Patricia, and Beatrice Medicine, eds. *The Hidden Half: Studies of Plains Indian Women.* Lanham, Md.: Rowman & Littlefield, 1983.

Aldrich, Gene. "A History of the Coal Industry in Oklahoma to 1907." PhD diss., University of Oklahoma, 1952.

Alexander, M. Jacqui, and Chandra Mohanty. *Feminist Genealogies, Colonial Legacies, Democratic Futures.* New York: Routledge, 1997.

Allen, Paula Gunn. *Grandmothers of the Light: A Medicine Woman's Sourcebook.* Boston: Beacon, 1991.

———. *The Sacred Hoop: Recovering the Feminine in American Indian Traditions.* Boston: Beacon, 1992.

———, ed. *Song of the Turtle: American Indian Literature 1974–1994.* New York: Ballantine, 1996.

Anderson, Kim, "Affirmation of an Indigenous Feminist/Feminism." In *Indigenous Women and Feminism, Politics, Activism, Culture,* edited by Cheryl Suzack, Shari M. Huhndorf, Jeanne Perreault, and Jean Barman, 81–91. Vancouver: University of British Columbia Press, 2010.

———. *A Recognition of Being: Reconstructing Native Womanhood.* Toronto: Sumach, 2000.

Anderson, Kim, and D. Memee Lavell Harvard. *Mothers of the Nations: Indigenous Mothering as Global Resistance, Reclaiming and Recovery.* Bradford, Ont.: Demeter, 2014.

Annual Report of the Board of Indian Commissioners to the Secretary of the Interior. Vol. 17. Washington, D.C.: Government Printing Office, 1885.

Archuleta, Margaret, Brenda J. Child, and K. Tsianina Lomawaima, eds. *Away from*

Home: American Indian Boarding School Experiences, 1879–2000. Phoenix: Heard Museum, 2000.

Awiakta, Marilou. *Seeking the Corn-Mother's Wisdom*. Golden, Colo.: Fulcrum, 1993.

Baird, W. David. "Are the Five Tribes of Oklahoma 'Real' Indians?" *Western Historical Quarterly* 21, no. 1 (February 1990): 4–18.

Baker, Terri M. "A Song for Two Voices and Four Worlds." *Nimrod: Oklahoma Indian Markings* 32 (Spring–Summer 1989): 78–79.

———. "Cherries in Wildcat." Essay, *Cultural Survival Quarterly*. April 9, 2012. www
.culturalsurvival.org/news/cherries-wildcat.

———. "Medicine Man Blues." Unpublished poem.

———. "The Hungry Ones." *Palo Alto Review: A Journal of Ideas* (Spring 1998).

Baker, Terri, and Connie Oliver Henshaw, eds. *Women Who Pioneered Oklahoma: Stories from the WPA Narratives*. Norman: University of Oklahoma Press, 2007.

Barker, Joanne, ed. *Critically Sovereign: Indigenous Gender, Sexuality, and Feminist Studies*. Durham, N.C.: Duke University Press, 2017.

———. *Native Acts: Law, Recognition, and Cultural Authenticity*. Durham, N.C.: Duke University Press, 2011.

———. *Sovereignty Matters: Locations of Contestation and Possibility in Indigenous Struggles for Self-Determination*. Lincoln: University of Nebraska Press, 2005.

Barsness, John. "Henrietta Whiteman: Keeper of Traditions." November 9, 1978. Unpublished work. Available at ScholarWorks at the University of Montana. https://scholarworks.umt.edu/newsreleases/29688/.

Bataille, Gretchen M, and Laurie Lisa, eds. *Native American Women: A Biographical Dictionary*. Lincoln: University of Nebraska Press, 1984.

Bataille, Gretchen, and Kathleen Mullen Sands. *American Indian Women Telling Their Lives*. Lincoln: University of Nebraska Press, 1984.

Bauer-Maglin, Nan, and Alice Radosh, eds. *Women Confronting Retirement, A Nontraditional Guide*. New Brunswisk, N.J.: Rutgers University Press, 2003.

"Beatrice Medicine." Women's Intellectual Contributions to the Study of Mind and Society. Accessed August 24, 2024. http://faculty.webster.edu/woolflm/medicine
.html.

Blackburn, Alex, ed. *Writer's Forum*. Colorado Springs: University of Colorado, 1997.

Blansett, Kent. *A Journey to Freedom: Richard Oakes, Alcatraz, and the Red Power Movement*. New Haven, Conn.: Yale University Press, 2018.

Bowers, Ethan W. "The Women of DRUMS and the Struggle for Menominee Restoration." MA thesis, Bowling Green State University, 2015.

Bradford, William. *History of Plymouth Plantation, 1606–1646*, edited by William T. Davis. New York: Scribner, 1908.

Bradford, William. "Of Plimouth Plantation." In *Of Plymouth Plantation*, edited by Samuel Eliot Morrison. New York: Knopf, 1952.

Brant, Beth, ed. *A Gathering of Spirit: A Collection by North American Women*. 2nd ed. Ithaca, N.Y.: Firebrand, 1988.

Broder, Patricia Janis. *Earth Songs, Moon Dreams: Paintings by American Indian Women*. New York: St. Martin's, 1999.

Buchanan, Kimberly Moore. *Apache Women Warriors*. Southwestern Studies Series No. 79. El Paso: Texas Western, 1989.

Bulbeck, Chilla. *Living Feminism: The Impact of the Women's Movement on Three Generations of Australian Women*. Cambridge: Cambridge University Press, 1997.

Carcamo, Cindy. "Fort Sill Apache Tribe Says Its Roots Are in New Mexico." *Los Angeles Times*. January 13, 2014. www.latimes.com/nation/la-na-ff-apaches-new-mexico -20140114-story.html.

Chalcraft, Edwin L. *Assimilation's Agent: My Life as a Superintendent in the Indian Boarding School*. Lincoln: University of Nebraska Press, 2004.

Charleyboy, Lisa, and Mary Beth Leatherdale, eds. *#NotYourPrincess*. Toronto: Annick, 2020.

Chavez, Aliyah. "LaDonna Harris 'Stumbled' into a Legacy of Impact." *Indian Country Today*. August 18, 2019.

Chavez, Will. *Cherokee Phoenix*. April 12, 2010.

Chenault, Venida S. *Weaving Strength, Weaving Power: Violence and Abuse Against Indigenous Women*. Durham, N.C.: Carolina Academic, 2011.

Child, Brenda J. *Boarding School Seasons: American Indian Families, 1900–1940*. Lincoln: University of Nebraska Press, 1998.

"Brenda Child." University of Minnesota. News and Events. Accessed August 24, 2024. https://twin-cities.umn.edu/news-events/expert/brenda-child#:~:text=Child%20is %20the%20author%20of,)%3B%20and%20Indian%20Subjects%3A%20Hemispheric.

———. *My Grandfather's Knockings Sticks: Ojibwe Family Life and Labor on the Reservation*. Saint Paul: Minnesota Historical Society, 2014.

———. "The Boarding School as Metaphor." *Journal of American Indian Education* 57, no. 1 (2018): 37–57.

———. *Indian Subjects: Hemispheric Perspectives on the History of Indigenous Education*, edited by Brenda J. Child and Brian Klopotek. Santa Fe: School for Advanced Research, 2014.

Child, Lydia Maria. *History of the Condition of Women in Various Ages and Nations*. Vol. 1. Boston: John Allen, 1855.

Choctaw Nation of Oklahoma State of the Nation. Durant, Okla.: Choctaw Nation of Oklahoma, 2019.

Chunestudy, Callie. Interview by Terri Baker via email, July 18, 2019.

Civilization Fund Act. U.S. Statutes at large, 3: 516b, chapter 85.

Cobb-Greetham, Amanda. "LaDonna Harris: Comanche Leader, Activist, Matriarch." In *This Land Is Herland: Gendered Activism in Oklahoma from the 1870s to the 2010s*, edited by Sarah Eppler Janda and Patricia Loughlin, 207–227. Norman: University of Oklahoma Press, 2021.

Cobble, Dorothy Sue, Linda Gordon, and Astrid Henry. *Feminism Unfinished: A Short Surprising History of American Women's Movements.* New York: Liveright, 2014.

Collins, Patricia Hill. *Black Feminist Thought: Knowledge, Consciousness, and the Politics of Empowerment.* New York: Routledge, 2000.

Congressional Record, 39th Congress, 1st session, 1866, CH (designation for bills before 1957) 240, 241, 236–239.

Conley, Robert, J. *The Cherokee Nation: A History.* Albuquerque: University of New Mexico Press, 2005.

Cooper, Karen Coody. *Oklahoma Cherokee Baskets.* Charleston, S.C.: History Press, 2016.

Cott, Nancy. *The Grounding of Modern Feminism.* New Haven, Conn.: Yale University Press, 1980.

Cotter, Bill. *The Wonderful World of Disney Television.* New York: Hyperion, 1997.

Crawford, Grant D. "Campus Protest." *Tahlequah Daily Press,* Saturday–Sunday, November 20–21, 2021, p. 1.

Crow Dog, Mary (Mary Brave Bird), with Richard Erdoes. *Lakota Woman.* New York: HarperCollins, 1991.

Debo, Angie. *And Still the Waters Run: The Betrayal of the Five Civilized Tribes.* 2nd ed. Norman: University of Oklahoma Press, 1973.

Deer, Ada, with Theda Perdue. *Making a Difference: My Fight for Native Rights and Social Justice.* Norman: University of Oklahoma Press, 2019.

Deer, Sarah. *The Beginning and End of Rape: Confronting Sexual Violence in Native America.* 3rd ed. Minneapolis: University of Minnesota Press, 2015.

———. *Maze of Injustice: The Failure to Protect Indigenous Women from Sexual Violence in the USA.* New York: Amnesty International, 2007. Available at https://www.amnesty .org/en/documents/amr51/035/2007/en/.

DeLong, William. "Ella Baker: The Unsung Hero of the Civil Rights Movement." October 2018, but edited and updated by John Kuroski, October 23, 2023, published December 2, 2021. www.allthatsintereting.com.

Deloria, Philip J. Athletics: "I Am of the Body: My Grandfather, Culture, and Sports." In *Indians in Unexpected Places,* 109–135. Lawrence: University Press of Kansas, 2004.

Denetdale, Jennifer Nez. *Reclaiming Diné History: The Legacies of Navajo Chief Manuelito and Juanita.* Tucson: University of Arizona Press, 2007.

———. *The Long Walk: The Forced Exile of the Navajo.* New York: Chelsea House, 2007.

DeRosier, Arthur H. *The Removal of the Choctaw Indians.* Knoxville: University of Tennessee Press, 1970.

Deval, Patrick. *American Indian Women.* Translated from French by Jane-Marie Todd. New York: Abbeville, 2015.

Donaldson, Laura E. *Decolonizing Feminism; Race, Gender, and Empire-Building*. Chapel Hill: University of North Carolina Press, 1992.

Donovan, Kathleen M. *Feminist Readings of Native American Literature Coming to Voice*. Tucson: University of Arizona Press, 1998.

Driver, Harold E., and William C. Massey. *A Statistical Analysis of the Driver-Massey Sample*. Philadelphia: Transactions of the American Philosophical Society, 1957.

Driver, Harold W. *Indians of North America*. 2nd ed. Chicago: University of Chicago Press, 1969.

Du Bois, W. E. B. *Souls of Black Folk*. New York: Dover, 1999. First published in 1903.

Dunbar-Ortiz, Roxanne. *An Indigenous People's History of the United States*. Boston: Beacon, 2014.

"Early History." National Women's Political Caucus. Accessed June 4, 2020. www.nwpc .org/history/.

Elbein, Saul. "The Youth Group That Launched a Movement at Standing Rock." *New York Times*. January 31, 2017.

Ellis, Clyde. "Look at 1920." *Biskinik* (Choctaw Nation of Oklahoma), March 2020.

———. *To Change Them Forever: Indian Education at the Rainy Mountain Boarding School, 1893–1920*. Norman: University of Oklahoma Press, 1994.

Ellis, Elizabeth N. *The Great Power of Small Nations: Indigenous Diplomacy in the Gulf South*. Philadelphia: University of Pennsylvania Press, 2023.

Emery, Jacqueline. *Recovering Native American Writings in the Boarding School Press*. Lincoln: University of Nebraska Press, 2017.

Erdrich, Heid E., and Laura Tohe. *Sister Nations: Native American Women Writers on Community*. St. Paul: Minnesota Historical Society Press, 2002.

Faludi, Susan. *Backlash: The Undeclared War against American Women*. New York: Crown, 1991.

Fariello Anna. *Cherokee Basketry: From the Hands of Our Elders*. Cleveland, Ohio: History Press Library Editions, 2009.

Fariello, Anna. *From the Hands of Our Elders: Cherokee Traditions, People: Rowena Bradley*. Cleveland, Ohio: History Press Library Editions, 2009.

Fear-Segal, Jacqueline. *White Man's Club: Schools, Race, and the Struggle of Indian Acculturation*. Lincoln: University of Nebraska Press, 2009.

Fear-Segal, Jacqueline, and Susan D. Rose. *Carlisle Indian Industrial School: Indigenous Histories, Memories, and Reclamation*. Lincoln: University of Nebraska Press, 2018.

"Feminism and Feminisms: American Indian Feminism." In *Reader's Companion to U.S Women's History*, 198, edited by Wilma Mankiller, Gwendolyn Mink, Marya Navarro, and Gloria Steinem. New York: Houghton Mifflin, 1998.

Fisher, Dexter, ed. *The Third Woman: Minority Women Writers of the United States*. Boston: Houghton Mifflin, 1980.

Foreman, Grant. *Down the Texas Road: Historic Places along Highway 69 through Okla-*

homa. Norman: University of Oklahoma Press, 1936. Reprinted in 1994 by the Atoka Historical Society.

Gilbert, Matthew Sakiestewa. *Education beyond the Mesas: Hopi Studies at Sherman Institute, 1902–1929.* Lincoln: University of Nebraska Press, 2010.

Glancy, Diane. "Death Cry for the Language." In *Visit Teepee Town: Native Writings after the Detours,* edited by Diane Glancy and Mark Nowak, 209. Minneapolis: Coffee House, 1999.

Goeman, Mishuana. *Mark My Words: Native Women (Re)mapping Our Nations.* Minneapolis: University of Minnesota Press, 2013.

———. "Notes toward a Native Feminism's Spatial Practice." *Wicazo-Sa Review* 24, no. 2 (Fall 2009): 169–187.

Goeman, Mishuana R., and Jennifer Nez Dinetdale. Guest Editors' Introduction, "Native Feminisms: Legacies, Interventions, and Indigenous Sovereignties." *Wicazo-Sa Review* 24, no. 2 (Fall 2009): 9–13.

———. Settler Aesthetics Visualizing the Spectacle of Originary Moments in the New World. Lincoln: University of Nebraska Press, 2023.

Goettner-Abendroth, Heide. *Matriarchal Societies Studies on Indigenous Cultures across the Globe.* Translated by Karen Smith. New York: Peter Lang, 2013.

Grande, Sandy. *Red Pedagogy: Native American Social and Political Thought.* Lanham, Md.: Rowman and Littlefield, 2004.

Grann, David. *Killers of the Flower Moon: The Osage Murders and the Birth of the FBI.* New York: Doubleday, 2017.

"Green Country: Writing from Northeastern Oklahoma (2016)." *Cultural Survival Quarterly.* April 9, 2012.

Green, Joyce, ed. *Making Space for Indigenous Feminism.* Black Point, Nova Scotia: Fernwood, 2007.

Green, Rayna. *Native American Women: A Contextual Bibliography.* Bloomington: Indiana University Press, 1983.

———. *That's What She Said: Contemporary Poetry and Fiction by Native American Women.* Bloomington: Indiana University Press, 1984.

Guerrero, Anna Marie Jaimes. "Civil Rights versus Sovereignty." In *Feminist Genealogies, Colonial Legacies, Democratic Futures,* edited by M. Jacqui Alexander and Chandra Mohanty, 101–122. New York: Routledge, 1997.

Guerrero, M. A. Jaimes. "Patriarchal Colonialism and Indigenism: Implications for Native Feminist Spirituality and Native Womanism." *Hypatia* 18, no. 2 (2003): 58–69.

Guerrero, M. Annette, ed. *The State of Native America: Genocide, Colonization and Resistance.* Boston: South End Press, 1992.

"Guide to the Beatrice Medicine Papers, 1914–2003." Smithsonian Institution: Smithsonian Online Virtual Archives. National Anthropological Archives. https://sova.si.edu/record/naa.1997-05?q=Inventions+—+21st+century&t=C.

Gurr, Barbara. *Reproductive Justice: The Politics of Healthcare for Native American Women.* New Brunswick, N.J.: Rutgers University Press.

Hallowell, Anna Davis. *James and Lucretia Mott: Life and Letters.* New York: Houghton Mifflin, 1884.

Hämäläinen, Pekka. *Comanche Empire.* New Haven: Yale University Press, 2009.

———. *Lakota America: A New History of Indigenous Power.* New Haven: Yale University Press, 2019.

Haozous, Emily. Interview with Terri Baker and Carolyn Ross Johnston, May 16, 2017, Santa Fe, New Mexico.

Haraway, Donna, "Primatology Is Politics by Other Means." In *Feminist Approaches to Science,* edited by Ruth Bleier, 77–118. New York: Pergamon, 1986.

———. "Situated Knowledge: The Science Question in Feminism and the Privilege of Partial Perspective." *Feminist Studies* 14 (1998): 575–599.

Harjo, Joy. *An American Sunrise: Poems.* New York: Norton, 2019.

———. *Crazy Brave: A Memoir.* New York: Norton, 2012.

———. "For Anna Mae Aquash Whose Spirit Is Here and in the Dappled Stars." *Nimrod: Oklahoma Indian Markings* 23, no. 2 (Spring–Summer 1989): 60–61.

———. *She Had Some Horses.* London: Thunder's Mouth Press, 1983.

———. Gloria Bird, Patricia Blanco, Beth Cuthand, and Valerie Martinez. *Reinventing the Enemy's Language: Contemporary Native Women Writings of North America.* New York: Norton, 1997.

Harmon, William, and Hugh Holman, eds. *A Handbook to Literature.* 9th ed. Upper Saddle River, N.J.: Prentice Hall, 2002.

Harris, LaDonna. *LaDonna Harris, A Comanche Life,* edited by H. Henrietta Stockel. Lincoln: University of Nebraska Press, 2000.

———. Interview for *New Mexico in Focus.* A production of MMPBS, July 27, 2018.

———. Interview by Terri Baker and Carolyn Johnston, Albuquerque, New Mexico, July 19, 2017.

Harris, LaDonna, and Jacqueline Wasilewski. *This Is What We Want to Share: Core Cultural Values.* Bernalillo, N.Mex.: Americans for Indian Opportunity, 1992.

Harris, LaDonna, Kathryn Tijerina, and Laura Harris. "Applying Indigenous Values to Contemporary Tribal Citizenship: Challenge and Opportunity." In *The Great Vanishing Act: Blood Quantum and the Future of Native Nations,* edited by Kathleen Ratteree and Norbert Hill, 316–330. Golden, Colo.: Fulcrum, 2017.

Hauser, Christine, and Isabella Grullon Paz, "U.S. to Search Former Native American Schools for Children's Remains." *New York Times.* June 23, 2021.

Healy, Jack. "Rural Montana Had Already Lost Too Many Native Women. Then Selena Disappeared." *New York Times.* January 20, 2020. www.nytimes.com/2020/01/20/us/selena-not-afraid-missing-montana.html.

Healy, Jack, and Adam Liptak. "Landmark Supreme Court Ruling Affirms Native Ameri-

can Rights in Oklahoma." *New York Times*. July 9, 2020. www.nytimes.com/2020
/07/09/us/supreme-court-oklahoma-mcgirt-creek-nation.html.

Hiemstra, William L. "Presbyterian Missionaries and Mission Churches among the
Choctaw and Chickasaw Indians, 1832–1865." *Chronicles of Oklahoma* 26 Winter 1948:
459–467.

Hill, Sarah. *Weaving New Worlds: Cherokee Women and Their Basketry*. Chapel Hill: University of North Carolina Press, 1997.

Hogan, Linda. "The Direction of Light." *Nimrod: Oklahoma Indian Markings* 23, no. 2
(Spring–Summer 1989): 32.

Holt, Marilyn Irvin. "'A New Thing in Our Country': The Cherokee Orphan Asylum."
Chronicles of Oklahoma 97, no. 3 (Fall 2020): 261.

[Home Page]. Americans for Indian Opportunity. Accessed August 21, 2024. www.aio.org.

[Home Page]. Change.org (The World's Platform for Change). Accessed 21, 2024. www
.change.org.

[Home Page]. National Congress for American Indians. Accessed August 21, 2024. www
.ncai.org.

Hopkins, Sarah Winnemucca. *Life among the Paiutes: Their Wrongs and Claims*. Reno:
University of Nevada Press, 1994.

Hoskin, Chuck, Jr. "Chief Chat: Perpetuating Mankiller's Legacy by Expanding Water
Projects." *Tahlequah Daily Press*. May 1, 2021.

Howe, LeAnne. *Shell Shaker*. San Francisco: Aunt Lute Books, 2001.

———. "Tribalography: The Power of Native Stories." *Journal of Dramatic Theory and
Criticism* 14, no. 1 (1999): 117–125.

Hyde, Hazel. *Maria Making Pottery*. Albuquerque: Starlkine, 1973.

"Indian Affairs." U.S. Department of the Interior. Accessed August 24, 2024. www.bia.gov.

Indian Country Today, "Twelve Ways to Be Inducted in Native American Hall of Fame."
October 5, 2018.

Jackson, Helen Hunt. *Ramona*. Boston: Roberts, 1884.

Jacobs, Margaret D. *Engendered Encounters: Feminism and Pueblo Cultures 1879–1934*.
Lincoln: University of Nebraska Press, 1999.

Jaimes, M. Annette. *The State of Native America: Genocide, Colonization, and Resistance*.
Boston: South End Press, 1992.

James, Ed T., ed. *Notable American Women of 1607–1950*. Cambridge, Mass.: Harvard
University Press, 1971.

Janda, Sarah Eppler. *Beloved Women: The Political Lives of LaDonna Harris and Wilma
Mankiller*. DeKalb: Northern Illinois University Press, 2007.

———. *The Intersection of Feminism and Indianness in the Activism of LaDonna Harris and
Wilma Mankiller*. Norman: University of Oklahoma Press, 2002.

Janda, Sarah Eppler, and Patricia Loughlin, eds. *This Land Is Herland: Gendered Activism
in Oklahoma from the 1870s to 2010s*. Norman: University of Oklahoma Press, 2021.

Janko, Melinda. "Elouise Cobell: A Small Measure of Justice." *American Indian Magazine* (Smithsonian's National Museum of the American Indian) 14, no. 2 (Summer, 2013).

―――. "100 Years: One Woman's Fight for Justice," video project. 2:57. Accessed 21 August 2024. www.videoproject.org/100-Years.html.

Jeffries, Marshall. "Re-membering Our Own Power Occaneechi Activism, Feminism, and Political Actions Theories." *Frontiers: A Journal of Women's Studies* 36, no. 1 (2015): 160–195.

Jennings, Chris. "Kidwell Earns Lifetime Achievement Award." *Biskinik*, November 2022.

Johnston, Carolyn, "In the White Woman's Image? Resistance, Transformation and Identity in Recent Native American Women's History." *Journal of Women's History* 8, no. 3 (Fall 1996): 205–218.

―――. *Sexual Power: Feminism and the Family in America*. Tuscaloosa: University of Alabama Press, 1992.

―――, ed. *Voices of Cherokee Women*. Winston Salem, N.C.: John F. Blair, 2013.

Johnston, Carolyn Ross. *Cherokee Women in Crisis: Trail of Tears, Civil War, and Allotment. 1838–1907*. Tuscaloosa: University of Alabama Press, 2003.

Josephy, Alvin M., Jr. *500 Nations: An Illustrated History of North American Indians*. Based on a documentary filmscript by Jack Leustig, Robert Grossman, Lee Miller, and William Morgan, with contributions by John M. D. Pohl. New York: Knopf, 1994.

Journal of Gilcrease Museum 23, no. 2 (a publication of the Thomas Gilcrease Institute of American History and Art, Tulsa, Oklahoma).

Justice, Daniel Heath. *Why Indigenous Literatures Matter*. Waterloo, Ont.: Wilfrid Laurier University Press, 2018.

Kappler, Charles J., II, ed. *Laws and Treaties*. Vol. 2: Treaties. Washington, D.C: Government Printing Office, 1904.

Karcher, Carolyn. *The First Woman in the Republic: A Cultural Biography of Lydia Maria Child*. Durham, N.C.: Duke University Press, 1986.

Katanski, Amelia V. *Learning to Write "Indian": The Boarding-School Experience and American Indian Literature*. Norman: University of Oklahoma Press, 2005.

Kidwell, Clara Sue. *Choctaws and Missionaries in Mississippi, 1818–1918*. Norman: University of Oklahoma Press, 1997.

―――. *The Choctaws in Oklahoma: From Tribe to Nation, 1855–1970*. Norman: University of Oklahoma Press, 2008.

―――. "How America's Destiny Became Manifest." *Chronicles of Oklahoma* 97, no. 3 (Autumn 2019): 260–277.

―――― "Systems of Knowledge." In *America 1492: The World of the Indian Peoples before the Arrival of Columbus*, edited by Alvin M. Josephy Jr. New York: Alfred A. Knopf, 1992.

Kidwell, Clara Sue, with Alan Velie and Robert Con Davis. *Native American Studies*. Edinburgh, Scot.: Edinburgh University Press, 2005.

Kidwell, Clara Sue, with Homer Noley and George E. Tinker. *Native American Theology*. Maryknoll, New York: Orbis Books, 2001.

King, Brian D. "Coalition Wants 'Misleading' Statue Removed at NSU." *Tahlequah Daily Press*. May 25, 2021, p. 1.

King, Martin Luther, Jr. *Strength to Love*. New York: Harper and Row, 1963.

Kowaleski-Wallace, Elizabeth, ed. *Encyclopedia of Feminist Literary Theory*. New York: Routledge, 1996.

Krupat, Arnold. *Boarding School Voices*. Lincoln: University of Nebraska Press, 2021.

"LaDonna Harris (Comanche) Biographical Profile." Americans for Indian Opportunity. Accessed 2 September 2024. https://aio.org/ladonna-harris-comanche -biographical-profile/.

"LaDonna Harris (Indian Powerhouse)." *Playboy* 19, no. 2 (February 2, 1972), 178.

LaDuke, Winona. *All Our Relations: Native Struggle for Land and Life*. Boston: South End Press, 1999.

Lakota People's Law Project. "Native Lives Matter: The Overlooked Police Brutality against Native Americans." November 21, 2017. www.lakotalaw.org/news/2017-11-21 /native-lives-matter-the-overlooked-police-brutality-against-native-americans.

Landsman, Gail H. "The 'Other' as Political Symbol: Images of Indians in the Woman Suffrage Movement." *Ethnohistory* 39, no. 3 (Summer 1992): 247–284.

Langston, Donna. "Wilma Mankiller: American Indian Feminist Thought." Paper presented at the annual meeting of National Women's Studies Association, at the Sheraton Denver Downtown Hotel, in Denver, Colorado, on November 27, 2014.

Langston, Donna Hightower. "American Women's Activism in the 1960s and 1970s." *Hypatia* 18, no. 2 (2003): 114–132.

———. *The American Indian Encyclopedia*. New York: Wiley, 2002.

"Laura Harris." Land Peace Foundation. Accessed August 21, 2024. https:// landpeacefoundation.net/?page_id=30.

Lavell-Harvard, D. Memee, and Kim Anderson. *Mothers of the Nations: Indigenous Mothering as Global Resistance, Reclaiming and Recovery*. Bradford, Ont.: Demeter Press, 2014.

LaVere David. *Contrary Neighbors: Southern Plains and Removed Indians in Indian Territory*. Norman: University of Oklahoma Press, 2001.

Lewallen, Ann-Elise, "Strategic 'Indigeneity' and the Possibility of a Global Indigenous Women's Movement." *Michigan Feminist Studies* 17 (2003): 105–139.

Lewis, Reina, and Sara Mills, eds. *Feminist Postcolonial Theory: A Reader*. New York: Routledge, 2003.

Linderman, Frank B. *Pretty-Shield, Medicine Woman of the Crows*. Lincoln: University of Nebraska Press, 1972.

Lomawaima, K. Tsianina. "Preface" to *The Story of Chilocco Indian School: They Called It Prairie Light*. Lincoln: University of Nebraska Press, 1994.

Lonelodge, Latoya. "American Circle of Honor Celebrates Dr. Henrietta Mann." March 15, 2018. www.tulsalibrary.org.

Lowery, Malinda Maynor. *The Lumbee Indians: An American Struggle*. Chapel Hill: University of North Carolina Press, 2018.

"Luana Ross." University of Washington. American Indian Studies. Accessed August 24, 2024. https://ais.washington.edu/people/luana-ross.

Mankiller, Wilma, ed. *Every Day Is a Good Day: Reflections by Contemporary Indigenous Women*. Golden, Colo.: Fulcrum, 2004.

———. *The Reader's Companion to U.S. Women's History*, edited by Wilma Mankiller, Gwendolyn Mink, Marysa Navarro, Barbara Smith, and Gloria Steinem. New York: Houghton-Mifflin Harcourt, 1998.

Mankiller, Wilma, and Michael Wallis. *Mankiller: A Chief and Her People*. New York: St. Martin's Press, 1993.

Mann, Barbara Alice. *Iroquoian Women: The Gantowisas*. New York: Peter Lang, 2011.

Mann, Barbara Alice, and Heide Goettner-Abendroth. "Matriarchal Studies." Oxford Bibliographies. 2015; updated and reissued 2020. www.oxfordbibliographies.com /view/document/obo-9780199766567/obo-9780199766567-0113.xml.

Mann, Henrietta V. Whiteman. *Cheyenne-Arapaho Education, 1871–1982*. Louisville: University Press of Colorado, 1998.

Maracle, Lee. *I Am Woman: A Native Perspective on Sociology and Feminism*. Toronto: Press Gang, 1996.

Markstrom, Carol A. *Empowerment of North American Indian Girls: Ritual Expressions at Puberty*. Lincoln: University of Nebraska Press, 2008.

"Matriarchy." Merriam-Webster (website). Accessed August 21, 2024. www.merriam -webster.com/dictionary/matriarch#:~:text=A%20matriarchy%20is%20a%20social ,woman%20or%20group%20of%20women.

McCoy, Dara. "Choctaw Gift from 1890s Inspires Generosity during Global Pandemic." *Biskinik* (Choctaw Nation of Oklahoma), June 2020.

McReynolds, Edwin C. *Oklahoma: A History of the Sooner State*. Norman: University of Oklahoma Press, 1964.

Medicine, Beatrice. *Learning to Be an Anthropologist and Remaining Native*, edited with Sue Ellen Jacobs. Lanham, Md.: Rowman & Littlefield, 1982.

Merriam Webster's Encyclopedia of Literature. Springfield, Mass.: Merriam-Webster, 1995.

Mihesuah, Devon Abbott. *Cultivating the Rosebuds*. Urbana: University of Illinois Press, 1997.

———. *Indigenous American Women: Decolonization, Empowerment, Activism*. Lincoln: University of Nebraska Press, 2003.

Millay, Edna St. Vincent. *One Hundred and One Famous Poems with a Prose Supplement*. Rev. ed. An anthology compiled by Roy J. Cook. Chicago: Reilly and Lee, 1958.

Milligan, James C., and Stacy C. Shepherd, eds. *The Choctaw of Oklahoma*. Abilene, Tex.: H. V. Chapman, 2003.

"Mishuana Goeman, Ph.D." University of California, Los Angeles. Institute of the Environment and Sustainability. Accessed August 24, 2024. www.ioes.ucla.edu/person /mishuana-goeman/.

Mohanty, Chandra. *Feminism without Borders: Decolonizing Theory, Practicing Solidarity*. Durham, N.C.: Duke University Press, 2003.

Momaday, N. Scott. *The Way to Rainy Mountain*. Illustrated by Al Momaday. Albuquerque: University of New Mexico Press, 1969.

Monga, Vipal, and Collin Eaton. "What Is the Keystone XLPipeline and Why Did the Developer Abandon It?" *Wall Street Journal*. Updated June 9, 2021. www.wsj.com /articles/what-is-the-keystone-xl-pipeline-and-why-did-president-biden-issue-an -executive-order-to-block-it-11611240342.

Morgan, H. Wayne, and Anne Hodges Morgan. *Oklahoma: A History*. New York: Norton, 1977.

Nabokov, Peter. *Native American Testimony*. New York: Penguin, 1999.

Narayan, Uma, and Sandra Harding. *Decentering the Center: Philosophy for a Multicultural Postcolonial and Feminist World*. Bloomington: Indiana University Press, 2000.

Native News Online Staff. "Indigenous Women Rise." Native News Online. January 24, 2017. Red Lake Nation News. www.redlakenationnews.com/story/2017/01/24/news /indigenous-women-rise-womens-march-on-washington/56539.html.

"Notes for Mankiller Autobiography." Mankiller Collection, Western History Collection, Norman, Oklahoma: University of Oklahoma.

Oklahoma Forts, Military History and Civil War Map. Part of the Oklahoma Heritage Association's Oklahoma Subject Map Series, Oklahoma Heritage Association, Oklahoma City, Oklahoma.

One Fire Development Corporation. "About." www.onefiredevelopment.org.

Oskison, John. *Unconquerable: The Story of John Ross, Chief of the Cherokees, 1828–1866*. Lincoln: University of Nebraska Press, 2022.

Osti, Jane. Interview by Terri Baker at the Cherokee Art Center, January 22, 2020.

Ouellette, Grace J. M. W. *The Fourth World: An Indigenous Perspective on Feminism and Aboriginal Women's Activism*. Halifax, Nova Scotia: Fernwood, 2002.

Our Climate Voices, "Jasilyn Charger | Cheyenne River Sioux Tribe." Available on Internet Archive's Wayback Machine. https://web.archive.org/web/20221208182540 /https://www.ourclimatevoices.org/2019/jasilyncharger.

The Paper, Albuquerque Independent Community News. Albuquerque, N.Mex., August 29, 2021.

Perdue, Theda, ed. *Sifters: Native American Women's Lives*. New York: Oxford University Press, 2001.

Perdue, Theda, and Michael D. Green. *The Columbia Guide to American Indians of the Southeast*. New York: Columbia University Press, 2001.

Pesantubbee, Michelene E. *Choctaw Women in a Chaotic World: The Clash of Cultures in the Colonial Southeast.* Albuquerque: University of New Mexico Press, 2005.

Peterson, Susan. *The Living Tradition of Maria Martinez.* New York: Kodansha, 1977.

Phillips, Katrina. "The Longtime Police Brutality Drove American Indians to Join the George Floyd Protests." *Washington Post.* June 6, 2020.

Phoenix Archives, "Cherokee Artist Wins Awards in North Carolina Competition." July 21, 2010.

Pratt, Scott L. *Native Pragmatism: The Roots of American Philosophy.* Bloomington: Indiana University Press, 2002.

Ramirez, Renya K. "Race, Tribal, Nation, and Gender: A Native Feminist Approach to Belonging." *Meridians: Feminism, Race, Transnationalism* 7, no. 2 (2007) 22–40.

———. *Standing Up to Colonial Power: The Lives of Henry Roe and Elizabeth Bender.* Lincoln: University of Nebraska, 2018.

———. "Writing as Granddaughter and Academic." UNP Blog. Accessed July 25, 2020. https://unpblog.com/2018/12/18/from-the-desk-of-renya-k-ramirez-writing-as -granddaughter-and-academic/.

Rapid City Journal Staff. "NEW: Human Rights Advocate Beatrice Medicine Dies." *Rapid City Journal.* January 2, 2006. https://rapidcityjournal.com/news/article_83eefd24 -370f-596d-b2c5-14661170eed1.html.

Rennison, Callie. *Violent Victimization and Rape, 1993–1998.* Washington, D.C.: Bureau of Justice Statistics, 2001.

"Renya Ramirez." Anthropology. University of California, Santa Cruz. Accessed August 24, 2024. https://anthro.ucsc.edu/faculty/index.php?uid=renya.

Resendez, Andres. *The Other Slavery: The Uncovered Story of Indian Enslavement in America.* Boston: Houghton Mifflin Harcourt Mariner, 2016.

Richardson, Heather Cox. [@heathercoxrichardson]. *Substack.* www.heatherrichardson @substack.com.

Rifkin, Mark. *When Did Indians Become Straight? Kinship, The History of Sexuality and Native Sovereignty.* New York: Oxford University Press, 2011.

Ringold, Francine, ed. *Oklahoma Indian Markings* 23, no. 2 (Spring–Summer 1989).

Ringold, Francine, and Joan S. Isom, eds. *Nimrod: Oklahoma Indian Markings* 11 (1990).

Rodriguez, Roberto Cintil. *Our Sacred Maiz Is Our Mother: Tonantzin Non Centeotl.* Tucson: University of Arizona Press, 2014.

Rose, Wendy. "For the White Poets Who Would Be Indians." In *The Third Woman, Minority Women Writers of the United States,* edited by Dexter Fisher. Boston: Houghton Mifflin Company, 1980.

Ross, Luana. *Inventing the Savage: The Social Construction of Native American Criminality.* Austin: University of Texas Press, 1998.

Roth, Nathan. NPR. May 15, 2021. www.npr.org.

Sakiestewa, Gilbert Matthew. *Education beyond the Mesas: Hopi Students at Sherman Institute 1902–1929.* Lincoln: University of Nebraska Press, 2010.

Sanday, Peggy Reeves. *Women at the Center: Life in a Modern Matriarachy.* Ithaca, N.Y.: Cornell University Press, 2002.

"Sarah Deer." University of Kansas. Women, Gender, and Sexuality Studies. Accessed August 22, 2024. https://wgss.ku.edu/people/sarah-deer.

Saunt, Claudio. *Unworthy Republic: The Dispossession of Native Americans and the Road to Indian Territory.* New York: Norton, 2020.

Schaller, K. B. *100+ Native American Women Who Changed the World.* Sarasota, Fla.: Peppertree Publishing, 2014.

Schoolcraft, Jane Johnston. *The Sound the Stars Make Rushing through the Sky.* Philadelphia: University of Pennsylvania Press, 2007.

"Secretary Deb Haaland." U.S. Department of the Interior. Accessed August 24, 2024. www.doi.gov/secretary-deb-haaland.

"Secretary Haaland Approves New Constitution for Cherokee Nation, Guaranteeing Full Citizenship Rights for Cherokee Freedmen." U.S. Department of the Interior. Accessed August 24, 2014. www.doi.gov/pressreleases/secretary-haaland-approves -new-constitution-cherokee-nation-guaranteeing-full.

Segal, Jacqueline Fear, and Susan D. Rose. *Carlisle Industrial School.* Lincoln: University of Nebraska Press, 2016.

Self, Frank J. "What Really Made a Goodland Indian Student Tick?" *Indian Arrow* (Hugo, Oklahoma, Goodland Presbyterian Children's Home), 1977, 1–2.

Sellers, Stephanie A. *Native American Women's Studies: A Primer.* New York: Peter Lang, 2008.

Schaaf, Gregory. *Pueblo Indian Pottery: 750 Artist Biographies.* c. *1800–Present.* Ciac Press, 2000.

Shaw, Ana Moore. *Pima Indian Legends.* Tucson: University of Arizona Press, 1968.

Shirley, Glenn. *Law West of Fort Smith: A History of Frontier Justice in the Indian Territory, 1834–1896.* New York: H. Holt, 1957.

Simpson, Leanne Betasamosake. *Dancing on Our Turtle's Back.* Winnipeg, Mani.: Arbeiter Ring, 2011.

———. *As We Have Always Done: Indigenous Freedom through Radical Resistance.* Minneapolis: University of Minnesota Press, 2017.

Smith, Andrea. *Conquest: Sexual Violence and American Indian Genocide.* Boston: South End Press, 2005.

———. "Feminism, Sovereignty and Social Change," *Feminist Studies* 31 (Spring 2005): 116–132.

———. *Native Americans and the Christian Right: The Gendered Politics of Unlikely Alliances.* Durham, N.C.: Duke University Press, 2018.

———. "Sacred Sites, Sacred Rites." Joint project of American Indian Community House and the National Council of the Churches of Christ in the U.S.A., Racial Justice Working Group, 1998.

Smith, Andrea, and J. Khaulani Kaunai. "Native Feminisms Engage American Studies." *American Quarterly* 60, no. 2 (June 2008): 241–249.

Smith, Stephanie Izarek. "Joy Harjo: An Interview." July–August 1993. Poets and Writers. Accessed May 25, 2020. www.pw.org.

Snell, Alma Hogan. *Grandmother's Grandchild, My Crow Indian Life*, edited by Becky Matthews. Lincoln: University of Nebraska Press, 2000.

Snell, Lisa. "Keeping the Traditions: Cherokee Artist Focuses on Mothers, Babies." *Native American Times*. July 19, 2010.

Snodgrass, Mary Ellen. "Tales of Burning Love," In *Encyclopedia of Feminist Literature*, 176. New York: Facts on File, 2006.

———. *Beating the Odds: A Teen Guide to 75 Superstars Who Overcame Adversity*. Westport, Conn.: Greenwood, 2008.

The Social Justice Group at the Center for Advanced Feminist Studies, University of Minnesota. *Is Academic Feminism Dead? Theory in Practice*. New York: New York University Press, 2000.

Soderlind, Sylvia, and James Taylor Carson, eds. *American Exceptionalism from Winthrop to Winfrey*. Albany: State University of New York Press, 2011.

Sonneborn, Liz. *A to Z of Native American Women*. New York: Facts on File, 1998.

Steinem, Gloria. "Leaders as Guides of Return: Wilma Mankiller." April 7, 2020.

———. *My Life on the Road*. New York: Random House, 2016.

Stoler, Anne Laura, ed. *Haunted by Empire: Geographies of Intimacy in North American History*. Durham, N.C.: Duke University Press, 2006.

Stremlau, Rose. *Sustaining the Cherokee Family: Kinship and the Allotment of an Indigenous Nation*. Chapel Hill: University of North Carolina, 2011.

Suzack, Cheryl, Shari M. Huhndorf, Jeanne Perreault, and Jean Barman, eds. *Indigenous Women and Feminism: Politics, Activism and Culture*. Vancouver: University of British Columbia Press, 2010.

Taylor, Drew Hayden, ed. *Me Sexy: An Exploration of Native Sex and Sexuality*. Vancouver, B.C.: Douglas & McIntyre, 2008.

Taylor, Michael P., and Terence Wride, "'Indian Kids Can't Write Sonnets': Re-membering the Poetry of Henry Tinhorn from the Intermountain Indian School." *American Quarterly* 72, no. 1, March 2020, 25–53.

Thornton, Russell. *American Indian Holocaust and Survival: A Population History since 1492*. Norman: University of Oklahoma Press, 1987.

Tijerina, Kathryn Harris. Interview by Terri Baker, Santa Fe, New Mexico, June 14, 2016.

Todrys, Katherine Wiltenburg. *Black Snake Standing Rock, the Dakota Access Pipeline, and Environmental Justice*. Lincoln: University of Nebraska Press, 2021.

Trafzer, Clifford E., Jean A. Keller, and Lorene Sisquoc. *Boarding School Blues: Revisiting American Indian Educational Experiences*. Lincoln: University of Nebraska Press, 2006.

Trafzer, Clifford E., Donna L. Akers, and Amanda K. Wixon, eds. *Indigenous Activism: Profiles of Native Women in Contemporary America.* Lanham, Md.: Lexington, 2021.

Trennert, Robert A. *The Phoenix Indian School: Forced Assimilation in Arizona, 1891–1935.* Norman: University of Oklahoma Press, 1988.

Valaskakis, Clifford, Gail Guthrie, Madeleine Dion Stout, and Eric Guimond, eds. *Restoring the Balance: First Nations Women, Community, and Culture.* Winnipeg: University of Manitoba Press, 2009.

Wade, Edwin L., Carol Haralson, and Rennard Strickland. *As in a Vision, Masterworks of American Indian Art, The Elizabeth Cole Butler Collection at Philbrook Art Center.* Norman: University of Oklahoma Press; Tulsa, Okla.: Philbrook Art Center, 1983.

———. *The Arts of the North American Indian: Native Traditions in Evolution.* New York: Hudson Hills, 1986, in association with the Philbrook Museum.

Wagner, Sally Roesch. *The Untold Story of Iroquois Influence on Early Feminists.* Aberdeen, S.Dak.: Sky Carrier, 1996.

———. *The Women's Suffrage Movement.* New York: Penguin/Random House, 2019.

———. *We Want Equal Rights! How Suffragists Were Influenced by Haudenosaunee Women.* Summertown, Tenn.: 7th Generation, 2020.

———. "Is Equality Indigenous? The Untold Iroquois Influence on Early Radical Feminists." *On the Issues* 5, no. 1 (January 31, 1996): 21.

Wamsey, Laurel. "Court Rules Dakota Access Pipeline Must be Emptied for Now." July 6, 2020. www.npr.org/2020/07/06887593775.

Waters, Anne. "Introduction: Special Issue on Native American Women, Feminism, and Indigenism." *Hypatia* 18, no. 2 (Spring 2003).

Weaver, Jace. *That the People Might Live: Native American Literatures and Native American Community.* Oxford: Oxford University Press, 1997.

Whelehan, Imelda. *Modern Feminist Thought: From the Second Wave to "Post-Feminism."* New York: New York University Press, 1995.

Wiget, Andrew, ed. *Dictionary of Native American Literature.* New York: Garland, 1994.

William, Samantha M. *Assimilation, Resilience, and Survival: A History of the Stewart Indian School, 1890–2020.* Lincoln: University of Nebraska Press, 2022.

Wingsard, Joel, and Joan S. Isom, eds. *Literature: Reading and Responding to Fiction, Poetry, Drama, and the Essay.* New York: Harper Collins College, 1996.

Zitkála-Šá, Gertrude Bonnin. *American Indian Stories and Old Indian Legends.* Minneola, N.Y.: Dover Publications, 2014. First published in Boston by Ginn and Company, in 1901.

———. *My Life: Impressions of an Indian Childhood; The School Days of an Indian Girl; Why I Am a Pagan.* Copyright, Hannah Wilson.

———. *Oklahoma's Poor Rich Indians: An Orgy of Graft and Exploitation of the Five Civilized Tribes, Legalized Robbery* (pamphlet with Charles H. Fabens of the Indian Defense Association and Matthew K. Sniffer and Indian Rights Association, 1924). Available at www.britannica.com/biography/Zitkala-Sa.

Intertribal Women's Organizations
Indigenous Women's Network
WARN (Women of All Red Nations)

Manuscript Collections
Fred R. Harris Collection 1963–1976, Carl Albert Center Archive
Personal Collection of Geraldine Hull McKinney, held by Terri McKinney Baker
Western History: Mankiller Collection

Federal Statutes and Legislation
Board of Indian Commissioners, *Annual Report*, 1902.
Congressional Record. Act enacted by the Thirty-Ninth Congress, 1866. "An Act granting
    Lands to the State of Kansas to aid in the construction of the Kansas and Neosho
    Valley Railroad and its Extension to Red River."

INDEX

Abourezk, James, 108–111
activism: Bay Area Indigenous, 69–72, 89; DAPL and, 146–152; goals of, 41; women's traditional power and, 9, 63, 69, 151, 157. *See also* feminism, Indigenous; feminism/feminist movement; *individual movements; names of individual women*
Adair, Mary, 135
Alcatraz occupation, 70–71
Allard, LaDonna Brave Bull, 147–148
Allen, Paula Gunn, 121, 160
allotment, 6, 15, 17–18, 19–21
American Association for University Professors (AAUP), 58
American Indian Movement (AIM), 70, 91, 103
American Indian Studies programs, 60, 161–162
Americans for Indian Opportunity (AIO), 91–93, 102, 116, 118–119
Apache Nation, 166–167, 190–191n56, 191n60
Army Corps of Engineers, 147–148, 151
art, Indigenous: Avanyu and, 124; basket weaving and, 133–134; curatorial work and exhibits of, 131–132; form and function in, 120; inclusion/exclusion and, 123; literature and, 34, 59–60, 80, 120–122, 136–142, 164, 179–180n2; music and, 142–44; painting and, 133, 134–136; pottery and, 123–129; sculpture and, 133
assimilation, 3–6, 22–24, 53, 163. *See also* boarding schools
Awiakta, Marilou, 141

Baird, W. David, 52–53
Baker, Terri McKinney: AAUP and, 58; background of, 8, 44–49, 63; on cultural ignorance, 50, 58–60, 64–66; on ethnohistory, 60–61; on gatekeeping, 52–53; on Geraldine Hull McKinney, 49; interest in activism/feminism, 45–47; on Jake Chanate, 54; Mankiller and, 44–45, 52, 64, 66–67, 78–84; on microaggressions, 59–60; NSU and, 50–57, 81–83; Philbrook Museum and, 49–50; publications and presentations of, 179–180n2; retirement of, 63–64; return to Oklahoma, 48–49; Summer Seminars and, 57–58
Baker, Tom, 48
basket weaving, 133–134
Bell Water Project, 73–75, 78
Belvin, Jimmy, 28, 39–40, 46
Biden, Joe, 151
Blackfeet Nation, 152
Black Lives Matter protests, 103, 105
blood quantum, xiii, 18, 126
boarding schools, 11–14, 22–31, 36–37, 163, 171, 189n43
Bradford, William, 64–65, 66
Bradley, Rowena, 133–134
Broder, Patricia Janis, 134–136

Cain, Shawna Morton, 134
California, Indigenous people of, 180–181n9
casinos, 21, 61–62, 123, 129, 191n62
Catt, Carrie Chapman, 5
Cattaraugus Reservations, 3–4
Chanate, Jake, 54

Charger, Jasilyn, 146, 148, 149–151

Chavarria, Pablita Tofoya, 124

Cherokee Heritage Center, 131–132

Cherokee Nation, 36, 72–73, 128–129, 130–131, 144. *See also* Mankiller, Wilma

Cherokee National Female Seminary, 21, 50–51, 81

Cherokee National Treasures, 128–129

Cherokee Orphan Asylum, 72–73

Child, Brenda, 162–163, 188–189n41

Child, Lydia Maria, 3, 4, 171

Choctaw Nation, 14–20, 24–25, 30, 33–34, 39–41, 60–61

Choctaw National Health Care Center, 30–31

Chunestudy, Callie, 129–132

Cloud, Henry Roe, 163–164

Cloud, Elizabeth Bender, 163–164

Cobell, Elouise Pepion, 152, 153–154

colonialism/colonization: consequences of, 122–123; gender roles and, 1–2, 160; Indigenous women and, 6–8, 13–14, 157–158; motivations/justifications for, 2, 5–6, 20–21, 64–66; property and, 13–16; race and, 16

Comanche Nation, 85, 93, 97–99, 101, 115, 119

Cooper, Karen Coody, 134

Cope, Marnie, 170

Council of Energy Resource Tribes, 110

cultural survival: art and, 134, 140–141; boarding schools and, 36–37; Indigenous women's traditional power and, 6–8, 26, 41, 169; invisibility and, 58–60, 64–66; resilience and, 122–123

Curtis Act, 6, 17

Dakota Access Pipeline (DAPL), 146–152

Dawes Act/Rolls, 5–6, 17–18, 35, 153

"Death Cry for the Language" (Glancy), 34

Debo, Angie, 6, 16, 21, 30

Deer, Ada, 154–155, 178n11

Deer, Sarah, 157, 158–159

Denetdale, Jennifer Nez, 165–166, 190n50, 190n54

Department of Energy, 110–111

Department of the Interior, 156

De Soto, Hernando, 13–14

Determination of Right and Unity for Menominee Shareholders (DRUMS), 155

Dictionary of Native American Literature (Wiget), 139–140

Diné, 165–166

disappearances of Indigenous women, 186–187n27

Doctrine of Discovery, 65

Dunbar-Ortiz, Roxanne, 65

"Earth Shakers" (exhibit), 131–132

Earth Songs, Moon Dreams (Broder), 133, 134–136

economic prosperity, Indigenous, 21, 61–62, 123, 129, 167, 191n62

education: art and, 124, 132, 139–140; boarding schools and, 11–14, 22–23, 25–30, 36–37, 163, 171; curriculum issues and, 56, 66, 72; importance of, 63, 162; "Indian 101" and, 93, 119; Indigenous scholars/teachers and, 47–48, 159–166

environmentalism. *See* Dakota Access Pipeline (DAPL)

Erdrich, Louise, 141–142

ethnohistory, 47, 49, 58, 60–61

exclusion, 123

Federal Indian Boarding School Initiative, 156

feminism, Indigenous: Ambassadors program and, 92; Baker and, 45–46; Chunestudy and, 130; cultural survival and, 76–77; diversity of, 7–10; goals of, 169, 171–172, 190n54; Haozous on, 167–168; Harjo and, 137–138; Jane Osti and, 128; "living feminism" and, x–xi, xiv, 9–10; Mankiller and, 72, 79–80; race and expediency in, 4–6, 90–91; traditional values and, 97–98, 115, 117, 161; tribal viewpoint and, 121; white feminism vs., 111–112; Winnemucca and Zitkála-Šá and,

Indigenous women's traditional power
(*continued*)
   legacy and transmission of, 8, 44, 170–
   172; Mankiller and, 84, 94; "medicine"
   and, 121–123, 170; precontact and post-
   contact, 1–2, 6, 13–14; roles and, 76–77,
   121; sacredness of, 10; scholars/teachers
   and, 160–166; student community and,
   55, 57; Tijerina on, 107–108; traditional
   narratives and, 166. *See also* Indigenous
   women's traditional power; *names of*
   individual women
International Indigenous Youth Council,
   147–148, 151
interracial marriage, 14
Iron Eyes, Kate, 151

Jeffries-Logan, Vivette, 76–77
Jenkins, Connie, 132–133
Justice, Daniel Heath, 163

Keystone XL Pipeline protests, 146–152
Kidwell, Clara Sue, 16, 41, 66, 161
Kiowa Five mural, 56–57

Lady of Cofitachequi, 13–14
languages, Indigenous, 33–34, 52–53
LaVere, David, 53
Lawton, Okla., 86–87, 106–107, 191n62
Lighthorse Patrol, 135–136
Linderman, Frank, 139
Linton, Laura Jane, 19
literature, Indigenous: Baker and,
   179–180n2; contemporary, 136–142, 164;
   languages and, 34; perception of, 59–60,
   80; women and, 120–122
Lomawaima, K. Tsianina, 36–37
Louisiana State University, 47

manifest destiny, 64–66
Mankiller, Wilma: activism of, 69–72; Alcatraz occupation and, 70–71; background
   of, 8–9, 68–69, 75, 94; Baker and, 44–45,
   52, 64, 66–67, 78–84; Bell Water Project

and, 73–75, 78; car accident of, 73; "Earth
   Shakers" exhibit and, 131; feminism and,
   69, 72–73, 76–77, 80, 171; Harris and,
   94; legacy as chief, 68, 75–76, 77–78,
   181–182n34
Mann, Henrietta V. Whiteman, 162, 188n38
Mapping Indigenous project, 164–165
Mark My Words (Goeman), 164
Martinez, Julian, 124
Martinez, Maria Montoya, 123–124
"Maze of Injustice" (Amnesty International
   report), 158
McAlister, Barbara, 142–144
McGirt v. Oklahoma, 159
McKinney, Geraldine Hull: background of,
   8, 17–20, 21–22, 37–39; boarding school
   experience of, 11, 13, 22–31, 33–35, 163, 171;
   Choctaw Nation and, 33–34, 39–41; health
   care and, 30; traditional power and, 44
McKinney, Raymond, 38–39, 41
medicine (talent), 60, 92, 121–122, 145, 170
Medicine, Beatrice, 161–162
"Medicine Man Blues" (Baker), 42–43
Menominee tribe of Wisconsin, 154–155,
   178n11
microaggressions, 59–60
Mihesuah, Devon A., 36
Mitchell, Anna, 125, 127, 131
Mother Earth, 63
Mott, Lucretia, 3–4
music, Indigenous, 142–144

National Native American Hall of Fame,
   95–96
National Symposium on the American
   Indian, 52–54
National Women's Political Caucus, 89–90
Native American Student Association, 51,
   55–57
Northeastern State University, 21, 44, 50–52,
   53–56, 81–83

Oakes, Richard, 89
Of Plymouth Plantation (Bradford), 64–65, 66

www.ingramcontent.com/pod-product-compliance
Lightning Source LLC
Chambersburg PA
CBHW020858270326
41928CB00006B/763